A World in a Grain of Sand

A World in a Grain of Sand

The Clairvoyance of Stefan Ossowiecki

MARY ROSE BARRINGTON,
IAN STEVENSON *and* ZOFIA WEAVER

McFarland & Company, Inc., Publishers
Jefferson, North Carolina, and London

Frontispiece: **Stefan Ossowiecki.**

LIBRARY OF CONGRESS CATALOGUING-IN-PUBLICATION DATA

Barrington, Mary Rose, 1926–
A world in a grain of sand : the clairvoyance of Stefan Ossowiecki /
Mary Rose Barrington, Ian Stevenson and Zofia Weaver.
p.   cm.
Includes bibliographical references and index.

ISBN 0-7864-2112-6 (softcover : 50# alkaline paper) ∞

1. Ossowiecki, Stefan. 2. Psychics—Poland—Biography. 3. Parapsychology—
Research. I. Stevenson, Ian. II. Weaver, Zofia, 1947– III. Title.
BF1027.O8B37   2005   133.8'092—dc22   2005007324

British Library cataloguing data are available

©2005 Mary Rose Barrington, Ian Stevenson and Zofia Weaver. All rights reserved

*No part of this book may be reproduced or transmitted in any form
or by any means, electronic or mechanical, including photocopying
or recording, or by any information storage and retrieval system,
without permission in writing from the publisher.*

On the cover: background ©2005 PhotoSpin; foreground ©2005 Image Source

Manufactured in the United States of America

*McFarland & Company, Inc., Publishers
Box 611, Jefferson, North Carolina 28640
www.mcfarlandpub.com*

To the memory of Stefan Ossowiecki,
who gave so much of his time
and energy to psychical research

Acknowledgments

The authors would like to express their gratitude to the following: the Institut Métapsychique International for permission to reprint material from *Revue Métapsychique*; to the Society for Psychical Research for use of material published in the *Journal of the Society for Psychical Research* and the *Proceedings of the Society for Psychical Research*; to Doctor Alexander Imich, for generously allowing us to use his archive material in this volume; and to Krzysztof Boruń, for supplying advice and much background knowledge. Permission to quote from original sources has been obtained wherever this has been possible; any acknowledgments inadvertently omitted will be included in subsequent editions.

Contents

Acknowledgments	vii
Introduction (*Ian Stevenson*)	1
1. The Life and Times of Stefan Ossowiecki (*Zofia Weaver*)	5
2. The Formal Experiments	26
Early Experiments by Geley and Richet	27
Reception at the Institut Métapsychique International	45
Geley Probes Deeper	55
Co-Operation from London	62
Reports by Various Other Researchers	70
3. Informal Experiments and "Fieldwork"	85
Demonstrations of Clairvoyance	87
"Fieldwork"	103
Telepathy?	117
Out-of-body Experiences?	118
Premonition/Precognition?	119
Influence at a Distance?	122
4. Answers and Questions (*Mary Rose Barrington*)	124
Afterword (*Ian Stevenson*)	151
Appendix I: Archaeological Experiments	159
Appendix II: Chronology and List of Cases	165
Appendix III: Biographical Profiles of the Experimenters	175
Glossary	179
Bibliography	181
Index	185

Introduction

IAN STEVENSON

> To see a World in a Grain of Sand,
> And a Heaven in a Wild Flower,
> Hold Infinity in the palm of your hand,
> And Eternity in an Hour.
>
> William Blake, *Auguries of Innocence*

"To see a World in a grain of sand." Could anyone ever do that? Has anyone actually done that? Not exactly, but Stefan Ossowiecki showed that someone might do it. Stefan who? Stefan Ossowiecki, whose name you pronounce like Ossovietzki. A Pole by birth and an engineer by profession, Ossowiecki demonstrated clairvoyance of a range and quality no one has exceeded, at least under experimental controls. He seemed—to quote William Blake again—to have had the doors of perception "cleansed," and to a degree unmatched by any other person whose clairvoyance has been tested by experts and reported in reputable publications.

Ossowiecki lived between 1877 and 1944, and his life may now seem to belong to a period remote from our own and perhaps of little interest. Why remember him with a book at this time? I will mention the least important reason first. With two exceptions, all the reports of his clairvoyance were published in French or Polish journals not readily accessible to modern readers, even those of France and Poland. More importantly, Ossowiecki made himself available to the best of investigators of his time. Some of these were also among the best of all time. He flourished, we might say, between 1920 and 1944. During those decades he was living and working in Warsaw. He had a busy professional and social life, but somehow found time to use his gift in aiding a large number of persons who sought his help. Many of these persons wrote informal reports of their experiences with Ossowiecki, all highly positive. Their testimony adds to the information we have about his extraordinary talent; but their statements by themselves would not warrant publishing a book about him. That comes from a smaller series of controlled observations most of which French investigators, principally Gustave Geley, Charles Richet, and Eugene Osty, conducted in Warsaw and Paris. Translations of their reports form the most important section of this book. Two controlled experiments by British investigators add substantially to the evidence of Ossowiecki's talent compiled by the French investigators. So do two experiments conducted by a Polish investigator, Prosper Szmurło.

The case of Ossowiecki has additional sources of interest and value to the modern reader. First, unlike many psychics, Ossowiecki wanted to know how he accomplished his feats of clairvoyance. He talked (in interviews) and he wrote (in an autobiography published in Poland) about his search for an understanding of his gift. He described how the process of clairvoyance seemed to him from the inside, so to speak. He attributed his clairvoyance largely to early training by a Russian seer called Wróbel (about whom we know almost nothing else). Ossowiecki, however, believed that experienced investigators could learn and teach him something more about the processes of his ability. This book describes what they learned. Read it to learn for yourself from original reports. Here I will say a little of what I have learned.

I think some unusual ingredient of Ossowiecki's character empowered him. It seems likely that Wróbel advised him never to ask for a fee or accept one, and he never did. He never turned away anyone who asked for his help in finding a missing person or lost object. (He could decline proposals for a demonstration when the person requesting it had no need for help.) This generosity sometimes left him drained, because he fitted requests for help into a life filled enough with the work of a businessman who also enjoyed social pleasures: he was not an ascetic.

Perhaps we can find another clue to his talent in the extraordinary benignity of his attitude toward everyone, including wrongdoers. He sometimes used his talent to detect criminals; but he always believed in their ability to reform. He himself believed that his clairvoyance derived from his goodwill. Of the state he entered when he demonstrated clairvoyance he once wrote: "I affirm that this condition is brought about by my unshakable faith in the spiritual unity of all humanity." Ossowiecki's universal charity toward others did not make him an undiscriminating observer of them. Indeed he developed strong attachments to certain persons he found congenial. Sometimes he would single out one person from a group and insist on experimenting with that person alone. The full exercise of his talent required a rapport with an investigator or with a person asking for his help. When he was trying to read a concealed message furnished by one person and other persons remained in the room, he asked them to ignore him; being the focus of attention by others diminished his capacity for clairvoyance. The exercise of his talent fatigued him and sometimes left him in a state of mild confusion with amnesia. If he did not think his condition was right for a trial, he would decline to make one. Alternatively, if he believed he was ready, he might impulsively ask for a test of his powers there and then.

I have summarized some of what we can learn from the reports in this book about the circumstances that facilitated Ossowiecki's clairvoyance. These tell us nothing about the state he entered when he exhibited it. If he felt right for a trial, he got himself into a condition in which he could, as it were, roll time backward. In this unusual state he could see not only the experimental target, but the circumstances of its preparation and, behind that, some anterior details of the life of the person who prepared the target. Readers familiar with theosophy may recognize in this feat the concept of the *akashic* record. I myself thought this idea a mere fantasy until I became acquainted with Ossowiecki's record.

I have used the word *clairvoyance* in referring to Ossowiecki's talent without meaning to preclude a careful examination of other explanations for it. Any explanation, however, will have to reckon with the complexity of the processes involved. For example, it will need to include the role played by Ossowiecki's touching, holding, and sometimes kneading the object of a trial. Ossowiecki preferred such contact, but did not always require it. Explanations must also account for the extraordinary range of Ossowiecki's paranormal abilities. The reports of controlled investigations in this book emphasize his ability to discern, with astonishing accuracy, writing or drawings concealed in opaque envelopes or other coverings. He appears, however, to have had an extensive repertoire of other paranormal powers, even though testimony for them lacks the certitude of control that the major investigations of concealed writings provide. Writers worthy of our confidence credited Ossowiecki with identifying criminal employees in businesses, with locating missing persons, including a corpse buried in a mass graveyard, with influencing particular persons to come to him, with locating small lost objects, and with moving a heavy piano ten meters without touching it. We have one report also of his appearing voluntarily as an apparition in the apartment of an acquaintance while his physical body was in his apartment.

The limits of his talent also deserve attention. He said that he could not read printed words, only handwritten ones. Although he knew French and German well, he knew no English and could not read a target written in that language. Above all, he could not, or perhaps would not, use his talent for his own benefit. He lost when playing cards, did not foresee the collapse of his first marriage, and seems also not to have known in advance how he was going to die—shot by the Germans in August 1944.

The study of Ossowiecki's remarkable accomplishments offers a rich opportunity for improved understanding of paranormal powers. It will not, however, provide by itself all the answers we need, and this brings me to my most important reason for recommending the study of his record. Trendiness affects and sometimes retards many fields of scientific inquiry, including that of paranormal phenomena. Investigators of these change their enthusiasms no less than scientists in other fields.

In the period of Ossowiecki's demonstrations, investigators believed that they could best study paranormal powers in certain specially gifted persons like Ossowiecki. In the later decades of the twentieth century, however, their successors became disappointed with the rareness of significant talent among the crowd of claimants to greatness; they abandoned the effort to find the few persons who had both a gift for paranormal cognition and the willingness to submit to controlled studies as Ossowiecki had done. Instead, they turned their attention to experiments with groups of subjects composed of ordinary persons who made no claims to special talents. Experiments with groups of subjects have certainly succeeded in their way, but they do not provide evidence of abundant paranormal communication, such as Ossowiecki did. Consequently, they tell us almost nothing about processes. Experiments with groups of ordinary people rest on the false assumption that the capacity for paranormal communication is evenly distributed among humans. We do not think this of other abilities. Many persons have some musical ability, but great musicians occur rarely. Schools of music know this; they look for a musician with exceptional talent and foster his or her development. They encourage unendowed lovers of music, but do not record their playing. We need this attitude in psychical research. Ossowiecki was outstanding, and he may have been the greatest clairvoyant of whom we have reliable knowledge. Moreover, he came as close as anyone has ever done to providing repeated demonstrations of clairvoyance under controlled conditions.

1

The Life and Times of Stefan Ossowiecki

Zofia Weaver

Historical Background

To a reader unfamiliar with Poland's turbulent history, the extensive gaps in the biography and the experimental record of Stefan Ossowiecki might appear to be a sufficient reason to regard with suspicion the claims made for him. Yet, in its incompleteness, Ossowiecki's story is like that of thousands of other Poles whose settled, sometimes very comfortable existence was suddenly shattered by the political upheaval brought about by the First World War (1914–18) and the Russian Revolution.

From 1796 to 1918, Poland disappeared from the map of Europe. Its territory was partitioned between the empires of Russia, Prussia and Austria, and attempts at regaining independence through insurrection were put down swiftly and followed by harsh reprisals. The history of Poland throughout the nineteenth century is the history of a nation fighting to preserve its identity without an independent state, with periodic decimation of its intellectual elite and its economic base, against the constant and often ruthless pressure to assimilate. While the preservation of national identity in the original Polish territory demanded courage, effort and sacrifice, the achievement of the many Polish families and communities scattered throughout the occupiers' lands in keeping their sense of Polishness alive seems perhaps just as remarkable.

Without an independent state, the main source of national awareness was family tradition, literature, a cult of the great past of the Polish nation and a sense of its historic mission passed on from generation to generation. On a practical level, possibilities for maintaining cultural identity within a community varied. The Russian empire itself was open to those Poles ambitious for a career and, away from the original Polish territory, the pressure to assimilate was less intense.

In the early years of the twentieth century, as Russia tried to reform itself, it was possible, for those in a position of influence, to work for the Polish cause through attempting to increase Poland's representation in the Russian parliament, the Duma, and through supporting Polish cultural, educational and charitable organizations. However, it would have been even easier for families like the Ossowieckis and their circle—wealthy, privileged and well-established in the heart of Russia—to become part of the mainstream establishment. It could be argued that the sense of mission, of service to a greater cause, which was a significant feature of a whole generation's heritage, forms an important aspect of Stefan Ossowiecki's personal philosophy and helps to explain his attitude to his gift as an almost sacred trust, only to be used for the benefit of others.

With the advent of the First World War and then the Russian Revolution, the leaders of Polish communities took the opportunity of advancing the cause of Poland's freedom as the occupying powers tried to win loyalty and support for their crumbling empires. Very quickly, that which for generations was only a dream—an independent Poland—became a realizable goal. Organizations were formed to work for this cause. Jan Jacyna, Ossowiecki's brother-in-law, who later became a general in the independent Poland's army and whose career is quite well documented, was on the Council of the Polish Chief Military Commission, and Stefan Ossowiecki was also active in this body. However, as the course of the revolution became more extreme, unpredictable and dangerous to anybody with a "bourgeois" background, "going home" to the independent Poland, re-created on 11 November 1918, became the obvious course for those who survived the ordeal of fighting, confiscations, interrogations and arrest.

Many of those "coming home" were seasoned freedom-fighters, for whom such experiences were commonplace. For many others, uprooted from sheltered and comfortable lives, the experience must have been traumatic. Ossowiecki's reaction seems to have been the fairly common one, of reluctance to remember his previous, "Russian" life. However, it is also important to bear in mind that, if there is a time to live in the present, it is when dreams come true. After 123 years Poland had regained its independence, with Józef Piłsudski, a charismatic military leader, its first head of state. Three geographical areas, each subjected for over a century to very diverse influences and administrative systems, came together, bringing their own problems as well as creating further problems in trying to unify. Their economies were weak and fragmented, as well as being plundered by the departing powers and ravaged by war; the external borders were uncertain; there were significant minorities with conflicting interests; and there were no structures of state, legislature or the military. Even though many of the problems did not find their solutions in the period between the two world wars it was, especially in its early days, a period of great creativity in all fields of public life, and a sense of commitment and purpose prevailed. Warsaw seen through the eyes of Ossowiecki's contemporaries reflects this sense of dynamism in the flourishing artistic, literary, social and business life, as people try to find their place in the constantly changing social and economic order. It is something to bear in mind when one reads of the unfinished, interrupted, poorly recorded and sometimes poorly controlled experiments, so frustrating to a modern researcher: Ossowiecki had a very full life to live and enjoy.

The destruction of Warsaw during the Second World War (1939–1945), following the uprising by the resistance movement in August 1944, meant that a great many national and private records, from manuscripts of historic value to treasured family photographs, have been irretrievably lost. Most of the original records relating to Ossowiecki's life and experiments met the same fate. His personal papers and archives burnt along with his apartment block; the manuscripts he carried with him when rounded up with the thousands of other civilians by the Nazis were probably burnt with his body and the bodies of those executed at the same time. The archives of the Polish organizations dedicated to psychical research did not survive either. There are thus many aspects of the Ossowiecki story which cannot be fully verified. However, the part of the story for which corroboration can be found is remarkable enough.

Ossowiecki the Man

Stefan Ossowiecki was born in 1877 in Russia, in Moscow, into a well-to-do family of high social standing. His father, who in his youth had been an assistant to the famous chemist Mendeleyev, was a successful industrialist with his own extensive chemical plant in Moscow, which produced paints and varnishes. His mother, whose roots came from the landed gentry of eastern Poland (now Lithuania), was a very beautiful woman (her portraits, painted by the famous artists of the day, testify to this), reputedly with great powers of intuition. Stefan had two elder sisters and three younger brothers, all of whom did well in later life.

According to some relatives, Stefan was his mother's special favorite as a child, which might have made him somewhat impractical and uninterested in material matters. This may also explain his trust in people, and the need to draw their attention and affection (Boruń & Boruń-Jagodzińska, 1990, p. 16). His mother and grandmother were reputed to be somewhat psychic, being subject to premonitions, and one of his brothers practiced automatic writing.

In his autobiography Stefan claims that he showed telepathic abilities from the age of 14, but does not say how they manifested themselves. Over the next three to four years his telepathy evolved into "mediumistic abilities," which included the ability to move objects and write in languages unknown to him.

His education followed a pattern predictable for a youngster born into a wealthy family with influential connections, being groomed to look after the family business. His later fluency in French and German is natural for somebody with his upbringing; one would expect foreign language tutors/nannies in his kind of household from the earliest age. At the age of 17 he graduated from the exclusive Third Cadet Corps in Moscow. He then went on to study at the St Petersburg Institute of Technology. In an interview given many years later (*Goniec Warszawski* [Warsaw Messenger] 25 April 1937, p. 6) Ossowiecki relates how, during the diploma exam he "read" his chemistry questions through the sealed envelope, went up to the board and started writing the chemical formulae. He got them all right and passed with flying colors.

It was around that time (1898–99) that the meeting with Wróbel, described by Ossowiecki in his autobiography as the most influential event in his development as a psychic, took place. Having time to kill while waiting for a train in the small town of Homel in south-east Belarus to take him to the paper mill where he was to undertake his work experience as a third year student, Ossowiecki asked about things of interest in the area, and was told about the local celebrity, the wise old Jew called Wróbel, who had spent his life in India studying esoteric sciences, and returned home to end his days.

According to Ossowiecki, "Wróbel lived in the suburbs in a small wooden house. By then the old man was bed-ridden—he was lying dressed in a black, monk-like robe. He had a beautiful Semitic face with a long gray beard. He saw immediately into my inner world and told me at once my name and the purpose of my visit. He moved mentally to Moscow, and described in the smallest detail my whole life, pondering over its more interesting stages. He was the first to explain to me the meaning of the aura and told me that I am among those who at times can see it. He also emphasized my supernatural abilities and foretold that my name will be well-known in later years. He spoke about my future and my past and I have to admit that so far everything has come true. He was an exceptional man" (Ossowiecki, 1933, pp. 93–94). Ossowiecki went to see Wróbel and learn from him at every opportunity whenever he was in the area; he also gives names of other acolytes who visited the old man regularly, but it has not proved possible to trace any information about him.

We have very little information about Stefan's life-style, friends and interests during that period. His autobiography consists mainly of accounts of experiments, and personal information is limited to remarks about the development of his psychic powers. We can get some idea of the social circles in which his family probably moved from the memoirs of Jan Jacyna (Jacyna, 1926), Stefan's brother-in-law. He was a military man working as a teacher of military subjects to the sons of Grand Duke Vladimir, brother of Tsar Alexander III (1845–1894). He and his wife were also on friendly terms with other members of the royal family. It is logical to assume that Stefan, who was close to his sister, would have been a frequent visitor at her home, just as he was later on in Warsaw. One of the few surviving photographs of Stefan Ossowiecki shows him with Grand Duke Michael (brother of Tsar Nicholas II). The tsar's immediate circle was deeply involved in religious-mediumistic pursuits dominated by Rasputin, but there is no evidence to suggest any involvement by Ossowiecki.

There must have also been many business and industrial connections in his life at this stage, in the early years of the twentieth century. Ossowiecki was busy working in factories, then serving on the boards of various enterprises, eventually becoming the head of the family business after his father's death in 1914.

There is no record of Ossowiecki's psychic feats during this period. He tells us in his autobiography how his powers of psychokinesis increased and developed, enabling him to move very heavy objects, and performing such feats in front of friends. He gives a number of names of friends who at that time could confirm the truth of his statements, but previous researchers found it impossible to trace them, and present-day researchers face an even greater time gap. However, one has the impression that his psychokinetic powers were being used as a "party trick," with no serious intent. At the age of about 35 these powers started to decline; since they were also having an adverse effect on his health, Stefan agreed to his father's request that he give them up.

The advent of the war brought with it the involvement of the military in the control of industrial plants, while the revolutionary upheavals which followed soon afterward must have spelt the end of the family business. At the same time, Ossowiecki was actively involved in politics. After the revolution of February 1917 he was elected vice president of the Poles' Military Union, and in June 1917 he became a member of the Chief Polish Military Committee, in which his brother-in-law, Jan Jacyna, was a member of the Executive Committee (Boruń & Boruń-Jagodzińska, 1990, p. 19).

At the end of 1918 Ossowiecki was arrested on suspicion of working with the French Military Mission, which had its offices in his house. He was accused of collaborating with the French, and imprisoned for six months under terrible conditions which he described to Geley (Geley, 1924, p. 32). He was kept in a dark, bug-infested cell, and fed on salted fish and one glass of water a day. During the day he was made to dig ditches for burying the victims of executions. Finally, he was sentenced to death and taken to the place of execution, only to be saved at the last moment through the intervention of a friend from his student days, who had become a high-powered official in the new regime. This account is largely corroborated by Ossowiecki's stepson in a letter to Alexander Imich (personal archives), with the additional information that it was Ossowiecki's mother who successfully begged for mercy from a Bolshevik dignitary—who may indeed have been an old friend. Ossowiecki did not like to talk about his experiences of that time; he did, however, say in a newspaper interview in 1937 that the experience of arrest, enforced isolation and the threat of death was a watershed in his spiritual development, and the development of his psychic powers. In his own words, "It was only then that I appreciated this gift, given to me by the Creator, and understood that I can help others using it" (*Goniec Warszawski*, 29 April 1937, p. 6).

It is logical to suppose that Ossowiecki left Russia as soon as he was able. His brother-in-law, Jan Jacyna, had already departed in haste earlier on, after receiving warning of imminent arrest. There was nothing left to stay for in Russia, while independent Poland was no longer a dream but a real place to go to and start again.

It may thus be the case that Ossowiecki's career as a psychic really did begin after his arrival in Warsaw, probably in 1919, fresh from the ordeal that intensified his powers. Many of his friends and family were already there, and he quickly found himself at home in the Warsaw milieu where, with so many people uprooted, friendships, as well as commercial and political connections were being established and re-established with great ease. It has been mentioned that Jan Jacyna became a general in the Polish army. At that time Jacyna was also adjutant to Marshal Piłsudski and it is logical to assume that the friendship between Stefan Ossowiecki and the Marshal, which flourished for a number of years, started through this connection.

We do have a number of accounts of Ossowiecki the man from that period; with his extraverted, friendly personality he quickly acquired many new friends, and his fame as a psychic made him even more popular. One contemporary, a writer, describes him as tall, athletically built, with a round, friendly, open face and the expression of a child trusting everything and everybody. He loved being with friends, he loved a good joke, good food, good wine, and the company and admiration of ladies. "It was enough to see this radiant full moon of a face, set on the shoulders of an Atlas, to become convinced that life is worth living" (Grzymała-Siedlecki, 1962, p. 286). There was a rumor, strongly denied by his family in Poland and never confirmed, that Stefan had been married a number of times in Russia. He is definitely known to have been married twice. His first marriage, to the Russian Alietta de la Carrierre, lasted from 1922 to 1930. It does not seem to have been a particularly happy union: the time he devoted to the metaphysical experiments was at least one cause of friction. Alietta's departure, which came as no surprise to those who knew them but was a shock to Ossowiecki, caused quite a lot of amusement over the predicament of a clairvoyant who could not predict such an important event in his own life (he himself always emphasized that he is "blind" in relation to himself and those close to him). His second marriage, in 1939, to Zofia Skibińska* *primo voto* Świda, who understood him and shared his attitude to his gift, was a success. However, the in-between years, according to some trustworthy accounts, were not bereft of female friendships. This is hardly surprising; he was acknowledged to have great personal charm, and was reputed to be particularly susceptible to damsels in distress. The damsels, on the other hand, followed him remorselessly demanding help and advice, which was given generously in Polish with a strong Russian accent and interspersed with whimsical terms of endearment.

According to Ossowiecki's widow (interview with Jerzy Jacyna, 42/70), the most accurate account of Stefan was given by Grzymała-Siedlecki, the writer already quoted. In his book about the unusual people he had known, he describes Ossowiecki in a chapter called *Traveler from the Fourth Dimension* in the following terms: "The most fundamental feature of his character was optimism, which brought with it an unbelievable degree of trust in people. He, who of all people could know more about human criminality, duplicity and hidden evil, kept giving moral credit to his fellow men. I have never known anyone who would be so surprised when somebody's misdemeanor or ugly side was revealed. He had an amazing belief in people and a need to empathize with people" (Grzymała-Siedlecki, 1962, p. 284).

This belief in people also meant that he never had any money; it just never occurred to him that he could refuse something to someone. His trust, as well as his enjoyment of life, made him a worse businessman than he liked to believe he was. His first job, as sales director for a manufacturing company, lasted some six years (1919–1925). He then worked as administrative director in another manufacturing company (1925–27). Following that he operated an employment co-operative for the benefit of officers of reserve (1930–1934). In the '30s he was involved in numerous business activities, becoming a founder member and vice president of a Bank for Foreign Trade, starting a partnership for trade in coal and construction materials and serving on the boards of various manufacturing and construction companies.

In Polish, it is often the case that the masculine and feminine versions of a surname are expressed differently; for example, Skibiński (masculine) and Skibińska (feminine).

He was also active in various charitable organizations, including the Polish Red Cross (Boruń & Boruń-Jagodzińska, 1990, p. 20).

Perhaps it was the enthusiasm with which he threw himself into so many projects which made it difficult for him to juggle them and achieve success in any particular one. Ossowiecki's absent-mindedness was in fact legendary. He was always forgetting appointments, making arrangements to meet different people in different places at the same time, losing things, forgetting names and faces. Jerzy Jacyna, a young cousin of Jan Jacyna and a frequent visitor to the Jacyna household, witnessed a number of situations where Stefan introduced himself to people he had already met a number of times. Having known the young Jacyna for about two years, Stefan one day introduced himself to him, asking his sister to tell him something about "our young guest" (Jacyna, 1970–71, 46/70). Ossowiecki himself attributed at least some of his lapses to the effect of the experiments, some of which left him disoriented for long periods, making him lose his sense of time and affecting his memory.

A number of reliable sources agree that Ossowiecki's financial position was misrepresented in the legends circulating about him. According to his stepson, Marian Świda, Stefan may have been well off in the 1920s, but later, in the 1930s, he was barely making ends meet. It was Świda's opinion (letter to Alexander Imich, personal archives) that Ossowiecki was too kind and trusting, lending money or getting involved in dubious enterprises. This opinion was shared by a number of witnesses interviewed by Boruń, who tended to agree that while Stefan was active and willing, his business acumen was not great and friends and relatives sometimes had to come to the rescue both with advice and financial help (Boruń & Boruń-Jagodzińska, 1990, p. 20).

In fact, the very number of high-powered posts which he held for short periods (two of them in companies of which he was a founder member and which did not last long) is indicative of the unreliability of these ventures. However, it is perhaps not very surprising in view of both his character and his background—he started out with a high position in a secure environment of a flourishing family business, which did not prepare him for being the kind of entrepreneur who can build up a business from nothing. Add his high expectations, his other interests, his sociable nature and there is a recipe for ensuring that the grandiose plans never materialize. But it does seem likely that his "business persona" was just as real and necessary to him as his other interests, and that he enjoyed projecting the contrasting images of the hard-headed "Monsieur l'Ingénieur" and the aloof mystic.

It is clearly apparent from reliable evidence from many sources that he truly was a very busy man. It is also confirmed consistently from every quarter that he never accepted payment for "clairvoyant services" or tried to use his gift for financial gain. When he was new to Warsaw society, many people refused to play bridge with him in case he could "read" their cards. According to a number of witnesses he was a poor player and usually lost. His explanation was that he made a special effort not to use his gift under such circumstances. What is certain is that as his fame grew, he had plenty of opportunities to obtain financial rewards from his special position—and yet he never did.

It would be facile to suggest that ruling out pecuniary gain rules out motivation for cheating. In the Ossowiecki experiments, regardless of their design, there is no evidence of any attempt at cheating. There is plenty of evidence to show that he sincerely and genuinely believed in the efficacy of his gift and used it in situations where cheating was impossible by virtue of the task, such as tracing the fate of strangers who were missing during the war. But, objective evidence apart, it is only through a better understanding of how he regarded his abilities and what his status meant to him that we can gain an insight into his true motivation.

What is most important about Ossowiecki's philosophical beliefs (of which more later) is that in their light he was entrusted with a special gift, to be used not just to help people on a practical level, but to show them the way which leads to a higher level of consciousness, to play a part in the spiritual development of mankind. To make material profit from this trust would have amounted to sacrilege. It would have been offensive to his religious convictions, just as it would have been demeaning for a gentleman to take money for clairvoyant services, like a common fortune teller.

He was quite vain and proud of his powers, he enjoyed the fame (it is no exaggeration to say that he was one of the most famous people in Poland during the years between the wars), adulation and the sense of importance which they brought him, but at the same time felt humbled by them.

On a number of occasions, when asked, Ossowiecki advanced descriptions and explanations of how he thought his gift worked, emphasizing the importance of pursuing esoteric studies and disciplines. However, he never claimed to really understand it and was himself very eager to have it investigated. He was very impressed by the new science of "metapsychics" and enthusiastically co-operated with the experimenters whenever he could. In view of all the other pressures on his time, it is hardly surprising that often he could not, which is why "experiments" are often done on the spur of the moment or carried over to another session, or left unfinished.

There are thus a number of seemingly contradictory images of Ossowiecki to reconcile: the hard-headed businessman, the sociable bon vivant, the powerful magus, the hermit student of esoteric knowledge. Some of these images he undoubtedly enjoyed and helped to build up, albeit not necessarily consciously. What is well attested are his qualities of kindness, openness and trust. And, of course, the experiments.

When the Second World War broke out in 1939, Ossowiecki and his wife stayed in Warsaw, even though they had the opportunity to go abroad, to Italy. Legend has it that Ossowiecki refused to leave because he would be needed to help people. Ossowiecki's stepson advances a more prosaic reason he heard from his mother, that nobody expected the war to last as long and be as horrific as it turned out to be, and the prospect of starting a new life among strangers in one's sixties must have been daunting.

Whatever his reasons for staying, Ossowiecki did help great numbers of people during the Nazi occupation. Anxious relatives came from all over the country, hoping he could "track" their missing loved ones, waiting sometimes for hours outside his apartment. He did not refuse anybody. Since on his own admission he sometimes lied, when the visions which came to him were too horrific, the evidential value of this period is variable and, of course, mostly unrecorded. It was also a tremendous emotional stress on his personality. Apart from occasional commercial deals, the main source of the family income during the war years was the café managed by Ossowiecki's wife.

During the occupation he also carried out many archaeological and other experiments with a number of professors from Warsaw University. Records of these remain incomplete, although some accounts have been published both in Polish and English.* Since their paranormality could only be judged by a historian of archaeology with the necessary knowledge of the periods and cultures involved, they have been omitted from this volume and await further investigation.

There are a number of versions of Stefan Ossowiecki's death, which most probably had no surviving witnesses apart from the anonymous killers. The most likely and the best authenticated one is that he was killed with thousands of other civilians in the early days of August 1944, soon after the start of the Warsaw uprising on 1st August. The Gestapo rounded up all the civilians hiding from the fighting in the area near his apartment block, dragged out those still remaining at home and separated the men from the women. Stefan's wife was separated from him when they emerged from hiding in the local vicarage with other civilians, and she was taken away with the other women. However, a friend who lived in the same area and who had been dragged out of her home at a later stage, claims to have seen Ossowiecki in the columns of men prisoners being guarded in the street, and even to have managed to exchange a few words with him before the guards broke up their conversation. The women were kept waiting for many hours, while the men were taken away in fours to an area behind some burnt-out buildings and shot. Although there were no eyewitnesses to the massacre, they could hear machine-guns, the screams of the wounded and the single shots indicating they were being finished off. The bodies were then burnt, together with a lot of papers, with ash floating down as thick as snow (Boruń & Boruń-Jagodzińska, 1990, pp. 42–3). Estimates vary as to how many thousands were killed at this spot, but there is no doubt that this massacre, like many others, did take place.

It is most likely that Ossowiecki was among those who perished there. Other, unconfirmed, accounts, report him being tortured at the Gestapo headquarters (which was close by) and then executed; yet others have him appearing at concentration camps at a later stage. It is certain that he was never seen again after early August 1944. He still had so many plans, so much he wanted to accomplish, not for himself but for humanity. Perhaps it would be fitting to let Ossowiecki the man explain what he wanted to achieve, with a quotation from the end of his autobiography:

---

*Archaeological experiments with Ossowiecki took place both before and during the war. When they were first attempted, the question of their usefulness was raised in the Polish psychical research journal Zagadnienia Metapsychiczne [Metapsychic Issues], since they seemed virtually impossible to verify except on a very basic level. The series of experiments conducted with Professor Poniatowski and other archaeologists from 1935 to 1944 seems to have been aimed at providing leads to archaeological research. See Appendix I.

I want to be one of those people ... who try to help raise the spirit of today's humanity, confused and oppressed by the struggle for survival. I want to be the servant of all those who seek reconciliation and a common platform for human hearts and minds.... And I ask you, Readers, as you read the thoughts presented in this book, to look upon all the people without exception as your brothers, tied to you with the same knot of birth and death—do it for a moment, but do it every day [Ossowiecki, 1933, pp. 365–66].

Psychical Research in Ossowiecki's Poland

At this stage it is important to mention the status of psychical research at that time. While Warsaw probably had the same size population of self-proclaimed psychics, fortune-tellers, astrologers, quacks, and the same proportion of the gullible as any major Western city, there were some important features which make the period and the place special.

In the Western world generally psychical research seemed to be held in greater regard than it is today, as a legitimate and perhaps especially significant branch of scientific enquiry. The names of Richet and Geley, who were the first to conduct experiments with Ossowiecki, were highly respected; the Polish academics who followed in their footsteps were no less so, even if less famous. The subject was thus academically acceptable. It was also socially acceptable, particularly since Piłsudski, the head of state, was himself very interested in the paranormal, and is reported to have had a number of psychic experiences. A charismatic, powerful and controversial character, Piłsudski was a legend in his own lifetime, and certainly at the time of the early experiments commanded universal respect.

Like many other areas of intellectual activity in Poland at the time, psychical research was undergoing a period of intense development. A number of societies were established with the aim of promoting research in that area; since their activities and membership overlapped to a large extent, they will be referred to in this volume as the Warsaw Psychophysical Society.* It modeled itself on the French Institut Métapsychique International, and its founder, Prosper Szmurło, edited a periodical, *Zagadnienia Metapsychiczne* [Metapsychical Issues], which reported experimental data and spontaneous cases. Unfortunately, its records do not seem to have survived and not all issues of the periodical are available. The surviving data suggests that the researchers were very thorough in their investigations, as well as being imaginative in the kinds of experiments they designed. It is a great pity that so much of their work has been lost, either through destruction during the war, or through neglect during the postwar period of intense materialistic indoctrination under communism.

For most of that time its president was Prosper Szmurło. Not much is known about his personal background, but the quality of many of the experiments he was

---

A brief history of the psychical research societies in Poland is given in Appendix III under the heading Warsaw Psychophysical Society.

involved with is impressive. So are the lengths to which the investigators were prepared to go to in order to establish the truth of mediumistic claims. There is, among others, an account to warm the heart of a conscientious researcher: Stefan Rzewuski, a very active member of the society, tells of a physical medium claiming to produce ectoplasm, whose fraudulent method was exposed by ignoring the dire warnings of the harm which might be caused by a sudden flash of light and photographing him without the warning "click." It turned out that the medium, having already been searched and restrained in various ways, relied on causing the phenomena with his teeth (*Zagadnienia Metapsychiczne*, Jul/Aug/Sept 1924, No. 3, pp. 161–172). It is thus worth bearing in mind that many of the people involved in the experiments spent most of the time devoted to psychical research investigating trickery or looking for normal explanations for paranormal claims; they were not naïve or credulous.

A publication that carried a regular biweekly feature on investigations into the paranormal and in which some of the Ossowiecki experiments were published was *Ilustrowany Kuryer Codzienny* [Illustrated Daily Courier]. It was a popular and respected daily paper, a household name with nationwide circulation whose editor, Ludwik Szczepański, as well as reporting on research and spontaneous cases, devoted a great deal of space to debunking fraudulent phenomena and providing rational explanation for the reported phenomena in the light of current scientific knowledge.

It is also important to note that psychical research in Poland ignores almost totally the question of survival. In fact, at the International Psychical Research Conference in Warsaw in 1923 a declaration was adopted to specifically register its protest against mixing psychical research with spiritism, stating that "no hypothesis can be regarded as proven, and survival of bodily death cannot be regarded as the only possible interpretation of psychic phenomena," and emphasizing that psychical research is not associated with any religious or moral doctrine (*Zagadnienia Metapsychiczne*, Jan/Feb/Mar 1924, p. 15). Scientific stance apart, it should be remembered that, while most religions say "yes" to life after death in some form, the Roman Catholic Church, with a very strong position in Poland, specifically forbids attempts to contact the dead, and yet another edict to that effect had been issued by Pope Benedict XV as recently as 1917. The position of the church is that contact with the dead is exceptional; it can be a gift from God, but it is an event so rare that claims of those who say they can call them at will must be dismissed as either false (fraudulent) or, in most cases, mistaken (originating from subconscious levels of the mind). Trying to evoke apparitions or communicate with the dead means that one is meddling with things little understood but not necessarily benevolent, which may bring forth manifestations definitely not originating with God. However, scientific investigation of *man's* gifts, such as telepathy or psychometry, is to be commended and encouraged.*

There has been little change in this attitude. A bishop writing recently in a magazine devoted to the paranormal (Nieznany Świat, March 2000) reminds the readers that one can only maintain contact with the dead through prayer, and the calling up of spirits is forbidden by the church. Also viewed with suspicion are claims by some persons who have come close to death and survived that they have had a glimpse of life after death; the preferred interpretation of such experiences is that all the features associated with them are the product of the human mind.

Such exhortations did not stop the socialites in Warsaw flocking to séances with mediums such as Jan Guzik, a physical medium frequently caught cheating, but these were fashionable "crazes" pursuing sensational thrills rather than seeking scientific or spiritual enlightenment. Very little is known about the personal religious beliefs of the researchers; however, a profound religious conviction which places the numinous on a level beyond the reach of human intellectual curiosity may be a better guarantee of objectivity than devotion to a model of a world regarded as scientific at a particular time. It is a particularly striking feature of the accounts relating to the period of war and occupation that the thousands who flocked to Ossowiecki for help only wanted to know whether their loved ones were alive or dead and, as happened in one striking case, wanted to locate the body to give it a proper burial.

Another feature which makes the Ossowiecki phenomenon different and special is the relationship between the investigator and the investigated. Ossowiecki is the social equal and usually a friend of the investigators and witnesses, and himself an eager participant in the investigation. So many of the characters who take part in the "experiments" are creative, charismatic personalities—not just academics but writers, journalists, musicians, actors and opera stars, leading politicians and military leaders. There is a often a closeness, intimacy and sheer high spirits, almost a party atmosphere, with everyone enjoying the display of Ossowiecki's special gift. Not all experiments took place under such conditions, but it may be the case that the rapport Ossowiecki shared with the investigators and witnesses played a part in some of his more spectacular successes.

Ossowiecki's Philosophical Ideas and Beliefs

Ossowiecki's personal philosophy is not helpful in trying to find an explanation of his gift, although he regarded it as crucial. However, it is very important to our understanding of his character and his view of the role of the true psychic.

In his autobiography Ossowiecki acknowledges his debt to Wróbel, but he also mentions Józef Jankowski as one of his teachers. Ossowiecki belonged to the movement led by Jankowski, a poet, journalist and translator, who passionately propagated the ideas of Hoene-Wroński, a nineteenth-century Polish philosopher working in France, whose life work was the attempt to create an absolute philosophy designed to solve all the basic problems of mankind. He did not define the Absolute, but the core of his system was the law of creation which involved constant movement between the Absolute and the concrete, as mankind strives for harmony and freedom. Hoene-Wroński's ideas included Russia leading the Slav nations in the salvation of mankind, but later Polish ideological and independence movements based on his philosophy rejected this element and saw Poland as the "Messiah of nations." The movement led by Jankowski had in it elements of Rosicrucian, theosophical and messianic ideas (Roszkowski, 1983). The main influences on Ossowiecki's beliefs are those of humanity evolving towards perfection (in spite of many setbacks and cycles of regression) helped by the coming together of science, religion and metaphysics.

In Ossowiecki's philosophy, the evolution of mankind progresses from the East to the West, and while Christianity is the pinnacle of all religions, the East is the cradle where the higher spiritual forces were born out of the human longing for God. The "One Soul" he often refers to when trying to explain his gift, is part of everything in the universe, unlimited by time and space. The "ether" is in a sense its body, with a variety of waves traveling through it.

The primitive man, connected to the world of plants and animals, has evolved to the point where he, his consciousness, is capable of "taking" the divine element. However, the current stage is not his final, finished state. We are creatures still inhabiting physical bodies, which are subject to destruction. Only when mankind has reached its "winged" (spiritually speaking) form, can it rejoin the One Soul. The "I" with its subjective forms of perception (which can be conquered through clairvoyance) will disappear forever. Thus all people are brethren, striving for the evolution of the soul toward the divine.

Ossowiecki distinguishes three spiritual phases in the human psyche: the subconscious, the conscious and the superconscious. The subconscious absorbs what it needs from the One Soul without being aware of it. As the soil accepts seed and makes it grow, so the subconscious grows into consciousness, producing flashes of understanding. The subconscious and the superconscious can be linked directly. Consciousness is the self-awareness, it is the "helmsman" in the cosmic ocean. The superconscious is linked to the consciousness of the One Soul, the source of all Wisdom coming from God.

Ossowiecki was deeply influenced by the concept of great men, the masters or leaders, sent by Providence to guide mankind. These people are able to cross the borderline which separates us from the superconscious. Scattered throughout the world, they act like aerials, connecting the ordinary folk to the superconscious. His own gift of *conscious* clairvoyance makes him aspire to be one of such leaders, but he sees the same principle operating in people of genius in moments of inspiration: great artists, scientists, inventors. However, true esoteric knowledge is not being studied sufficiently and is in need of a great synthesis. It is a subject requiring great mental discipline and steady effort, and Ossowiecki deplores the debasement of psychic powers by those who use them without preparation (Ossowiecki, 1933, pp. 71–73).

In their general outline, Ossowiecki's ideas share some common ground with those in circulation today, described using the more modern expressions like "cosmic consciousness," or "emergent properties." However, when one examines the "evidence" put forward to support these ideas, one finds a somewhat embarrassing mixture of stories clearly culled from a variety of popular sources, such as a garbled version of the Tutankhamen curse exemplifying the power of talismans, or inaccurate accounts of inventions owed to flashes of inspiration from the superconscious in totally unprepared individuals. But he rather disarms the more demanding reader by admitting that he has no pretensions to any philosophical knowledge, while his confidence that he was in control of his clairvoyant feats may well have been an important condition of his ability to perform. The introduction to Ossowiecki's autobiography, in which he presents his ideas, might be thus regarded as providing further evidence of his trusting nature and child-like enthusiasm, in the unquestioning acceptance of the wonders of the world.

The Psychic Process

Ossowiecki's philosophical beliefs influenced his interpretation of the processes involved in his psychometric feats, giving them a spiritual and volitional dimension. Comments about what he actually experienced while "crossing the boundaries of consciousness" are few and scattered but they do provide, to some extent, some insight into why he felt these experiences took him into a different dimension.

In a newspaper interview in 1937, he explained one aspect of the "initiation" he underwent when studying esoteric secrets under his chosen Master, Wróbel. Wróbel taught Ossowiecki above all to concentrate thought and willpower. As a lively young man, Stefan found it very difficult to concentrate all his attention on one point, one object. At first he saw nothing, then swirling colored circles, such as one sees when one shuts one's eyes tightly. This would make him dizzy, but his Master thought this was a promising sign. One day he told Ossowiecki to visualize his, Wróbel's, face without looking. This turned out to be very difficult—to visualize a familiar face in every detail and make it come alive. He carried on trying to do this with other faces, then whole persons, and came to feel that during those visualizations he seemed to lose his own personality. It was as if he, his own self, would cease to exist. He understood then that he crossed the border of ordinary human consciousness. His visions were "superconscious," controlled by the exercise of trained will, as opposed to uncontrolled images supplied by the subconscious.

To the question about the role of the objects he needed to hold during psychometric experiments, Ossowiecki's answer was that these were the leads which guided him towards contact with the given entity, alive or not.

During the "visions" themselves, he had no sense, no awareness of being close to the person he was "seeing." He had no sense of "self" at all. He saw a live film, with all the internal and external detail, being aware of what was happening both to the people and inside their minds and souls. That is why tragic visions were so traumatic to him. It was as if he was seeing everything from a bird's-eye view, from somewhere in space, although he could not pinpoint his position—but, finally, he found it impossible to find the appropriate words to describe the experience (*Goniec Warszawski*, 26 April 1937, p. 4).

In his autobiography published four years earlier, Ossowiecki tried to describe this process of creative visualization in the following terms:

> Above all I try to recreate the object in my imagination, and once I have it in front of me as it is in reality, this desensitizes my consciousness, makes it subject to autosuggestion. I try to keep this object in front of my eyes all the time, and once I see the object or the landscape or the man I am interested in, then the form of the object I held before my eyes begins to disappear, and then I feel great psychical satisfaction, moving further and further into the cosmos of the universe.

> Enormous horizons and visions arise before my eyes: it is enough to pick up an object, and instantaneously it transports me to those places on which I am concentrating, and which it has just touched. During moments like this I lose the sense of time and space, my temperature is raised, my heart beats faster and when I look I have the impression that I am already there, in that place. The more effort I make to see, the more blurred becomes the reality which surrounds me [Ossowiecki, 1933, pp. 56–57].

The effect of such powerful visions seems to have been a blurring between the impressions created by them and the surrounding reality, which affected his sense of time and his memory. According to Ossowiecki, it was also easier to carry out the experiments when those present did not think about them, as this avoided "false leads" (Ossowiecki, 1933, p. 57).

In his autobiography and in the interview already referred to, Ossowiecki talks about his ability to see auras:

> I used to see it when I was still a student at the Technological Institute and at the time I could not understand it, I even thought that it must be defective vision. I consulted a number of ophthalmologists in Moscow. One of the very well-known doctors, Professor Gilius, claimed that I suffer from color-blindness. I even started treatment. I was scared, but I felt that they were all wrong and stopped the treatment. Quite accidentally I noticed that when I see the white aura emanating from someone, this person dies on the same day, the next day at the latest; I verified it frequently with the same result [Ossowiecki, 1933, p. 65].

Unfortunately, while there are many accounts of Ossowiecki seeing auras, it has so far proved impossible to find an "uncontaminated" one originating from a reliable source.

One of the "gray areas" in the accounts of Ossowiecki's powers is the power of precognition. Numerous prophecies have been attributed to him, particularly regarding the advent and the outcome of the Second World War, but those close to him denied that he ever predicted great events. Both Boruń and Borzymowski quote the reminiscences of Ossowiecki's widow, according to which the clairvoyant told an artist friend that he "saw" "dreadful things over Warsaw" and a "terrible death" for himself (Boruń & Boruń-Jagodzińska, 1990, p. 41; Borzymowski, 1965, p. 274). However, it must be remembered that 1st August 1944, the day on the morning of which Ossowiecki allegedly reported the vision, was the date of the beginning of Warsaw uprising, due to start at 4 pm. The many first-hand accounts of that day remark on the explosive atmosphere of tension, fear and exultation which seemed to fill the air, and the expectation of terrible events both on a general and personal level was shared by many thousands. It is thus safer to bear in mind Ossowiecki's claim to Jerzy Jacyna, made on a number of occasions, that the "gift" did not work in relation to himself or people very close to him (Jacyna, 70/5). There are, however, examples of specific predictions regarding particular events (e.g. the sex of the forthcoming baby, pp. 33–34, *Experiment 8*), and at least one occasion which might be interpreted as Ossowiecki seeing "in real time" the results of an event which has not yet taken place (p. 121, *Premonition/Precognition? Case 3*).

The Quality of the Evidence

Stefan Ossowiecki truly was a legend in his own time. Many stories endowing him with superhuman powers beyond belief circulated during his lifetime; after his death the legends multiplied and took on a life of their own. This makes it all the more necessary for the researcher to proceed with caution in dealing with the sources.

On the other hand, there is enough good quality evidence from a variety of sources to regard his gift as indeed remarkable.

Most of the accounts of Ossowiecki's powers presented here can be regarded as genuine, either because they were published contemporaneously, or because there are persuasive reasons to regard them as reasonably accurate. All of the experiments involving the French researchers Richet and Geley were published shortly after they took place. The best-documented period of experimentation is 1921–24, up to the death of Geley. Accounts of many of the experiments involving Polish researchers and witnesses were published in Ossowiecki's autobiography which first appeared in 1933; some of them were also published in contemporary Polish publications.

A number of accounts of Ossowiecki's feats were sent to his widow Zofia after the war. She tried to collect all available material about Stefan, and she impartially gave access to the same items to all researchers. Further evidence was provided by people writing to the Polish press in the 1970s, after the publication of reminiscences about Ossowiecki by Jerzy Jacyna in a national weekly. Each account reported in detail in this volume is regarded as deserving consideration on a number of grounds.

The important criteria taken into account are whether the reports are first-hand, how far they could be corroborated, and the degree of reliability gauged from the application of an informal "fantasy-proneness index" to the personalities of the witnesses. There are many stories, some very dramatic, provided by people who did know Ossowiecki but whose accounts seem "too good to be true" and which cannot be corroborated. There are also stories which seem to originate from one source but then become a "personal witness account" from different participants, times and locations, or are repeated as reliable evidence by a succession of authors. Such is the story which tells of a member of a famous banking family flying to Warsaw in 1938, to ask for Ossowiecki's help in finding important family documents, including a vital will, which had mysteriously disappeared. Ossowiecki is supposed to have described to his amazed visitor the exact circumstances of the theft, the appearance of the thief, as well as the current hiding place of the missing documents. On the basis of this information the documents were found, and the grateful banker offered the clairvoyant a fortune as a reward—a fortune which Ossowiecki declined. Unfortunately, although many authors writing at a later date quote it (one of them chastises Ossowiecki for not accepting the reward on behalf of a charity), the earliest appearance of this story cannot at present be traced further back than a Polish émigré newspaper published in 1945. Future researches may find corroboration for it but, because of the uncertainty as to the source, this story, like many other spectacular feats ascribed to Ossowiecki, is not included in this collection.

The range of phenomena considered in detail here falls within the same fairly narrow area. Ossowiecki found missing objects and people, read sealed messages, described places he never visited and guessed the histories of objects hidden from him. The information he gathered about people and their circumstances because of his social position could not have helped in these tasks, and he did not give "readings" or tell fortunes. Some of the evidence may point to his gifts being greater than that of "just" tracking the targets he was given (such as the ability to influence the outcomes of the investigations he was involved in), but the actual objectives of the experiments are quite clearly defined and independent of the experimenters' interpretations. The varying nature of conditions, experimenters and quality of the reporting can thus be regarded as a virtue. The volume and variety of reports mean that, while one group of experiments or experimenters can be accused of a particular bias, no accusation can apply to the whole body of the experiments.

Everything said about Ossowiecki so far, his social position as a gentleman, his self-image as an independent businessman, his belief in the sanctity of his gift and his open, even naïve, nature, all militate against trickery as an explanation for the phenomena. However, regardless of the psychological arguments, the question needs to be examined explicitly and in detail from the practical point of view.

Regarding spontaneous, real-life situations, it has already been noted that Ossowiecki would readily offer to help people in situations where trickery was not possible, such as "tracking" people whose fate was unknown and unknowable at the time. While it is impossible to determine his success record in this area, the confidence with which he undertook such tasks testifies to his genuine belief in the powers at his disposal. We do not have enough information to determine his overall success rate, and it is well known that enthusiastic sitters often read personal meanings into general statements applicable to anybody. However, when one examines the factual content of some of the well-corroborated accounts presented here, this explanation does not seem adequate.

Locating missing objects is another category of spontaneous events, one where trickery cannot be ruled out *a priori*. The obvious explanation (and one which could not be ruled out if the evidence was limited to a few cases of the same kind) would be that of having accomplices who arrange for the objects to disappear and turn up in agreed locations. The problem with this explanation is the sheer variety of incidents and participants, largely caused by Ossowiecki's special position in Warsaw society. Once his fame had spread, people would activate whatever contacts they could to obtain the clairvoyant's help, and "Stefanek" would always do his best to indulge his friends and his friends' friends. Whatever the shortcomings in the recording of such incidents, their spontaneity precludes the possibility of their being pre-arranged.

When we come to the experiments specifically set up to test Ossowiecki's powers, different criteria apply. In this context, it is useful to draw on a discussion of the possible tricks employed by psychic claimants presented in a book by Marks and Kammann (1980) which spells out the obvious pitfalls an investigator needs to avoid.

In experiments involving "viewing" through a sealed envelope, it is clearly unsatisfactory to have the drawing/writing done in the presence of the psychic, since this does not eliminate the possibility of clues being supplied by observing the movement of the pen or the sound of pen on paper, even if precautions are taken to avoid this. Most controlled experiments of this type done with Ossowiecki use sealed envelopes prepared beforehand. Where the experimenters arranged for the targets to be prepared by other people and presented at random, the possibility of Ossowiecki guessing the target by "fishing" for information is also precluded.

In order to guard against the possibility of the target being seen through an envelope stretched through handling, the specimens would be folded over, wrapped in additional sheets and/or placed in a number of envelopes, the outer one being marked in such a way as to make any attempts at unsealing it detectable. Ossowiecki would often handle the envelope for prolonged periods, and while it is possible, even likely, that at times the experimenters' attention may have been distracted away from him, they record the state of the envelope after the "viewing" is completed.

The success of the famous experiment at the International Psychical Research Conference in Warsaw in 1923, for which E.J. Dingwall produced the target (pp. 62–65), forced the latter to consider the complicity of the other investigator involved, Schrenck-Notzing, as the only alternative to the paranormal interpretation. Indeed, the *ad hominem* argument, which places inordinate value on the evidence of witnesses mainly because of their social or academic standing, is one to guard against. On the other hand, applied in reverse and to its logical conclusion, the same argument makes it impossible to trust any evidence, regardless of its source, since one can always question the integrity of those involved in the collection and interpretation of the data.

It is thus valid to examine the credentials of the experimenters and the witnesses, without attaching too much importance to their status but paying careful attention to such qualities as willingness to believe, objectivity and ability to observe and report without embellishment. As has been noted before, the "experiments" presented here have been selected partially on this basis, which means that preference is at times given to accounts of "outsiders" instead of those of people who were Ossowiecki's friends. The outsiders also usually have a different emotional commitment to the "experiment" from psychical researchers, since their prime consideration is finding a solution to their problem.

The credentials of Geley and Richet, who were introduced to Ossowiecki in April 1921, are discussed elsewhere (pp. 26, 175 and 177). Some of the Polish researchers, such as Stefan Rzewuski and Prosper Szmurło, seem, judging from the material published in *Zagadnienia Metapsychiczne*, to have spent a lot of their time coming up with normal explanations for "paranormal" reports from overenthusiastic readers, exposing fraud, investigating psychic claimants with modest psychic ability or none at all, or trying to improve the quality of the experiments.

A witness whose name appears frequently on the reports of spontaneous experiments is Olgierd Missuna. He was related to Ossowiecki, being a grandson of Ossowiecki's mother from her second marriage. A lawyer by profession, he was a State Prosecutor from 1930. Since this function in Poland's legal system of the time involved working closely with the police, investigating criminal cases and securing evidence, he was well-equipped to observe and judge the quality of the evidence.

In the 1960s he published a number of books recalling various cases he was involved in, which demonstrate a great deal of level-headedness and a good understanding of human nature. We are also indebted to him for the only available account of Ossowiecki's psychokinetic powers.

Missuna witnessed one of Ossowiecki's psychokinetic séances as a small boy in Russia in 1913, in a manor house. Various members of the Ossowiecki, Jacyna, Krieger and Missuna families and their friends were present. The séance seems to have taken place in an enormous hall, perhaps a ballroom. Before the séance all the furniture and carpets were removed, which caused some delay and annoyed the guests. The audience stood along the walls, a heavy chair was placed in the middle of the room, and Ossowiecki was tied to the chair by experts, both arms and legs. In the corner of the room there was one object left—a heavy piano. This was the object the young psychic was to move by psychokinesis.

Unfortunately, after witnesses verified that Ossowiecki was properly tied down, everyone had to leave the room in total silence. He was left alone with the piano, which was 10 m away. Five minutes later people were asked back. Ossowiecki was still in his chair, pale with effort, and the piano stood next to him. Although the above account shows a disappointing lack of reliable evidence of paranormality, it does demonstrate a commendable lack of creativity on the part of the witness.

While it is inevitable that some giving away of clues, subjective validation and misreporting would have occurred at times, when there were so many witnesses under such variety of conditions, the actual reproductions of drawings and written text, or precise locations of missing objects, cannot be subject to such accusations. It is a great pity, however, that Ossowiecki's actual mentation in the spontaneous cases is not, in the majority of cases, subjected to the kind of statement-by-statement analysis demonstrated in the Besterman experiment (pp. 65–70). It would be of great interest to investigate in detail Ossowiecki's visualizations and find out just how specific and accurate they were. Ossowiecki himself had no doubt that he clairvoyantly transported himself to the appropriate destination, and many of his mentations sound very real and dramatic. Since on many such occasions he successfully "viewed" the target, it would perhaps help us gain some understanding of the processes involved to know just how accurate the details of his visualizations were. While witnesses often say that his descriptions totally corresponded to reality, it is difficult to accept such claims without analyzing the statements in detail.

It is also worthwhile to note that a great many of the targets presented to Ossowiecki are highly individualized, and could not be guessed by chance, as would be the case with population stereotypes (a house, a tree, a boat, etc.*).

Descriptions of cases where Ossowiecki gets it wrong are rare. Lack of success is reported by researchers where it occurs; however, it is very likely that selective reporting is at play where informal experiments are concerned, and it is impossible to say just what the proportion would be. One of the sources quotes a story of Ossowiecki spontaneously telling a young woman that she had three children and

---

Marks & Kammann (1980, p. 218) report an ESP experiment with a control group and a set of non-stereotypical targets, where there were four target matches out of 1,642 trials.

was exceptionally happy in her marriage, with a husband who would live long, when in fact she was a widow (Jacyna, 14/2/71). There are also two anecdotal cases quoted by Józef Marcinkowski, a practicing clairvoyant himself,* involving missing valuable objects where the author claims to have corrected Ossowiecki's mistaken diagnosis as to the identity of the thief. However, in neither case did Ossowiecki point to a particular person; rather, it was the case of the people involved drawing their own conclusions on the basis of his descriptions. In any case, since for most of the time we are dealing with real-life situations, and Ossowiecki's "hits" are not the kind one experiences by chance however long the run, statistical analysis of the kind employed in large scale studies does not seem to have a place here.

There are, however, at least two situations where "control groups" were provided. One is the experiment where the other participants write down their impressions of the sealed target (pp. 38–39, *Experiment 2*); the other is the Jonky experiment (pp. 80–84), where a total of 17 clairvoyants tried to divine the contents of a package which were unknown to anyone living. In neither case was the performance of the control groups comparable to that of Ossowiecki.

Like many other psychics and psychic claimants, Ossowiecki was affected by the atmosphere in which he was performing. Sometimes, when in the mood, he would ask for an experiment to be performed; at other times he would try to avoid it or the people who wanted to be involved. The attitude of some researchers, especially during the earlier days, has been to dismiss the claims of "negative vibes" as excuses or ways of maneuvering the experimenters into introducing conditions which make cheating possible. This attitude sometimes seems reminiscent of Dickens's novel *David Copperfield*, where David's stepfather is angered by David's perverse reluctance to learn his lessons in spite of the frequent beatings. It would appear obvious that most people behave and perform differently when faced with a hostile as opposed to a friendly environment, whether at a political meeting, a stage performance, a classroom or a dinner party. Fortunately, modern researchers no longer expect psychic claimants to be immune to such influences and try to create a favorable environment for their experiments without compromising the control conditions. This seems to have been the approach of the researchers working with Ossowiecki, although they did not always provide a formal procedure protocol.

It is also the case that Ossowiecki sometimes deliberately withheld information or told lies. This he did for compassionate reasons: to give the perceived offender a second chance, or to spare the relatives the visions of horrific deaths which came to him (Jacyna, 1/71). Such cases obviously lose a lot of their evidential value but they are infrequent and his attitude is natural and understandable. However, for the most part he told the truth as he saw it, and the excerpt from a letter given below describes what was probably a fairly typical reading among the many he gave during the war :

He was a practicing clairvoyant, using the pseudonym Akhar Jussuf Mustafa, whose memoirs were published in 1976. They present a realistic and very skeptical account of the psychic scene from the point of view of a young man using human gullibility as he struggles to survive.

Just imagine, we even went to see him with Maga [the correspondent's sister]. It must have been 1940. We were both in love, and our boyfriends had been transported by the Germans. It so happens that a friend of my Dad knew Ossowiecki well. We begged Dad to ask Ossowiecki through his friend to agree to see us, to find out if our boyfriends were alive. Ossowiecki agreed. It was somewhere in the center [of Warsaw], but I cannot remember exactly where: an elegant apartment, an elderly butler opened the door. Ossowiecki—an elderly gentleman—received us with a smile. He took the—I don't remember photographs or letters—I think photographs, and said with the same smile "don't worry, they are both alive." That was the end of our visit. After two or three years, when it was well established that Maga's love (who was our cousin) was in the camp in Mathausen-Gossen, and Maga even managed to establish contact with him, she received a telegram notifying her of his death. She was shattered by this news, and some people tried to comfort her by saying that it may be a mistake, as such errors did happen from time to time. Maga asked through Dad again and Ossowiecki agreed [to see her]. When she came to Ossowiecki she gave him the photograph and asked if the subject was alive. Ossowiecki said to her: "but you have a telegram in your handbag, notifying you of his death" [which was true]. She then explained that she had hoped the news was a mistake, but Ossowiecki told her it was the truth.*

---

*The account quoted here comes from a letter written in 1998 to the third author's (ZW) mother by a close friend, also known to ZW, who had learned about ZW's research on Ossowiecki. While the time gap is considerable, it is consistent with other reports published at earlier times and conveys the atmosphere of these interviews. It is of course impossible to establish how much information may have been given away by the intermediary, but in other circumstances Ossowiecki supplied information unknown to anyone. Another first-hand unsolicited account from a trustworthy source, received through simply telling friends about the research, involves Ossowiecki telling ZW's informant that her sister, who was arrested and disappeared, was alive in Ravensbrück. This was confirmed at a later date.

2

The Formal Experiments

The earliest recorded experiments in clairvoyance with Ossowiecki are those conducted with none other than Marshal Piłsudski, the Polish head of state. It is, however, with the arrival in Warsaw of two eminent French researchers, Dr. Gustave Geley and professor Charles Richet, Nobel prize-winning physiologist, that we see the start of the systematic investigation on which his solid reputation rests today. Geley was a physician who had turned his considerable talents to the field of psychical research and become both the Director of the Institut Métapsychique International (IMI) in Paris and the editor of its journal, the *Revue Métapsychique* (RM). He later wrote two books of outstanding interest, *Clairvoyance and Materialization*, in which some of his work with Ossowiecki was described, and the more theoretical *From the Unconscious to the Conscious*. Initially he worked closely with Richet, though later he was the principal experimenter, devising ever more imaginative protocols aimed at distinguishing and defining the processes which might be responsible for the Ossowiecki phenomenon. One of the concerns shared by most of the researchers is that of excluding the possibility of telepathy coming into play, and some experiments are designed with this in mind.

The following reports from the RM are presented in the order in which they appeared (approximately in date order) so that the reader can share the perspectives of the IMI researchers as they progressed through the stages of amazement, verification, conviction and finally to various attempts at elucidation. Geley's habit of switching from retrospective narration to the immediacy of the present tense is preserved in all its ungrammatical enthusiasm.

It should also be noted that the experiments often take place in informal settings, with interruptions for meals, visitors and other engagements. In view of the limited time Ossowiecki could devote to the researchers, and his status as a friend and an equal, this is hardly surprising.

A noticeable point is that the researchers are sometimes anxious to avoid boring the readers; at one stage, Geley remarks that he carried out more experiments than he thinks his readers will wish to hear related. Modern researchers in pursuit of truth are more often heard to complain that the report does not tell them nearly enough.

In one important respect Geley was untypical of the IMI researchers, in that he was anti-materialist and inclined to a belief in immortality. He envisaged the gradual coming to consciousness of those hidden depths of the mind that make up the unconscious. Unfortunately his hope or expectation that lucidity might become more prevalent has not so far been supported by subsequent developments. On the evolutionary scale it is, however, early days.

We start in April and May, 1921, when Geley, Richet and Dr. Geo-Lange, a scientist who was also skilled in conjuring, took the first steps toward verifying the seemingly incredible stories told about Ossowiecki. At this stage Ossowiecki was cautiously described by Geley as M.O., perhaps in deference to his professional status as a chemical engineer and businessman, but in later reports Geley must have realized that Ossowiecki's psychic powers were so very well known in Poland that there was no need for his identity to be kept confidential.

Early Experiments by Geley and Richet

Experiment series 1 April–May 1921 [related by Geley]

During our unforgettable stay in Warsaw we witnessed the truly astonishing faculties of M. Ossowiecki.

Ossowiecki, an engineer and industrialist, a man leading a very active life, has since early childhood had the gift of clairvoyance.

This faculty, which we hope soon to study in all its aspects, thanks to M. Ossowiecki's unbounded co-operation and dedication, manifests in different ways.

For the moment we shall leave aside the astounding stories told by sincere witnesses, and we shall content ourselves with reporting the main experiments carried out by Prof. Richet, M. Geo-Lange and myself.

After a private dinner where we had had the pleasure of meeting M. Ossowiecki for the first time he invited us to try an experiment. He suggested reading a sealed letter.

I was sitting about three meters away from the clairvoyant, at the other end of the table. I took a letter from my pocket and folded it so as to place the signature on the inside; I put it in an envelope, I sealed it up and handed it to M. Ossowiecki, who took it in his hand.

With some difficulty he told me the approximate contents of the letter. But he made some mistakes, describing the writer of the letter as "an elegant man, handsome, feminine in character" when the writer was in fact a woman. On the other hand, he read with total accuracy the first five letters of the signature, and said that there were four more letters that he could not read. The total number of letters was correct.

The experiment was encouraging. M. Géo-Lange, sitting opposite me, very far from the clairvoyant, wrote on a piece of paper the following sentence, in English:

I consider you are wonderful.

It is impossible for the clairvoyant by normal means to have had any knowledge of what was written on this paper, which was immediately folded and put in an envelope, which was stuck down.

M. Ossowiecki, kneading the envelope in his hand, walked a few steps up and down the room, and said, "It's in English! I can't read it, I don't know any English."

M. Géo-Lange exclaimed, "That's marvelous."

M. Ossowiecki continued, "I see one isolated letter, then a word of eight letters that starts CON, then two short words, then a long word that is like Vendredi, but it can't be vendredi because it's English."

The second session was conducted by Prof. Richet, alone in his hotel room, next day. Taking all necessary precautions not to be seen, the Professor wrote the following sentence, which he put into a closed envelope. "Never does the sea look grander than when it is calm. Its furies diminish it."

Here is the professor's written note: Ossowiecki said: "I see a lot of water!" (I said: very good!) "It's something difficult. It's not a question, it's an idea of yours that you've taken up." (I said: very, very good.) "The sea was never so grand as … I can't grasp this whole thing." (I say: it's perfect, it's wonderful.) "The sea has such grandeur apart from its movement."

The professor then wrote a four digit number, which was read without any error (as ever, it was put into a closed envelope).

The professor had prepared two sealed up envelopes, identical in appearance, and he had put in each of them a letter he had just received. He took one at random from his pocket and handed it to M. Ossowiecki. But he was too tired, said nothing definite and asked the professor to defer the experiment. The professor, who had to leave the next day, handed the letter to me, without telling me what it contained.

The third session, carried out by me, alone, at M. Ossowiecki's residence, on 1st May 1921.

First experiment: I gave the clairvoyant the sealed letter that Prof. Richet had left with me. Here are the words I noted down as he spoke them, promptly and without hesitation:

"There is talk about a lady called Berger. It's a gentleman 50 years of age who wrote this letter, which is a reply to a letter from Prof. Richet. This letter does not come from Paris; it comes from a place near the sea. It's about various matters. It's an invitation. There is something about this lady called Berger. She is 33 years of age. She is married. I can't read this. It was written very quickly, it's confused, it digresses. It's a musical man who wrote it."

In this long monologue, there was just one mistake: "A place near the sea." All the rest is correct: it is an invitation to give lectures on behalf of various societies. It says "you will be Mrs. Berger's guest of honor." The letter includes the words "[written] in great haste" It is very badly written and rather incoherent. The age and characteristics of Mr. and Mrs. Berger are correct.

Second experiment: I sit facing the clairvoyant. Between us is a very wide rectangular table. There is no mirror and there are no reflective surfaces behind me.

I write on a card, under the table, without moving my arm (supported by a book resting on my knees). "Nothing is more stirring than the muezzins' call to prayer." I put the card in a large, opaque envelope (still under the table). I stick down the envelope and give it to Ossowiecki, who takes it in his hand and rubs it. Here is what he said:

"It's not a question. These are your ideas. There is something…. A feeling of prayer, something very deep … a call…. From men who are killed, wounded … no, it's not that…. Something affecting, emotional."

Then, straight off, the clairvoyant said:

"Nothing is more moving than the call to prayer; nothing in life is more tender, that moves the soul like prayer…. Towards … what … who … it is a certain caste of men, mazzi … madz … a caste … I can't see any more."

These experiments, very simple, seem to us conclusive. In a series of sessions to take place soon at the Institute, we shall try to study some of the theoretical problems that arise from M. Ossowiecki's mysterious and admirable faculties.

[RM 1921 No.5]

These were early days, and the only test carried out under truly rigorous conditions was due to Richet having had to leave Warsaw, so that the content of his prepared letter was unknown to Geley, the experimenter present at the time.

While the possibility of cueing cannot be excluded in some cases (as, for example, in this last test, when Ossowiecki may well have divined from Geley's demeanor that the target sentence had nothing to do with men being killed or wounded), it would be far fetched to posit that the clairvoyant was able to pick up the English sentence by cues from Géo-Lange.

In general Ossowiecki responded more immediately to visual targets and factual statements; so that these initial tests, in which ideas starting "Never is the sea grander...' and 'Nothing is more stirring..." were very difficult targets for him.

In the next group of experiments a lot of thought went into planning tests under varied conditions, most of them excluding any possibility of cueing.

Experiment series 2—September 1921 [experimenter: Geley]

New experiments in clairvoyance with M. l'Ingénieur Stefan Ossowiecki
[The French title has been left intact, as there is no way of conveying in English the respect implied by according Ossowiecki his title of Chartered Engineer]

I tendered to M. Ossowiecki a series of documents, all prepared in advance, in his absence. These documents consisted of sealed up envelopes each containing a paper prepared for clairvoyant reading. Each specimen was itself folded over and wrapped in several sheets of opaque paper. So it was impossible for anyone to know what was there by normal means.

In one case, in fact, the target paper was not in an envelope, but was encased in a thick lead pipe.

Among the documents submitted to M. Ossowiecki, some were prepared by me; the others had been given to me by friends of mine who were not acquainted with the clairvoyant, and I was not aware of their content.

The experiments took place in quite varied conditions. M. Ossowiecki, a very busy man, could not give me regular sessions. So I seized any opportunity to meet with him, whether at the house of mutual friends, or at a restaurant, or at a materialization séance, to offer him one of the sealed targets.

While an experiment was in train I never let the clairvoyant out of my sight. He would take the envelope in his hand, concentrate his thoughts, walk up and down the room, then, after 5, or 10 or 15 minutes, he would usually tell me the exact contents.

He took longer to become aware of the paper contained in the lead pipe; he needed two sittings, and he had to make considerable efforts.

Out of 10 experiments I obtained—
Eight complete successes,
One incomplete success.
One failure.

I shall first of all relate a full report of the experimental procedure and results, in chronological order; then I shall add some brief remarks about M. Ossowiecki's mysterious gift.

Experiment 1: 12th September, c. 11 p. m.

Following a private dinner party with some mutual friends, I offered M. Ossowiecki, in the presence of those same people, the collection of envelopes prepared in advance that I had brought with me.

There are eight sealed up envelopes, two of which were made up by me, and I know their contents; one is from M. [René] Sudre, one from M. Magnin and four from Mme. Geley. I know nothing at all about the contents of these six envelopes.

I offer the envelopes to the clairvoyant; he takes one, apparently without making any deliberate choice. I know that it is either the one from M. Sudre or from M. Magnin, because the two envelopes are different from the others. But that is all I know. M. Ossowiecki takes the envelope in his hand. He strides across the room. He sits down, gets up again. He makes a visible effort to think. Finally he says the following words, which I write down as he speaks.

"It's very short ... just a few words."
(A few minutes of silence)
"This has been written by a man."
(Short silence)
"It is question about Poland."
(Very short silence)
"It consists of good wishes." [Ce sont des souhaits'.]
(Very short silence)
"That's all. It's not signed."

I open the envelope and, from a sheet of paper folded twice over (the writing folded inside) I read out:

"Best of luck at Warsaw." [Bon succès à Varsovie.]

I may say that I was expecting something quite different from this simple good wish. This letter was the one supplied by M. Magnin.

***

Experiment 2: 14th September 1921, chez Prince Lubomirski, 6 p. m.

After a materialization séance with [Jan] Guzik,* I offered the collection of letters that I had brought with me to M. Ossowiecki. He took an envelope, which I recognized as being from M. Sudre. I had no idea of its contents.

Here are the contents of the target envelope, which was opened immediately after completion of the test, and the words spoken by M. Ossowiecki, written down as he said them.

TARGET LETTER:
Man is but a reed, the weakest thing in nature, but he is a thinking reed.
WORDS SPOKEN BY M. OSSOWIECKI:
"This is about humanity; or rather about man.
"He is the stupidest of creatures. It is something about man. I have an impression of stupidity. It's a proverb. These are the ideas of one of the most important men of the past. I should say Pascal. Man is weak; a weak reed, but ... weakness ... and also the most pensive reed" (sic) [Ossowiecki used the word "pensif," and Geley remarked in a footnote that he obviously meant "pensant." To use an English equivalent, one could say that Ossowiecki obviously meant "thinking"].

These first two experiments tell us two things:

1. I have said that I had absolutely no idea of the contents of the target material that had been lodged with me by M. Magnin and M. Sudre. The clairvoyant was therefore not able to acquire his knowledge by reading my thoughts. Further, since my colleagues are quite unknown to M. Ossowiecki, it is very difficult to envisage any mind to mind communication as the origin of his cognition.

2. These two experiments seem moreover to show that, in M. Ossowiecki's case, there is no question of his "seeing" through opaque material. In fact, the clairvoyant often has a clear idea of the contents of the envelopes, but this idea does not precisely conform to the written text. His interpretations are remarkably

---

**Jan Guzik was a professional psychical medium, frequently caught cheating.*

close, but nevertheless there are approximations or errors. This duality of M. Ossowiecki's clairvoyance is confirmed in the following experiments.

***

Experiment 3: 21st September Chez Prince Lubomirski, in the same conditions as in experiment no. 2

I recognize the envelope as containing one of the two letters prepared by me. I did not know which of the two it was. I opened it up only after M. Ossowiecki had finished speaking.

TARGET MATERIAL
1. An oriental landscape; some camels.
2. [drawing of a fish, facing right]
3. The ringing of bells.
4. The scent of Mimosa.
5. Long live Poland!

WORDS SPOKEN BY M. OSSOWIECKI
"This thing, it's long.

"This was written by a man. It's chaotic! It's so chaotic I can't grasp it! It's four or five ideas, a broth of ideas!

"Something of a certain size. Something that swims. I see some work on a fish that reminds me of a corassin [a very large Polish fish]. It's not writing, but there is a fish. What's the connection between this fish and Poland? I can't understand it. It's an exclamation: Long live Poland!

"Why Poland?

"I smell something, perfume, delicious perfume." (M. Ossowiecki seems to breathe in these scents.)

"There is also something to do with nature.

"There is one more thing, three things in this broth. I see the fish, I am going to draw it." (He makes the drawing shown below.) "Why these scents?

"There is a numbering system, 1st, 2nd, 3rd, 4th, 5th. After the No. 2 there is nothing written.

"Something to do with nature ... I don't see any more."

To sum up, out of the five different ideas comprising this target, M. Ossowiecki fully grasped those behind Nos. 2, 4 and 5. He perceived nothing for No. 2, and had a very incomplete idea of No. 1.

He had a clear, dominant and persistent notion of fish; but, curiously enough, his drawing is not at all like mine. His fish is wide across and looks to the left. Mine was long in the body and looked to the right. For target No. 3, he was aware of delicious perfumes, without specifying that it was mimosa that was in question. The idea behind No. 5 was given in its entirety.

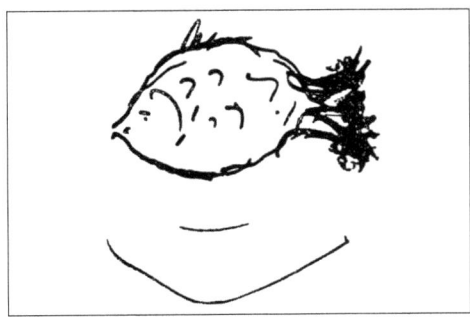 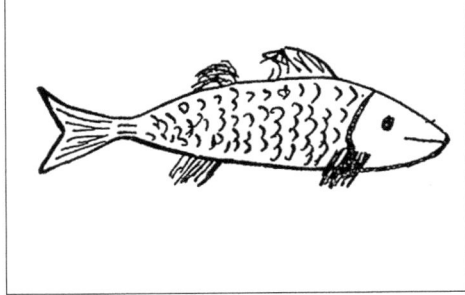

Left: **Drawing by Ossowiecki.** *Right:* **Drawing by Geley.**

During the whole of the evening that we spent together M. Ossowiecki remained obsessed by the drawing of the fish.

***

Experiments 4, 5 and 6
While the International Conference on Medicine at Warsaw was in progress, a certain number of conference delegates who had heard about M. Ossowiecki's gift asked for an opportunity to test him.

Eight of them accepted an invitation from Prince S. Lubomirski, and came together in his drawing room one evening (I forgot to make a note of the date) around 1700 hours.

M. Ossowiecki, sensitive to atmosphere like all psychics, seemed agitated at being in the midst of this bevy of doctors. He definitely had "the jitters." That no doubt accounts for the part failure of the 4th experiment, and the complete failure of the 5th.

Dr. Piery, from Lyon, handed M. Ossowiecki an enveloped target paper, which he had prepared while by himself in an adjoining room. The paper contained, as we saw after the experiment:

China is a charming country.

M. Ossowiecki had a lot of trouble. It was only after some 10 minutes that he said:

"It's very short.

"It's not a question; but it is your opinion.

"It's on the subject of Poland.

"Poland is a charming country."

M. Ossowiecki, questioned about the cause of this confusion between Poland and China, attributed it to his being put off in the presence of this "medical jury" and also to his having allowed his conscious thoughts to intervene instead of simply relying as he usually did on his intuition alone. He had a clear impression of "is a charming country" and, pondering on that, thought that it must apply to Poland.

M. Ossowiecki then went with Dr. Bergeret, from Paris, into an adjoining room. Dr. Bergeret gave him a sealed envelope. He did not tell us what this envelope contained. But he said simply that M. Ossowiecki had got it entirely wrong.

After this setback, Dr. Gliksman, from Warsaw, in the same conditions as Dr. Bergeret prepared a target paper enclosed in a sealed envelope. Just at the moment when he was going to give it to M. Ossowiecki, the clairvoyant said: "Keep your letter, and hold it in your hand." He then placed his right hand on the hand of Dr. Gliksman, who went on holding the document, and, speaking rapidly, said:

"It's about love. It's about the child. It's about worldly love. Like the Bohemian child … in the main."

The target paper read: *Love is a Bohemian child.*

***

Experiment 7, 23rd and 24th September
Following dinner at a restaurant I gave M. Ossowiecki one of the letters that Mme. Geley had prepared for him, contents unknown to me. He said:

"This is a letter from a lady. It's your wife. It consists of compliments and an invitation. I'll tell you more exactly tomorrow. You keep this letter."

The next day, at Prince Lubomirski's, I gave it to him again. Here are its contents and the record of M. Ossowiecki's words:

MME GELEY'S TARGET LETTER
Monsieur Ossowiecki

Monsieur

I congratulate you on possessing such marvelous gifts, and I cordially thank you for giving the Doctor an opportunity to study you.

I hope that you will soon give us the pleasure of coming to see us in Paris.

Meanwhile please accept with my compliments my sincere good wishes.

Yours sincerely

A. Geley

Paris, 22nd August 1921

M. OSSOWIECKI'S REMARKS

"A lady … years of age (here Mme. Geley's exact age) wrote this letter.

"The letter is addressed to me. It is an affectionate sort of letter. It expresses her feelings of admiration and good wishes.

"One of her daughters was at her side while she was writing. It was written on the second floor. The lady looks tired.

"She wrote this in the office where there are chairs covered in dark leather.

"The letter was written on 22nd August. This lady, in her admiration for me, is happy to know me, and expresses the hope that she will see me soon. The letter was written between 4 and 5 o'clock in the evening."

Everything was exactly right, except for the chairs covered in dark leather. These chairs exist, though in an adjoining room. But it is to be noted that Mme. Geley had spent the greater part of the day in that room. The letter was indeed written between 4 and 5 p. m. on 22nd August, on the second floor, in the presence of one of my daughters.

Mme. Geley was in fact very tired that day.

***

Experiment 8: 25th September 1921, at 2300 hours, chez friends.

M. Sudre had sent me a new sealed letter, contents unknown to me. He had simply warned me to expect a novel sort of experiment. I gave the letter to M. Ossowiecki. After 10 minutes, M. Ossowiecki, who had been squeezing the letter in his hand, said:

"This is about me. It is someone who wants to get to know me." Long silence, fidgeting. M. Ossowiecki makes intense efforts. He starts again after 10–15 minutes.

'It's very difficult today. There is something very…. My vision is obstructed because I have the impression that it's printed.

"I was wrong just now. It's not about me; but the man who prepared it was thinking about me when he wrote it, and hence my mistake. He wants to try a special test. He wants to see if I can read this printed material. I can't read things that are printed."*

This took place (the preparation of the letter) at 6 or 7 o'clock in the evening. He was sitting at a table. There was a woman at his side.

"It's printed in tiny little letters."

I unsealed the envelope and found a leaf torn from a book and on which were printed, in very small print, some verses. I then said to M. Ossowiecki, "Describe the man and the woman you saw."

M. Ossowiecki said: "It's a second floor, on the left. He has no beard but has a little moustache. It's a man of 38–40 years of age, rather slim, delicate features. He is not bald. He has a parting in his hair.

"She is large, but not very tall. She is not blonde. She talks a lot. It is she who gave him the idea for this test. They have two children, a boy and a girl."

---

*The inability to read print is very curious given the visual quality of Ossowiecki's clairvoyance, and it must be said that later in life he said that he had learned to read it. He had the same inhibition about typescript.

I say, "All that is exactly right, except that there is only one child, a daughter; the lady is large because she is soon to give birth."

M. Ossowiecki exclaims vigorously "It's a boy, I'm sure of that. You can write and tell them."

In fact, Mme. Sudre had a baby boy three days later. She got my letter, posted on 26th, the day after her confinement.

***

Experiment 9: 27th September, at 1800 hours, at Prince Lubomirski's
I gave M. Ossowiecki the second of the two letters that I had prepared, and of which I therefore knew the contents, which were:

An elephant, which was bathing in the Ganges, was attacked by a crocodile, which bit off its trunk.

To see if my conscious thought could influence M. Ossowiecki's clairvoyance I made a strenuous effort to imagine the scene described. The result was just the opposite. M. Ossowiecki experienced obvious difficulty: he walked up and down, very agitated, and it was only after about 20 minutes that he said:

"I have the impression that I am in a zoological garden. There is a struggle. I have the impression of a zoological garden. I see a big animal. It's an elephant. Is this elephant not in the water? I see it swimming in the water. There is an incident to do with its trunk. I see blood."

At that point M. Ossowiecki, very fatigued and agitated, asks me, "Is there anything else?"

I reply, "It's very good, but it's not complete." M. Ossowiecki cries, "Wait! Isn't it wounded in the trunk?" I say, "Very good!" and I add, "You said that there was a struggle, that's very good." M. Ossowiecki interrupted me and exclaimed, "Yes, with a crocodile!"

Experiment 10
This last experiment is the one that was made with the lead pipe. This idea and the procedure for carrying it out came from Count Guy du Bourg de Bozas. He had a length of 3 cm lead pipe made up. He asked one of our friends, M. Stanislas de Jelski, to get a third person, a lady who was leaving Warsaw the same day, to put a letter inside it, to be kept secret from all of us. Then he had the opening soldered and gave it to me.

The first attempt at a test took place on 28th September, in a restaurant, after a heavy meal. This is what M. Ossowiecki said:

"This was written by a lady.

"It is something about nature, in relation to man and feeling. He is at the center of creation. This was written in very unusual circumstances."

I asked the clairvoyant, "Shall we unseal the pipe?" He replied, "No, wait, I am not satisfied. I should like to have another session."

This second session took place chez Prince Lubomirski, at 6 p. m. on 30th September, in the presence of [five other named persons]. With a lot of initial effort but then more readily M. Ossowiecki said:

"Creation ... the whole creation ... nature." (long silence)

"It's about a powerful man. It's the feeling of the people that he is one of the great men of the century.

"I can't understand. I see two things: there is something written, written by a woman; and there is a drawing.

"The drawing shows a man who has large moustaches and large eyebrows, but no nose.

"He is in military uniform.

"He looks like Piłsudski.

"The writing is in French. It says: 'This man, he is afraid of nothing, not afraid of anything political or of any ideas ... like a knight.'"

Then the lead pipe (see photograph, p. 58) is cut open, in the presence of the witnesses. I take out the paper and unfold it. It contains a sketch drawing of Marshal Piłsudski, with large moustaches, large eyebrows, no nose drawn, in military uniform.

Under the drawing is written: Le chevalier sans peur et sans reproche [The perfect gentle knight; literally translated: The knight without fear and without reproach].

What theoretical conclusions can we draw from these facts?

In this summing up we take account not only of these last experiments but also of the first ones carried out last April by Prof. Richet and myself (See RM No. 5).

Target: drawing of Marshal Piłsudski.

The first question that presents itself is the following:

Do our experiments demonstrate the reality of M. Stefan Ossowiecki's gift of clairvoyance? The only possible answer has to be an unequivocal "Yes."

The facts that we have related are simple and very convincing, and they leave no room for deception or illusion.

The sessions took place in full light of day. All the precautions were taken to ensure that there could be no way of gaining knowledge of the target material by normal sensory means.

During the whole duration of the experiment the clairvoyant was never out of sight. He never looked at the sealed envelope; he held it in his clenched hand. When his clairvoyant reading is finished, the experimenters unseal the envelope themselves after confirming that it is intact.

Further, in our last ten experiments the targets were all prepared out of M. Ossowiecki's presence. There can therefore be no grounds for suspecting a reading based on some sort of visual hyperaesthesia or by analysis of gestures made by the writer or clues from his physiognomy etc.

Moreover, the clarity of the results obtained from sessions involving multiple tests and varied experimental procedures totally rules out any hypothesis of chance coincidence.

The reality of M. Ossowiecki's gift of clairvoyance is therefore absolutely certain.

Finally let us emphasize that these experiments can be repeated at will and that they succeed almost invariably. The tiresome objection, repeated incessantly, that paranormal phenomena are not scientific because they cannot be reproduced at will, is therefore completely refuted so far as M. Ossowiecki's gift is concerned.

Geley then discusses the results:

Let us now try to interpret this gift, so far as it may be possible.
    The first idea that comes to mind is the hypothesis of eyeless reading through opaque bodies.
    If one takes into account the details of our experiments it will follow that this hypothesis does not fit the facts.

M. Ossowiecki grasps the ideas contained in the written material very well, but he never reads the text word for word.

There are divergences between the text of the documents and his words, showing that it is not a case of reading by some supernormal process.

To cite just one example, let us take experiment No. 3.

M. Ossowiecki has the idea of a fish, or a drawing representing a fish. He is sure of that. But he does not see the drawing on which his idea is based. He sees it so little that he himself draws a completely different fish.

Note however that in one of the April sessions M. Ossowiecki was not able to "read" words written in English. We have there a curious contradiction; for if the clairvoyant has the concept of the idea rather than sight of the graphic expression of the idea, he ought to have had cognition of the letter written in English as easily as of a letter in French.

That is a mystery that remains to be elucidated. Nevertheless I believe that from the totality of the observed facts we can draw the general conclusion that it is not a case of M. Ossowiecki simply reading through opaque materials.

Is it a case of thought-reading or mind-to-mind communication?

This is obviously the most attractive hypothesis: the one that most researchers will encounter. But let us take a closer look and we shall see that it presents some serious drawbacks.

First of all, it is certainly not a case of reading conscious minds.

M. Ossowiecki was able to "read" just as easily text unknown to me as those of which I was aware. More than that, the target he "read" with the greatest difficulty was in fact the one in experiment No. 9 [the struggle between elephant and crocodile]. I remember that I concentrated my thoughts strenuously on the scene described. Well, this mental effort of mind only served to obstruct his. [In a footnote Geley comments, "During the sessions M. Ossowiecki would often say 'Talk! Don't think!'"]

If it is a case of thought reading, it must be said that the limitations of time, space, and a relationship or lack of relationship with the target donor have no importance. M. Ossowiecki's gift operates as powerfully whether it is something written by me, by someone closely connected with me (Mme. Geley) or by two friends in Paris at the time and totally unknown to the clairvoyant.

Another consideration: If it is thought reading, why can M. Ossowiecki not gain knowledge of a letter written in a language he does not know?

Why can he not "read" print? In experiment No. 8 no one knew the contents of the printed page. M. Sudre had put the page into the envelope in complete darkness and without knowing what it contained, a page torn at random from a book of poems.

One might conclude that M. Ossowiecki could not "read" it because the contents of the envelope were not in M. Sudre's mind. But other facts rule out this simplistic opinion.

For example, one day a friend of mine, in my presence, gave M. Ossowiecki a sealed envelope containing a letter he had written himself on a typewriter.

The donor therefore knew the contents. But despite that the test was a total failure. M. Ossowiecki said simply, "It's a typed letter. I can't read anything but living writing!"

It can be seen that the hypothesis of thought reading is neither as simple nor convincing as it may at first have seemed.

Is it then pure clairvoyance? This is a very difficult question to answer.

His clairvoyance would have to be a faculty above all contingencies of time, space and material obstacles. It would be outside all the physical and mental laws, it would encompass omniscience; in a word, it would be a divine gift.

Needless to say M. Ossowiecki's clairvoyance has neither this breadth nor this power. Marvelous though his faculty is, we have seen that it is confined within strict and sometimes narrow bounds: there are the limitations of writing in a foreign language or the printed word.

In reality the clairvoyance of M. Ossowiecki is, beyond doubt, a form of that restricted type of clairvoyance we call psychometry. The process of perception can be analyzed as follows:

There comes a certain idea of what the writing consists of. It is not properly described as reading; but M. Ossowiecki seems to have a global concept of the content, and he works on that perception.

For example, for the sentence written in English, M. Ossowiecki said: "It's in English. I don't know English; but I can tell you that I see one isolated letter then a long word that starts with CONS. Then two short words, then a long word that is like Vendredi." The words were "I consider you are wonderful."

The clairvoyant has certain land marks that serve as guide lines. This initial incomplete perception establishes a rapport between him and the person who has written the words.

Then he is able to describe this person, his characteristics, his surroundings. At the same time, he takes himself back to the time and place where the written material was prepared, and then he obtains a more or less complete intuitive knowledge of the contents.

In short, M. Ossowiecki's gift is to be ascribed mainly to psychometry. Though that, it is true, does not amount to an explanation.

Despite the excellent work reported on psychometry, especially those of M. Bozzano and M. Oestereich, this form of clairvoyance remains a total enigma.

For the time being we shall abstain from any attempt at an interpretation; but we have reason to hope that M. Ossowiecki's wonderful gift will enable us, one day, to throw some light on the mystery.

[RM 1921 No. 6]

Experiment series 3—April 1922

Experiment 1 [reported by Richet]—Wednesday, 19th April, at Warsaw; we carried out the experiment in my rooms at l'hotel d'Europe, Geley, Ossowiecki and myself.

We bandaged Ossowiecki's eyes, and Geley drew something. Ossowiecki made some efforts to reproduce it, but in vain. But we did not persevere with this; we told Ossowiecki that this experiment (with a bandage over the eyes) that we had been advised to carry out to test his lucidity proved nothing even if it succeeded, because one is never sure that the blindfold has been completely effective in blocking sight. Much better to work with sealed envelopes.

Ossowiecki then asks me to make a drawing, well away from him, and put it in a sealed envelope. He goes to the end of the room (6m in length). I am at the other end. Geley is between us. I turn my back on Ossowiecki and I make a drawing on a sheet of paper, with my pen, making a design that happens to come into my head.

Nothing that had gone on before this had suggested it. From where he was standing Ossowiecki could at most have known that I had taken about 25 seconds to make the drawing. My back still turned, I fold the paper in half and then over again (the drawing had been made on the four quarters of the paper, so that it is not folded on itself). Then, still remaining well away from Ossowiecki and separated by Geley, I take the folded

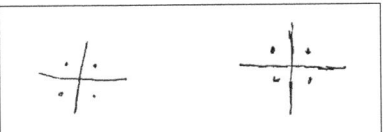

Drawings by Richet, left, and Ossowiecki.

paper and put it in a gummed envelope which I carefully seal up, and I give it to Ossowiecki.

After about a minute, during which time he has been kneading the envelope in his hand, he says that it is a cross. I say, "Very good." He adds, "It's a cross with some points, some stars; I am going to draw it."

He then draws the design above. I take the envelope, which is still perfectly intact, I open it and I confirm that the two drawings correspond.

It is utterly impossible for Ossowiecki to have seen what I drew. Even if he had had the complicity of Geley (!!) this would explain nothing, because Geley would not have been able to see either. There are then three hypotheses:

(a) The transparency of the paper. That won't do, because the paper was folded in four; and then there is the envelope. Moreover there was very poor lighting in the room from a ceiling lamp. There were no mirrors in the part of the room where I was. Anyway, Ossowiecki did not look at the envelope, or hardly; he held it in his hand, he fingered and squeezed it, almost behind his back.

(b) Chance. Yes, one can always, for all experiments, without exception, invoke chance. But that leads to absurd conclusions.

(c) The existence of cryptaesthesia must be acknowledged, call it lucidity, clairvoyance, or hyperaesthesia. Whether it is telepathic or not cannot be ascertained from this experiment, and obviously it is an open possibility. But the later experiment will prove definitely that telepathy is not operative in experiments with Ossowiecki.

***

Experiment 2—[reported by Richet, 20th April]
The following experiment is very remarkable and calls for some important observations.

Before my departure for Warsaw, Mme. A. de Noailles [Anna de Noailles was a celebrated poet] had sent me, to my home address in Paris, three envelopes (sealed up by gummed flaps, as with ordinary envelopes) opaque, containing a few lines in her own writing, all the contents being totally unknown to me. They are numbered 1, 2 and 3. On 19th April I show them to Ossowiecki, and he chooses No. 3, though telling me that he would not be able to do anything that evening. I put the three envelopes back in my briefcase, and next day, 20th April, I hand him back envelope No. 3.

Ossowiecki kneads the envelope feverishly for some time, without Geley or myself letting the envelope out of our sight. He knows that it is a letter from Mme. de Noailles, but he does not know her at all.

First he talks about Mme. de Noailles and gives various details about the conditions under which the letter was written, which on the whole are correct but do not go much further than the conjectures of any intelligent person.

The experiment was carried out in the presence of Mme. A, M. and Mme. Z (Mme. Z and Mme. A are sisters; and Mme. A is Ossowiecki's fiancée), in their apartment at l'hôtel d'Europe.

Three quarters of an hour passes. Ossowiecki spends the time kneading the envelope, which is still carefully sealed up [In a footnote Richet says he had taken the precaution of making ink marks over the flap of the envelope to be sure that it would not be possible for it to be opened and the ink marks realigned], while Geley and I kept our eyes on him and the envelope. Here is what Ossowiecki said, exactly as he spoke the words:

"There's nothing here for me. [He means that there is no reference to him in the letter.] It is something by a very great French poet, it's something about nature. It is the inspiration of a great French poet. I should say it is Rostand. Something from 'Chantecler.' When she speaks about 'Chantecler' she is writing something about the cockerel. There is an idea about light during the night. I see a great light during the night. Then Rostand with the beautiful poetry of 'Chantecler.'"

All that is said very quickly; then, after a long silence, and prolonged kneading of the envelope, Ossowiecki says: "The mistake about myself happened because there is talk about me in one of the other letters. The letters were all kept together. But there is something else."

Here there is a long silence and prolonged effort. During this renewed squeezing of the envelope a small piece of the envelope is torn, the tear being about a centimeter in length. But this does not matter, because (1) nothing inside the envelope can be seen through this tiny opening, (2) nothing can be removed from it, (3) Ossowiecki never looks at the envelope: he seems to operate only through handling it and (4) the essentials have already been said before this small tear in the envelope was made.

After about another half-hour Ossowiecki says:
"The ideas about the night and the light come first, before you get the name of Rostand. There is still something (in this letter) there are some lines: two lines, a word with two lines below."

Then Ossowiecki gives back the envelope. It is intact, except for the tiny tear referred to. For the facsimile of this letter see below:
It is during the night that it is good to believe in the light.
Edmond Rostand
Verse to be found in Chantecler and spoken by the cockerel.

This was a splendid experiment, scrupulously reported in all its details, incomparable in its precision.

[Richet's footnote:] As a curiosity, here are the phrases written down by way of a sort of competition with Ossowiecki by the five persons present:
(1) Criticism is easy and art is difficult.
(2) I should like to go back to Menton.
(3) One must be not too pleased nor too displeased with oneself.
(4) How sad it is that objects last longer than men.
(5) It is really a great pleasure to be a friend of Stefan Ossowiecki.

So, as one could have foreseen without this unnecessary trial, chance did not allow five people to offer anything similar to the words written by Mme. de Noailles. If we had enlisted ten thousand people the result would probably have been the same.

Richet now recapitulates the various precautions taken against trickery, illusion and complicity, including the question of whether one of the other persons present could have collaborated with Ossowiecki by substituting an envelope, an ineffectual idea that he has no difficulty in demolishing. He concludes:

Rostand quotation, by Anna de Noailles

For me, as for Geley, the certainty that there was no fraud is as strong as would be required to condemn a man to death.

Richet dismisses explanations in terms of hallucination or illusion, and proceeds to a historically original if rather arbitrary attempt to invoke statistics as an aid to judgment.

It was not likely that the target phrase was a quotation from poetry: let us say a ½ probability.

That it would be from Rostand one might assign a chance of 1/100.

That the verse would be from Chantecler, 1/10.

That it would be the verses about "Night and light" allow 1/2000.

That there would be below the quotation the name of Rostand followed by two lines, 1/100

That the two lines would be about Chantecler and the cockerel, 1/100.

We arrive at a probability of $(1/10^{11})$, which is equivalent to moral certainty.

***

Experiment 3 [related by Richet]

At my request (by telegram) Mme. Sarah Bernhardt sent me a letter to Warsaw for Ossowiecki to read without opening it. This letter was delivered to me by the postman, in the reception hall of l'hôtel d'Europe. I did not open it; I did not unseal it and I showed it to Ossowiecki, telling him that it came from Sarah Bernhardt.

This was a very difficult reading, and it lasted almost an hour and a half.

First of all Ossowiecki gave details about Mme. Sarah Bernhardt and the conditions in which she wrote this letter; they were not specific, and were not beyond the scope of ordinary good sense. What he said about the target writing was, on the contrary, very precise.

"Life. Life. Life." (He repeats this word three times.) "There are four or five lines, and beneath that the signature Sarah Bernhardt, a signature that slopes upwards." That was quite right, but perhaps he had seen a facsimile of Mme. Bernhardt's signature somewhere in a magazine.

"Life seems humble." (He repeats this word two or three times). "Humanity is there, life and humanity, but the word humanity is not written. There is an idea that is linked to the idea of life and humanity … because there is a lot of hatred. No, it is not hatred; there is only … only … it's a very difficult word, a very French word that I do not know: it's a word of eight letters. Exclamation."

Then, before opening the envelope, which is still completely closed (I had already established that it was absolutely opaque to light, direct or reflected) I write this down, to serve as the definite text of Ossowiecki's final reading:

"Life seems humble because there is only hatred [not hatred, but a word

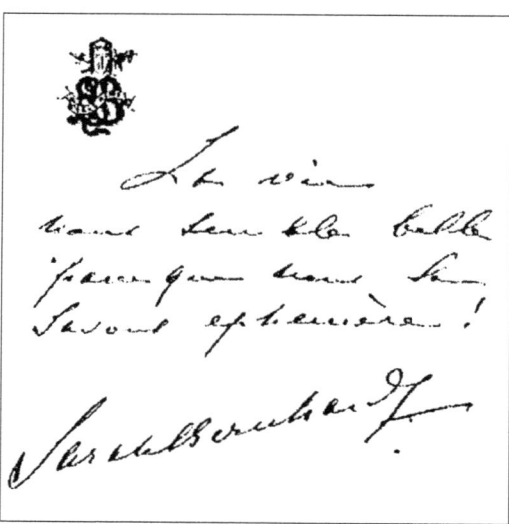

Letter from Sarah Bernhardt

that is not understood and which has eight letters]; signature Sarah Bernhardt."

The following words shown in facsimile were written:

Life seems good to us, because we know it to be ephemeral!—Sarah Bernhardt.

Richet then performs a calculation of probabilities on the same lines as for experiment 3, complicated by the mistaken "humble"—due to a confusion with a badly written "semble" (seems)—and the word "éphémère" that Ossowiecki did not know. The odds against chance are reckoned to be $(1/10^{10})$.
[RM 1922–23]

***

Experiment 4 [related by Richet]
This was done in rather different conditions.

Several people were present, and we were reduced to giving Ossowiecki words and numbers in very poor conditions of scientific control. Generally speaking he was very successful.

So, at a good distance from Ossowiecki, using a scrap of paper, taking all necessary precautions to ensure that no one saw what I was doing, I wrote the word TOI [the familiar form of "you" linguistically equivalent to "thou" or "thee"]. Then I screwed up the paper so as to make a little ball; Ossowiecki took it in the palm of his hand, his hand being placed in mine.

After three or four minutes he said, "It's a number." I remain impassive. "It's very short." Same impassivity. "It's a word." I make no gesture and say nothing. Then he adds, "I see a T." And then adds some details "There are two little strokes on the cross-bar of the T," which was absolutely true, because I had added two little vertical strokes to make the T more legible. I said, "That's very good."

Then he says, "There is a digit, a zero." I say, "Very good." He adds, "There is a 1." Then he adds, very quietly, "Ce n'est pas MOI." (It's not ME.) I try to give the impression that I have not heard that. Then Ossowiecki says, "Give me a piece of paper and I'll write it down." And he wrote "T 0 1."

Only then I unfolded my piece of paper, very crumpled, still in Ossowiecki's hand.

Richet then calculates the probabilities, and argues how Ossowiecki could not possibly have been guided by his own gestures. Richet once again reviews and dismisses chance, collusion, telepathy and visual hyperacuity as explanations.

Everything indicates that awareness of things comes to Ossowiecki by touch. Ossowiecki makes repeated efforts at handling, kneading, chafing the envelope. It is through his fingers and his skin, not by his eyes, his ears or sense of smell that he exercises his divining sense.

We must therefore associate cryptaesthesia with touch; it is a tactile hyperaesthesia, but an immensely potent hyperaesthesia that we do not understand.

One must even postulate that the written letters carry in themselves some property other than the external properties perceptible by our normal senses. There is something more (its properties utterly unknown) in a line of our handwriting than the marks made on the paper. [In a footnote Richet adds that this is supported by Ossowiecki's inability to read print or typescript. He goes on to speculate about "emanations" and "vibrations of some unknown order."]

In any event, what seems quite certain is that there is no transmission of thought attached to the letter, but a knowledge of the graphic forms. The arrangement of the lines, of the signature, the exclamation mark, were mentioned. The TOI was read as if there had been a zero and the number 1. Humble [humble] has no resemblance in meaning to *Belle* [beautiful]: the only resemblance lies in their graphic form. The word *éphémère* [ephemeral] was not understood because Ossowiecki did not know this French word: he said that it had eight letters; so he knew its graphic form, but had no idea of its meaning.

In other words, due to an emanation coming from the writing, and by means of an unknown tactile sense (cryptaesthesia) with which he is endowed, Ossowiecki acquires knowledge of graphic forms but not of ideas.

Experiment series 4—May 1922 [related by Geley]

After Prof. Richet's departure [from Warsaw] in April 1922, I carried on having further sessions, all very successful.

But with the limited time at my disposal for one thing and, for another, a reluctance to demand too much of M. Ossowiecki's good will, burdened as he was with work and various preoccupations, these considerations did not allow me to carry out all the tests that I had planned.

I shall confine myself here to reporting just one of the experiments I made after Prof. Richet left, because it is the logical successor to those that he published in the last issue of the *Revue Métapsychique*.

My colleague [Professor Richet] had left me one of the sealed envelopes that Mme. de Noailles had prepared for him. This letter was double-enveloped. The outer envelope had been slightly torn when Prof. Richet took it out of his pocket to give it to me. He advised me to keep this envelope, which contained the target writing, as it was and seal it up in a second envelope.

I followed his advice and did as he suggested. The sealed envelope never left my inside jacket pocket until the moment when I gave it to M. Ossowiecki.

A first assay took place in my room at l'hôtel d'Europe, on 4th May 1922, at 1600 hours. M. Ossowiecki concentrated, holding the envelope in his hand, and then after a quarter of an hour, said "I see it, I know what it is. This evening I shall tell you what is inside this envelope." Then he handed it back to me. It was intact and I replaced it in my pocket.

The same day, at 2100 hours, there was a meeting of the Polish Society for Psychical Research* at which 80–100 persons were present. In agreement with M. Ossowiecki, I suggested, before the meeting began, that the experiment in question should take place in front of the society members. This idea was accepted with enthusiasm, and I handed the envelope to M. Ossowiecki. Very quickly, after five–seven minutes, he started to speak. He described Mme. de Noailles and her apartment. On this subject he mentioned several details that I have not verified, and then he said

"She speaks, in this letter, about a great contemporary genius. It is Richet. She likes him very much. She says that the genius of Richet is as great as his heart. She signs with her first name and with her family name and she underlines the signature. This all took place in the evening at around 5 or 6 o'clock."

Then, before the whole assembly, I open the envelope:

---

*See Appendix III.

"Professor Charles Richet is as impressive in the sublime qualities of his heart as in his scientific genius. Anna de Noailles"

As can be seen, the test was entirely successful. My other experiments were just as good, and I should only be writing at unnecessary length if I extended this report by detailing them.

M. Ossowiecki's clairvoyance displays itself not only in the ability to know the contents of sealed packages or documents enclosed in an envelope or an opaque cover. It also manifests above all in the exercise of "psychometry," a faculty that surpasses by a long way everything that has been recorded in the annals of psychical research.

I have been present at some of the experiments of this sort and I have marveled at the results. My own experiments in psychometry are as yet too incomplete to be published at this time. I shall reserve publication until I have been able to carry out some new studies.

Finally, M. Ossowiecki has on various occasions located lost or stolen articles. Once put in touch with the person who has lost an object he can, after a few minutes of concentration, say where the object is to be found, in what conditions it was lost, describe the person who found it or stole it, etc.

Geley then relates a dramatic incident related by Aline de Glass, a judge's wife, whose report about her lost brooch appears on p. 104, *Missing Property, Case 1.*

Some pointers to interpretation.

In trying to understand M. Ossowiecki's gift it is essential to take account of all the different varieties of his clairvoyance and to consider all the facts.

From the study that we have managed to carry through in our three series of experiments, the following findings stand out:

Positive findings:

1. M. Ossowiecki can easily become aware of the contents of sealed envelopes inaccessible by normal sensory means. His lucidity seems the same whatever the obstacle that stands in the way of sensory channels.

It works equally well through a thick covering of lead (3 cm) or through several layers of opaque paper as well as for a simple envelope. The nature of the obstruction seems therefore unimportant. Though M. Ossowiecki had to make two attempts at discerning the document enclosed in the lead pipe, he had exactly the same difficulty in "reading" through the simple envelopes of Mme. de Noailles.

2. M. Ossowiecki acquires knowledge of documents prepared at a great distance from him just as readily as of those prepared in his presence.

3. It is of no importance for the functioning of M. Ossowiecki's lucidity whether or not people who are present know the contents of the concealed targets that are given to him.

4. In certain cases, such as those reported by Prof. Richet, M. Ossowiecki's lucidity seems to give him awareness of the graphic form rather than the idea of the document. In other cases, it seems to be focused on the idea, rather than the graphic form, as in the experiment with the drawing of a fish.

5. M. Ossowiecki's lucidity is brought into play not only in connection with a written and concealed document, but by any object (as in psychometry). Sometimes it manifests without any material intermediary (as in finding lost objects).

Negative findings:

So far as concealed writing is concerned, M. Ossowiecki is incapable of reading the contents of anything printed or typed. This restriction is curious and very difficult to explain, given the powerful psychometry that comes into play in other cases.

Could it be purely a matter of habit? One might speculate that one day he had a failure when trying to do a reading with print, and now anything he perceives to be printed has the effect of inhibiting his clairvoyance?

From these findings, what conclusions can one draw?

First of all, they point to the definitive exclusion of an interpretation in terms of thought-reading or telepathy as the basis of M. Ossowiecki's lucidity.... If the reader will re-read the account of all the experiments he will surely deem the question well and truly settled.

Is it a case of straightforward perception of graphical forms by an extraordinary sensory hyperaesthesia, probably tactile, as Prof. Richet has come to believe?

For my part I cannot see my way to accepting this hypothesis: the experiment with the lead pipe, the phenomena of psychometry cannot be explained in this way. So in any event, the hypothesis can apply only to certain experiments. Well, it is clear that an explanation that is not comprehensive is not a true explanation.

Better to admit our impotence at the present time to understand the mechanisms of lucidity. We have however sought to obtain the opinion and impressions of M. Ossowiecki himself. Here are the very interesting observations that he has sent us about himself:

I shall try to answer your question: "What do you experience while you're giving readings of material in sealed envelopes?"

It seems to me that Prof. Richet's conjecture does not cover the ground. It is possible that, without my being aware of it, I am influenced by a sort of hyperaesthesia; but there is certainly something else. This is what goes on in my mind:

I start by inhibiting the reasoning process and, concentrating all my inner forces, I throw myself into a world of spiritual feeling. I am sure that this condition is brought about by my unshakable faith in the spiritual unity of all humanity. Then I find myself in a new, special state, where I see or I hear things right outside time and space.

As you know, I sometimes find lost articles by clairvoyance. An incident of that sort happened only a fortnight ago. [This was the narrative of Mme. de Glass.]

Whether I read a concealed target, or find a lost article, or do psychometry, my sensations are almost the same:

Apparently, I lose a certain amount of energy; my temperature goes up and my heartbeat becomes irregular. A feature that confirms this impression is that as soon as I stop thinking, it feels as if a surge of electricity flows through my extremities for a few instants.

This lasts a moment, then a true state of lucidity takes hold of me; pictures rise up in front of me; usually of the past. I see the man who wrote the letter and I know what he has written. I see the object at the moment when it is lost, with all the details surrounding the event; or I know, I sense the history of some object that I have in my hands. The vision is clouded and demands great concentration. Great effort is needed to see some of the circumstances and details displayed.

Sometime this lucid state is evoked in a few moments, and at other times one has to wait for hours. It depends to a large extent on the ambience: incredulity, skepticism or even attention concentrated too closely on my person can block a quick and successful result or cripple the perceptions. When you were present at the session I gave at the Metaphysical Institute in Warsaw, I am sure that the facility and rapidity with which I read the two targets were due to a general harmony and to the friendly state of mind of the people present, which made things favorable for me.

This, my dear Dr. Geley, is all that I have been able to analyze about what I feel happening to me during my experiments. You have noticed that I am sometimes wrong. I am indeed still far from perfection, but I hope to get to that point one day. Believe me: everything that I am telling you is the product of considered reason working together with the mind and the heart.

May this guide you in your work, dear friend. It will lead to the wide road of the future.

I am yours very sincerely
Stefan Ossowiecki

These further observations are extremely valuable. They confirm us in our opinion that lucidity is absolutely independent of sensory capacities; in the same way as it is outside all powers of reason.

Lucidity is like all other psychic faculties, it cannot be attached to any of the physiological mechanisms of the conscious mind. It is beyond and above all organic limitations. It has nothing to do with the functioning of the cerebral neurons.

Geley deals with the objection that this "divine faculty" is of little practical use; though at present it may be confined to rare individuals, and be uncontrollable, a time might come when everyone would have lucidity and exercise it voluntarily. These ideas, and the argument that lucidity is extant throughout the animal kingdom, are developed in *From the Unconscious to the Conscious*.

If these propositions are true, lucidity is not just a psychic curiosity. It appears, on the contrary, to be one of the most important factors in human progress and turns one of the essential wheels of evolution *[RM 1922 No.4]*.

Reception at the Institut Métapsychique International

Dr. Stephen Chauvet, the author of the substantial article that follows, was an active member of the IMI, though he was a busy practicing physician. He was so astounded by his encounters with Ossowiecki that he immediately wrote an article about him in *La Vie*, 1 September 1923 (*Les Possibilités mystérieuse de l'être humain*) and contributed a personal study of him to *Le Mercure de France*, 1 October 1923 (*Le Merveilleux humain*). We take up his account of the memorable evening at the point where he relates his experience of the first experiment.

The mysterious possibilities of man
An account of some remarkable experiments with M. Stefan Ossowiecki
CLAIRVOYANCE—THOUGHT-READING
A. Experiments 12th June 1923
At 5 p.m. on that day I received a telegram from Dr. G. Geley informing me that M. Stefan Ossowiecki was to come here, quite unexpectedly, and would spend some time that same evening at the Institute. Geley asked me to attend if possible. At the time when the telegram was given to me, the wife of a colleague was in my consulting room. Well, as I was suffering a lot of pain at the time from a war wound, my first thought was to telephone and give my apologies. Then, realizing that this was a unique opportunity for me to see this outstanding clairvoyant and hoping to assuage my suffering with an extra dose of aspirin, I changed my mind and decided to go. A little later, thinking that an opportunity

for an experiment might arise during the evening, I decided to prepare a document for this purpose.

The consultation with my patient finished, I asked her (having explained the situation) if she would be kind enough, not in my presence and without my participation, to write some lines on a sheet of paper, then to wrap it in tinfoil that I had found, then to enclose it in a small envelope and seal it using a seal that I had put within reach. I then left the consulting room and did not return until everything was completed. My patient then explained, as she handed me the little packet, that she had failed to notice the seal I had left for her, so she had had the idea of sealing the two blobs of wax on the envelope with the heads side of a one franc piece.

I thanked her and she left. I must add (anticipating the outcome) that I learnt from her subsequently that, casting about for something to write on the paper, something in the way of a general, impersonal idea, she had finally decided to select a maxim from a book containing the thoughts of Epictetus, a book that she found in the room together with some medical textbooks, two books on ancient history and five others on the Moi people, Elamite art, the Hittites, the Incas and finally the explorations of Lake Chad.

Be that as it may, looking at the little package made up by my patient I was annoyed at the rather common look of the opportunist seals. I decided to cover them up with a new layer of molten wax, and I sealed it with a seal showing the neo-Babylonian design of a Chaldean priest worshipping the moon (Sin) and the sacred maces. I emphasize that the new layer of wax completely covered the old seals, to the point where it was impossible to see that there had been two successive applications of wax....

When I arrived at the Institute there were a dozen people already there, and in due course I was introduced to M. Stefan Ossowiecki. While waiting for other people to arrive we were seated round a large table. M. Ossowiecki was placed beside someone and had a lady whom I did not know on his right. I was at the other end of the table on the opposite side. There was talk among the several groups of people round the table. As for me, I had the good luck to be sitting next to Prof. Vallée, and we engaged in lively conversation. After a little while we were told that all the guests were now assembled on the floor below, and we all stood up and one by one left the room by the door near the end of the table where M. Ossowiecki was sitting. Instead of going through the door first, as he had been invited to do, he stood beside it—despite repeated exhortations—as if he wanted to be the last to leave the room. And because of where we had been sitting, Prof. Vallée and I were indeed the last to approach the door.

To my astonishment, at the moment when I was about to pass through the door, M. Ossowiecki made for me, grasping my arm and saying: "Sir, I don't know you and I know nothing about you. But from the start of the reception I noticed you and I felt myself irresistibly drawn to you. I can't describe what I felt. Several times I asked the people sitting next to me what they could tell me about you, but they don't know you. Then suddenly I read your thoughts and saw into your mind, your very being, your whole life." (At this point he enlarged on my intellectual merits and moral values and on my personality, which are matters of no interest here).

"I also feel towards you a total sense of intellectual and moral empathy. Everything interests you, and you work much too hard. For years and years you have pursued a goal. You would have achieved it and risen to great heights, but your life has been shattered from the viewpoint of health. You have had to endure a lot of suffering, continually, and for many years, and you resist it with fierce strength. Just now, while you were talking, I felt that you had terrible pain, though nothing showed. You mustn't overwork yourself as you do, because you will wear yourself out. Though your life is so painful, and in spite of your progress being slowed down by your state of health, you will nevertheless fulfill your destiny, but you must not kill yourself by carrying on the way you do. I think your health may improve. I should like to help you. I feel what you are suffering; let me take your head in my hands; I shall tell you what has happened and where you feel it most."

I agreed to this, and he then took my head between his hands and massaged the exact place on my neck and the occipital region, doing this in front of several people who had come back into the room and formed a circle around us. M. Ossowiecki was very strung up; his hands trembled; he had a far away look. Then suddenly he called out:

"I'm there; I see what's wrong; you were wounded in the war by an exploding shell; you nearly died; wait, wait; I shall tell you where you were wounded; it's there, on the neck; and you have a lot of pain there; there is a lot of congestion and thickening there. It's there that you need to be operated on, it's there." And he indicated the whole lower occipital region.

I have to say that I was astounded; leaving aside M. Ossowiecki's kind appraisal of my spiritual qualities and his predictions about the future, everything that he had just told me was absolutely right.

M. Ossowiecki did not know me; he had never heard anyone talk about me; did not even know that he was going to meet me that evening; no one (I later made painstaking inquiries) had told him anything about me; also, he could not have been guided by an obvious scar from the wound, bearing in mind that I had been injured by a shell case that had penetrated very little and its sole effect had been by way of shock from the impact, and in fact the very small scar was in any case covered up by my high collar.

I knew anyway, questioning a few minutes later the person who had been sitting on his right, that M. Ossowiecki had asked him, as well as his other neighbor, who I was ... and that she had not been able to tell him; she told me later that from that moment M. Ossowiecki had kept his eyes on me [in a footnote Chauvet says that he was unaware of this, and was concentrating on his conversation with Prof. Vallée] and he had continually talked about me and said that I had a lot of pain and that he "had full knowledge of my mind," that he wanted to know me, etc.... That is why he had stopped by the door and waited for me.

While M. Ossowiecki was saying all this to me Dr. Geley came to tell him that everyone was down below waiting impatiently for him. But an agitated M. Ossowiecki did not want to listen and replied, "No, no, let me be for a moment. I feel strongly drawn to this gentleman and I want to do an experiment with him first." Other people, including the pleasant and distinguished Mme. Ossowiecka tried to persuade him, but without success. Brusquely M. Ossowiecki said to me, "Give me your card." I gave it to him, he read it, then gave it back to me telling me: "Take it in your hands and rub it with your fingers; good; now go into the next room and make a drawing on this card. Then you must envelope it, seal the envelope and then call me. I shall stay here."

I went into an adjoining room where there was a footman whom I asked for an envelope. Then, alone in the room, I tried to decide what to draw. Unfortunately it is a fact of life that one is never short of ideas except when you suddenly need to have one, or simply to think of a few words, e.g. to try out a new pen. On top of that, I heard from the other side of the door, which I had only just closed, M. Ossowiecki calling out, "Hurry, doctor, hurry; they are coming to fetch me; they want me to go downstairs; draw anything at all, it's just for an experiment between the two of us." And, a few moments later, "Hurry; add a few personal words to the drawing."

At this point Chauvet enlarges on what might be a suitable target....

> Be that as it may, at the moment when I was going to draw a boat, M. Ossowiecki called out, "Draw something personal, something that relates to you." This just harassed me all the more. While I cast around for something—it was in fact only a matter of seconds—I was suddenly afflicted with the old pain. This paroxysm brought me down to a low state and set in train some unconscious ideas, and the thought came to me to draw a cross. No doubt what I had in my subconscious mind was something like the following: "How unbearable it is to suffer pain all the time; and not to be able to do the things I had planned to do or things that interest me. It is a matter of endless disappointment and endless suffering. It's not a life, it's a Calvary." And the idea of the cross surfaced in my mind.
>
> I set about the drawing; but instead of making a cross with full side bars I made it with an upright and a crossbar superimposed. I finished the drawing with the horizontal bars. Instead of drawing two bars either side of the upright I drew the horizontal with two lines, one above and one below, crossing the vertical. As a drawing, it was heretical; I decided on it, nevertheless, to bring a little extra challenge to the experiment. After I finished the drawing, with great haste, M. Ossowiecki called out, "Add a few personal words. Quick, hurry, anything will do, hurry." Still motivated by the train of thought noted above I wrote the following words to serve as a title for my drawing: "My life." I should like to have found some other theme, but M. Ossowiecki was still urging me to make haste. I had to act quickly, so quickly in fact that I scrawled the words illegibly; but I told myself that it did not matter, as this was only a personal experiment that would remain a private matter between the two of us.
>
> I put my card in an envelope, having ascertained that it was perfectly opaque, and I sealed it. At that moment, alerted by me that I was ready, M. Ossowiecki came into the room and asked for needle and thread. When these had been brought he made a knot in the thread and, without saying what he was going to do, stitched up the envelope, pulling the needle from back to front five or six times. Imagine my amazement when, following the comings and goings of the needle, I saw that after several excursions of the needle back and forth the black thread had traced on the envelope (and in the same recessed style as in my drawing) the lines of the vertical post of my cross, then the right cross member, then the upper line of the left one.
>
> I wondered if M. Ossowiecki had already seen the drawing and if he would reproduce it with black thread. But having arrived at the end of the left branch of the cross, the thread, instead of crossing the vertical horizontally (which would have completed the cross) moved off to the lower extremity of the vertical. I said nothing about these first proofs of his skill; it was disturbing, and quite strange to see that though he had not yet got down to the task of "reading" the drawing, he had, using the thread, almost completely reproduced the drawing in question, no doubt as if his subconscious mind already knew something and had autonomously guided his hand.
>
> At this moment M. Ossowiecki took the envelope with his right hand, put it behind his back and started to walk up and down the room, in a state of agitation, his features drawn, his eyes far away. Then speaking rapidly he said, "I am beginning to see; it's going to go well; quick, quick." But as he said these words people came once again begging him to go downstairs to the other guests. He replied at first, "But I am doing an experiment with the doctor; I am busy at the moment, let me be." Then they remonstrated, "Come on, they're waiting for you; you can finish this experiment with the doctor later. Come just for a short time." He agreed to go down, and before going handed me back the envelope.

In the great drawing room of the Institute he was introduced to numerous people and responded, in a very friendly way, to everyone. But you could see that really in his mind he was "elsewhere." Next, Dr. Geley brought him to meet M. Marcel Prévost, who was holding in his hand a mysterious little bag, and asked him if he would try an experiment with one of the documents contained in the bag. But M. Ossowiecki declined, both then and later, so that the little bag kept its secret.

One curious aspect of this remarkable clairvoyant should be noted in passing. When he feels tired, or when he simply feels out of sorts (and in this respect he is very much influenced by the impression made on him by certain individuals) or, come to that, if he wants to do an experiment with someone he has met and he has begun to get positive results with that person and he feels he has not exhausted those potentialities, there is no way of persuading this very likeable man (who after all wants to be of service and please people) to change his mind and try an experiment with another designated person. In just the same way at another meeting that I shall describe later he fixed on one guest, M. d'Anglard, for the whole evening, and would not do experiments with any other person.

So to all the friendly blandishments of Dr. Geley M. Ossowiecki replied that he first of all wanted to do the experiment with me. In fact he slipped away after a short time, having signaled to me to go into another room. Fearing that this experiment would be the only one to take place that evening, Dr. Geley asked if some other people could be present at it. I was slightly put out, because my drawing and the wording had been made on the basis of a strictly personal test and not for a formal experiment. Nevertheless M. Ossowiecki was impatient to get to a conclusion and did not want me to waste time preparing another document; besides, I felt that I did not have the right to deprive our scientific inquiry of a positive experimental result on the grounds that it touched on personal matters that I did not want to see exposed. I therefore resigned myself to accepting Dr. Geley's request. I was actually convinced, or nearly so, that M. Ossowiecki would not be able to see what I had drawn! At any rate, the request granted, M. Ossowiecki still did not want a great number of spectators. At first he wanted only Prof. Vallée and Dr. Osty. He had in fact been somewhat intimidated by the large number of guests, a crowd he had not expected. Still worried by this, he did not feel at ease and wanted only a few people around him. They had to insist that M. Prévost should be with us, though he himself wanted Dr. Geley.

When all the comings and goings, which irritated Ossowiecki, were finished, he asked me for the envelope again, and immediately put it behind his back; then he walked up and down the room. His face was contorted, and rather anxious; the temporal veins were strongly dilated; his eyes looked very strange; his hand trembled a little. As we were all silent, he relaxed his mental concentration for a few moments and told us "Talk among yourselves, even loud talk; it won't worry me; it worries me when everyone is silent, and even more when you stare at me. That worries me and puts me off getting myself into an altered state so that I can 'look in at myself' and have my clear sight." From then on we talked a little, but we never stopped watching his movements.

Speaking very quickly, M. Ossowiecki said: "There it is; I see it; yes, I see it. You wanted to draw something before this. You gave up that idea [that was correct] and you made a different drawing. It's strange. It's a cross but an unusual one. Give me a pencil, I shall draw it."

Armed with paper and pencil M. Ossowiecki, without hesitation, drew the whole vertical part of the cross, then the two horizontal arms. At that moment he hesitated and said: "That's not all; it's not the way it is usually; it seems to me that this one goes across like that" and he joined the upper line of the two arms by another line crossing the vertical post; then he started to do the same for the lower line. That done, he took the envelope again, and turning it round and round in his hands said: "Below the cross there is a two-word phrase; no, three words; they're not words, you could say they are just letters; no, it's not that; I can't see it, it's not clear enough."

The experiment finished, I broke the thread and opened the letter. On my visiting card there was the drawing, absolutely like the one drawn by M. Ossowiecki (and the same size) an openwork cross. One need only glance at the photograph of the two documents, which I have stuck side by side and which are reproduced natural size (without any retouching) to confirm the similarity.

I should point out that M. Ossowiecki did indeed indicate the lower cross bar, without finishing it off, not because he was not sure about it (because he had just drawn the upper bar without any hesitation) but out of a sort of laziness, the sort of thing you find in many painters who, rapidly making a sketch, content themselves with a quick movement or line to show the effect they are aiming at. Moreover, when he had just drawn the upper line he said, before starting the lower line: "And there too" indicating and there, too, it crosses!

As to the phrase I had written in such haste in the conditions I have already described, I must say that several people who were present at the experiment could not decipher it. So it is not surprising that M. Ossowiecki could not read it. Moreover, in the course of later experiments in which the text was better written he was always able to reproduce it completely. Finally, it should be noted that M. Ossowiecki had in fact grasped to some extent the layout of my little phrase because ... "My, li, fe" ["ma, v, ie"] are separated and make three groups, and these are indeed "words that are not words" and "like letters." The reading of this phrase was all the more impossible in that M. Ossowiecki, while speaking French with fair facility, has nevertheless not needed, in Poland, to get used to day-long deciphering of badly written texts, as he would certainly have had to do if he lived in France.

After this Ossowiecki, fatigued, went into an adjoining room to rest. After a short time he seemed recovered, and Chauvet told him that he had brought a prepared target envelope with him. At once Ossowiecki asked to have it.

Drawing and phrase (obscured) submitted, left, and drawing by Ossowiecki.

I gave him the little package, in such a manner that he did not see it; he closed his hand round it and put it behind his back. Then immediately he said:

"I see two coins; they are one-franc pieces; French money; yes, French; these coins give me a feeling of embarrassment; but still I see a sheet of paper with a phrase written on it; it was written by a woman, 30—35 years of age; tall; dark; distinguished; intelligent; she has been divorced, she is a doctor's wife; she looks at the desk, there are very varied things from foreign countries; some antiquities; she tries to think what she should devise; she has decided on a concept; it is something impersonal, something elevated, an ideal."

We had reached that point when we were interrupted. M. Ossowiecki handed me back the little package, saying, "We'll finish this later." Well, it turned out that that evening he was taken away for another experiment, and at the second meeting he carried out a series of experiments with one person (M. d'Anglard), so there was no way M. Ossowiecki could complete this remarkable demonstration of clairvoyance. For this reason I decided to open the envelope and acquaint myself with the concept of Epictetus that it contained.

I have to report that everything M. Ossowiecki said was exactly right, except for one small point: my patient's age (38 rather than 30–35). Apart from that small correction he saw everything as it was: the divorce; the essential quality; the appearance, the spiritual character; the fact that she had handled and glanced at several books on science and art (this relates to the various countries and past times); the choice of an elevated concept; and even the original sealing of the wax with a French one-franc piece;. You have only to re-read what I wrote at the beginning of this article to confirm the absolute precision of M. Ossowiecki's clairvoyance. It is easy to see from the photograph below the two seals that beyond all doubt they [the one-franc pieces] were covered by the other seals. Besides, I would emphasize that M. Ossowiecki did not even glance at the package I gave him. And I might add that no one seeing the seals with the image of a Chaldean priest worshipping Sin would imagine that the same person would use a common coin as an alternative seal. Also one must note that M. Ossowiecki saw the seal used by the person who had prepared the writing, not the second seal placed over it by me. All that, one has to say, is particularly intriguing.

I said above that people came and interrupted us during the course of this second experiment. A few moments later M. Ossowiecki was introduced to Mme. la marquise de B. (called here Mme. X for convenience); with her he carried out another perfectly successful experiment. In view of what I have already said about the experimental conditions I can describe this new experiment quite briefly.

M. Ossowiecki asked Mme. X to write a phrase on a sheet of paper. Withdrawing into another room Mme. X tried to think of a phrase. Directly after the successful outcome of this experiment she told me: "You never realize how short

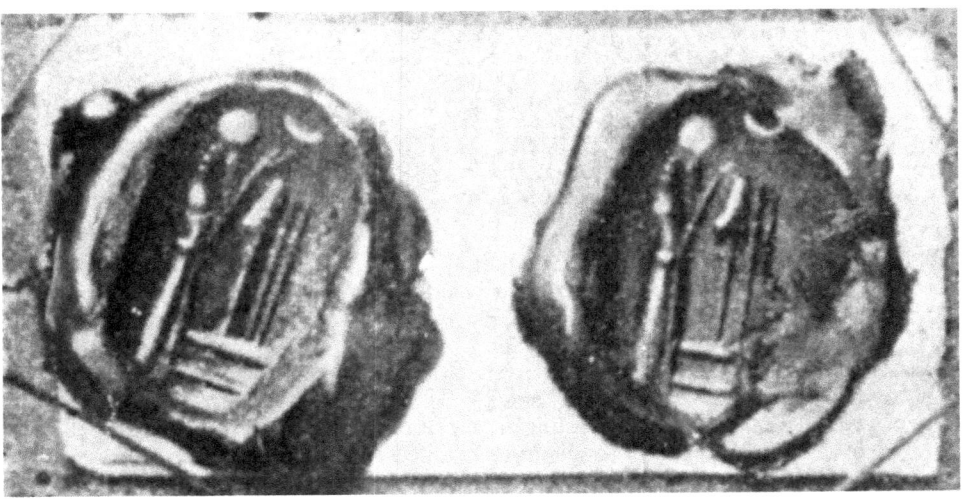

Photograph of the seals

of ideas you are until you are suddenly called upon to think of something in this sort of situation. I admit that I was going to write something quite insignificant: 'What is your wife's name?' when M. Ossowiecki, who was the other side of the door, called out: 'No, not that; write something personal, something that has meaning for you.' I, who did not believe in clairvoyance, was nonplussed for a few seconds, realizing that M. Ossowiecki had instantaneously become aware of my idea. So I wrote another phrase: 'This winter shall I go on the grand voyage that I want to make?'"

Let us come back to the experiment. As soon as M. Ossowiecki had taken possession of the envelope, he said:

"Yes, Madame, you will go on your voyage."

And as Mme. X looked at him questioningly he continued:

"Here is the sentence you wrote: 'Is it right that this winter I shall go on the grand voyage that I want to make?'"

Apart from a small variation in language at the beginning of the sentence [note that in French *ferai-je* is identical in meaning with *Est ce que je ferai*], the experiment was absolutely successful and Mme. X was both delighted and amazed, thanking M. Ossowiecki when he said that he could also tell her many other interesting things. He told her that she "wanted to go to Egypt; that she had already stayed there three years ago and remembered an unforgettable experience; that she had wanted to go back there several times but had never been able to do so because of various illnesses affecting her son; that he would get better and that her plans would come to fruition."

Apart from this last point, which relates to the future, everything M. Ossowiecki said was perfectly true. And he did not know Mme. X and knew nothing about her. Moreover he did not leave it at that. He took Mme. X aside for a time and told her a whole series of facts, quite personal ones, about her own past, which plunged her into a state of utter stupefaction. Coming away from this encounter Mme. X, still dumbfounded, told me that Ossowiecki told her not only some things that were known only to herself, but also some thoughts that had not developed beyond a state of desire. All this part of the experiment cannot unfortunately be divulged because of its very private character.

Chauvet concludes his article with the observation that it would be very desirable to have some idea as to what went on unseen in the mind of Ossowiecki as he performed his feats.

[RM 1923 No.5]

Incidentally, it appears from a much later report in RM 1925 No. 6 that on the same afternoon, 12 June 1923, Ossowiecki had already carried out a successful drawing experiment with Richet's wife and son.

B. Experiments carried out 15th June 1923

Three days after the experiments just described another session took place, also at the Institute. That evening M. Ossowiecki was very tired. He had agreed to attend the session only on condition that no one would ask him to do any experiment. Nevertheless, it turned out that after becoming acquainted with one of the members, M. d'Anglard, he wanted to try a test. M. d'Anglard, at his request, and in his presence, wrote a line on one of his visiting cards and put it in an envelope. Very quickly M. Ossowiecki said: "Where shall I be this time next year," which was the sentence that had been written.

Exhilarated by this success, excited and no longer feeling tired as he had before, M. Ossowiecki then asked M. d'Anglard to write another phrase and to

Drawings by d'Anglard, top, and by Ossowiecki

make a drawing on a piece of paper, and to put the drawing in an envelope. M. d'Anglard, by himself in one of the other rooms, did as he had been asked. Then M. Ossowiecki came into the room where he was, followed by other people [Chauvet names seven persons]. The envelope had hardly been given to him when M. Ossowiecki exclaimed to M. d'Anglard,

"I see, but is it possible? I see the same sentence as before: 'Where shall I be this time next year?' Yes, that's it; is it possible?" M. d'Anglard, momentarily disconcerted and amazed, recovered himself and said: "Indeed, that is the sentence that is there."

This is what had happened. M. d'Anglard had made the drawing (to be examined later) [see p. 53] on his visiting card (having first of all thought of a different drawing); then, heavily preoccupied with this new part of the experiment had, perhaps almost subconsciously, again written the same phrase as in the first experiment. This, one might well think, increased the difficulties for M. Ossowiecki and makes the success even more impressive.

This little incident concluded, M. Ossowiecki continued his work. After a few seconds he said:

"I see a drawing that you wanted to do first and which you decided to abandon; they are triangles; triangles ... intertwined. The drawing you made then is very odd. It's a man's head. A very funny head. And then there is a hat; no, it's not a hat, it's like a helmet; and it's not a real helmet. It looks rather like a Tyrolean hat. It's like this."

M. Ossowiecki then took a pencil and, without hesitation, drew first the head, then the hat. The envelope was opened. It contained the visiting card and on it the sentence mentioned above and the drawing. It can be confirmed that:

1st the two drawings are identical and manifestly to the same scale;

2nd the target drawing is very difficult, especially as its execution leaves much to be desired;

3rd the hat, as M. Ossowiecki explained, is a cross between a Tyrolean hat and a helmet, and both in its concept and in its unskillful execution made the task very difficult for M. Ossowiecki;

4th finally, it should be noted that before making the drawing M. d'Anglard had indeed thought of drawing intertwined triangles.

After this excellent experiment the experience we had been through three days earlier in connection with Mme. X and with myself happened all over again. M. Ossowiecki assured M. d'Anglard that he could tell him a lot more, and would not relinquish him. Mme. Ossowiecki, Dr. Geley and various other people entreated him to be good enough to do another experiment with someone else, but in vain. Though he remained perfectly amiable, he would not respond.

In a case such as this he probably feels, in a confused way, that he is in a sort of mysterious psychic communion with the experimental subject, and he feels certain that he will succeed again; and he wants to carry on ... just like a writer carried away with his thoughts who cannot be prised from his writing.

These drawings are accompanied by various notes made by Chauvet, who repeats his earlier remarks on the trouble inherent in target drawings purporting to show human features. He also draws attention to some needle holes made by Ossowiecki apparently sewing up the envelope as in the earlier test, though in the body of the report this is not mentioned.

Be that as it may, he went off with M. d'Anglard and, for a whole half-hour, told him a whole lot of facts about the past, present and future. So far as predictions are concerned the time has not yet come when these can be verified. As to statements made about the past and the present, M. d'Anglard could not tell us what was said, because they were too personal, but he said that they were all true, and he was all the more astounded in that some of them "could not have been known to anyone but himself."

These, faithfully reported, are the remarkable demonstrations of clairvoyance given by M. Ossowiecki on 12th and 15th June 1923 at the Institut Métapsychique International, and which I can confirm.

Dr. STEPHEN CHAUVET
[RM No.5, 1923]

Geley Probes Deeper

If Geley's researches had ceased at the end of 1922 his reports up to that point would have demonstrated the reality of Ossowiecki's psychic abilities beyond all reasonable doubt. What remained above all was to find out more about the *modus operandi*. But, alongside the excitement of forging ahead on a personal level of satisfaction, Geley also had to bear in mind the importance of bringing the opinions of his colleagues and of the general inquiring public along with him, and a public demonstration involving researchers of other nationalities was one way of accomplishing this. In this class comes the demonstration given in Warsaw in 1923 (pp. 62–65).

Later in the same year Geley was able to go to Warsaw, having prepared some very ingenious procedures designed to test Ossowiecki's powers to breaking point.

Experiment series 5—June–July 1924 [experimenter: Geley]

[Note: The French "encre sympathique" has in the following account been rendered as "sympathetic ink" though the normal English equivalent would be "invisible ink." This is to make intelligible the conversation in which Ossowiecki asks Geley how "an invisible ink" is expressed in French.]

Envelope prepared. On a half sheet of white paper I write, using sympathetic ink, the following phrase: "It is neither philosophy, nor atheism, nor materialism, nor spiritualism that counts. It is a question of facts—PASTEUR."

(The sympathetic ink had been provided by my collaborator and friend, M. [René] Warcollier, chemical engineer).*

I fold the half-sheet in such a way that the whole phrase falls under a fold.

I tear a sheet of dark gray paper, which I fold in two and place the target document between the two leaves.

I put it all together into an envelope bearing the crest of the IMI.

I stick down the flap and seal the envelope with wax (using my personal seal).

Then I stick some gummed paper strips (10 in all) on the back of the envelope. These strips are irregularly placed across the envelope flaps. Across all of them I make some marks using sympathetic ink.

Thus prepared, the envelope cannot be opened surreptitiously. All I have to do after the experiment is to expose the invisible ink marks. If they line up with one

---

*René Warcollier, Geley's collaborator, became eminent in the research field in the 1930s and '40s.

another I can confirm that the gummed strips have not been unstuck and re-affixed.

Needless to say, I remain absolutely silent during this procedure. Warcollier knows that I am preparing an experiment; but that is all.

There is no way that Ossowiecki can know anything about this. All these preparations have been made by me and no one else, in my office, several days before leaving [for Poland]. The target, once prepared, is shut in my suitcase up to my departure.

The experiment took place on 22nd June, at 17.30, at Ossowiecki's house.

After 10 minutes, Ossowiecki, holding the envelope in his left hand, said:

"There is something colored. There are several colors." (He kneads the envelope).

"I have the impression of a second colored envelope. This second envelope has been deliberately introduced. It is not shaped like an ordinary envelope. It is made simply by folding a sheet in two. The edges are irregular. In the middle there is a sheet of white paper, folded in half. The second envelope is a funny color: dark, gray, greenish, khaki."

(At this moment, Ossowiecki exchanged a few words with a friend who was present but was just leaving. Ossowiecki accompanied him, after having placed the envelope on the table in front of me. He came back, took it up again and started kneading it again).

"There is something that's obstructing me. It's not ordinary writing. It is something.... I see nothing. You could say that there is nothing to see. There is a man, it's not you, another man who collaborated in this experiment. You talked with someone. I see this man; he has moustaches and a lot of hair. He reminds me a little of [René] Sudre. You had a conversation with him towards evening time, at 5, 6 or 7 o'clock. He is a little taller than Sudre."

(All these details are correct. At this point however we have to leave the house to keep an appointment elsewhere. I stop the experiment, take the envelope back and put it in my pocket.)

Two days later, while we are having dinner, Ossowiecki suddenly said:

"I didn't see any writing on the piece of paper enclosed in the opaque envelope. It is just like a blank sheet, but I have the impression that there is something written there with an invisible ink ... how do you say it in French?" I reply "In sympathetic ink?" "Yes, yes," Ossowiecki cried, "It's a phrase written in sympathetic ink."

I say: "Well done! Now you have to read what it says."

For reasons outside my control, the experiment could not be taken up again until 6th July, at 4 p.m.

Several people were talking in the room; Ossowiecki's brother-in-law was playing the piano.

After a prolonged kneading of the envelope Ossowiecki said:

"It's not a drawing. There are two or three lines of writing. It is not a question. It is an exclamation, if one can put it like that. There is an exclamation mark at the end. It is something serious, something about humanity....

"The man who gave you the sympathetic ink is very young; he looks younger than he is" (correct). "He interrupted you while you were preparing the experiment. I see you leave your office; then come back."

(This detail is correct. I was interrupted and called to the library. I remember that I was annoyed at the idea of leaving the envelope, which had not yet been sealed. But I told myself that no one would go into my office, and that even if someone did go in he would not be able to read the invisible ink.)

Ossowiecki made intense efforts, placing the envelope on his forehead. I asked: "Is the piano distracting you?"

Ossowiecki replied, "On the contrary.... I see the movements you made when you were writing, and when you made the exclamation mark. But I can't manage to see what was written. I have never had such trouble. It's too difficult.

"It's not an idea of your own. It's borrowed from a writer. It's a quotation taken from a book. It was not prepared in advance. You just copied it, after a minimal pause for thought, from a book within hand's reach. Perhaps I shall be able to read it from the book I can see."

(He indicated the dimensions of the book, its height and width, with gestures. He was right).

Almost to himself: "God ... something about God."

I said "Good, good ... now see the rest of it."

Ossowiecki tries his best, makes visible but vain efforts.

At last, he said: "It's very Christian, very big ... the creation."

At this point, exhausted by the length of the session (more than an hour) and feeling that he has gone off course, thrown by the idea of God, I said:

"No. You're not speaking now from your intuition, you are thinking, rationalizing, and going wrong. Look at the signature."

He replied: "You are right. But I don't see it; I can't do it. But I sense that it's not a living author. It's a short name ... six letters."

I say: "Almost right."

Ossowiecki continued: "Five—no, seven letters—yes, seven letters." I said "Yes." Ossowiecki continued: "Seven letters, yes, definitely, the first letter is an R." (I do not answer.) "I see you writing but I can't grasp the sense of what you are writing. God is not the first word. God is there without being linked to humanity or to nature. It's more about human sentiments. There are two ideas in this sentence."

At this moment I was obliged by another appointment to interrupt the session.

7th July, at 1600 hours

Despite prolonged efforts (more than an hour) Ossowiecki could not discern the contents of the target paper. He insists that he can see me writing, that he sees the book from which the passage has been copied; but he cannot see the invisible writing or grasp the sense. He just has the idea of God and the two ideas, and that is all.

The experiment having a negative result and with no prospect of progress, I decided that there was no point in continuing with it.

I went into the adjacent room and wrote on a sheet of paper: It is not a matter of deism or atheism, of spiritualism or of materialism; it is a question of facts.— PASTEUR. I folded the paper four times, put it in an envelope, which I stuck down, and came back into the room and gave it to Ossowiecki.

Very quickly, holding the newly presented envelope in his left hand behind his back, he said:

"There is the word atheism. It is not a matter of atheism or of God" (he seemed to read from space, the letter still behind his back, spelling out each word; he lost the thread, caught it again). "It is not a matter of atheism or of God, spiritualism, materialism. The word God is not there, but deism." I said "Very good." But Ossowiecki was exhausted and could not finish it.

[RM 1925 No. 2]

***

The next experiment presented Ossowiecki with a far less formidable task, especially bearing in mind that he had already shown on more than one occasion that he could "see" targets inside rigid containers (e.g. the lead pipe experiment). As in the invisible ink test, Geley was aware of the target, and the experiment shows once more that the presence of someone who knows the identity of the target does not appear to facilitate Ossowiecki's response.

Experiment on 13th July, at 20.00
I had prepared the following packet, before leaving Paris.
1. Wrapped in a sheet of white paper, folded three times, I place two scales from a very large carp (fishing souvenirs). The two scales each measured 2 cm x 2 cm;
2. I refold the paper three times;
3. I enclose it in a small metal box that used to contain a pharmaceutical product;
4. On the side where the box opens I stick three gummed tapes. These tapes stick to the two faces of the box with their proprietary labels. Using invisible ink, I make numerous marks over both the tapes and the labels. (I shall activate the ink before opening the box so as to have proof that the marks correspond properly and that the tapes have therefore not been unstuck).
5. I enclose the box in a triple wrapping of white paper which I fold and seal the ends with three wax seals, using my personal seal.

The Experiment
On 13th July, at 20.00, I hand the package over to M. Ossowiecki, after satisfying myself that the seals are intact. I am seated beside him, and can observe his demeanor. Ossowiecki takes the packet in his left hand.

After five minutes, he says:

"This one was prepared by you. I see something rather odd. I get the idea of a pharmacy.

"It's a medicine box, in metal.

"But this box doesn't contain any medicine now.

"I can see the pharmacy laboratory. Young men dressed in white.

"It was a medicine for the stomach. No, it was for a cough.

"There's something white in the box. Some cotton wool, I think, and a little object. You have stuck something on the opening of the box. There are letters printed on the box....

"I read: medicament in printed letters.

"I also read the name of the medicine: mic, mac.

"In the cotton wool, a little object, little, little.

"I see you stick some labels round the box.

"I read Myk or Mykr.

"In the box something thin, white, in bone ... or in ivory.

"The printed letters on the box are blue. There are letters of different sizes.

"The object is not white.... It has a metallic sort of look."

Ossowiecki makes lengthy efforts but in vain. He does not see the object clearly. Then he asks if he might take the box out of its white envelope. As the box is inviolably sealed (see above) I agree to this. I break my seals and bring out the box. On the label on the lid of the box is written: *MYRRH*.

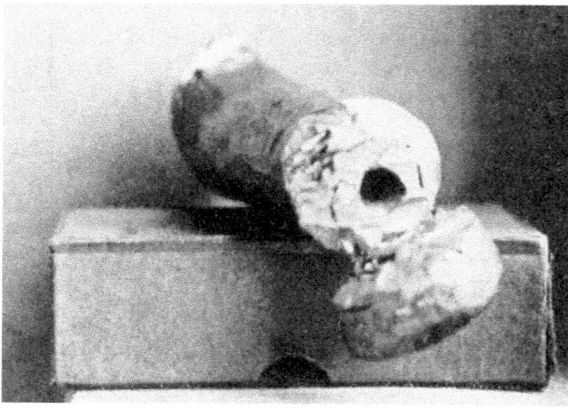

Lead pipe cut open, see experiment on pages 34–35.

And underneath in smaller print, very small letters: *Medicinal fiber*.
Below, in larger print: *Free sample*.
One sees that Ossowiecki perceived, to a large extent, the words *Myrrh* (which he read as *Mykr*) and *medicinal* [medicament]. He said that there were other printed letters of different sizes, which was correct.

It is the first time, in my experiments with Ossowiecki, that he has shown paranormal cognition of printed letters.

Just now, the experiment is interrupted by dinner. It starts again immediately afterwards.

Ossowiecki makes lengthy efforts.

At the end of 20 minutes he says:

"There is something in some white paper. It's not a hard object. It is something lying there. It is not an object for drawing.

"It's enclosed in white paper.

"It's not cotton wool. I made this mistake when I saw the white. The white is paper. In the paper, there is something placed on it, very thin.

"I see it; but I can't understand what it is. It's hardly visible, like something transparent.

"It's a very thin plate. It looks like a plate in ... in.... Something that sometimes takes the place of glass; something that gets used like glass.

"It's like, like ... I cannot remember the French name" (he says a Polish word).

I reply: "No doubt you mean 'mica.'"

Ossowiecki, excited, "Yes, yes, it's like a thin plate of mica, an attenuated plate lying in the paper."

I say "Very good, very good."

I activate the invisible ink. I see that the marks on the tapes and on the label are intact, corresponding exactly. It is certain that the box has not been opened.

I cut the tapes with a knife; I open the box, I unfold the jacket of paper and I show Ossowiecki the two scales end to end. He asks me: "What is it?" and I reply, "Two carp scales."

Ossowiecki says: "I have never seen such things; I saw this thin plate quite well. I thought it was mica." I reply: "The experiment was completely successful. But I was wrong to use such amorphous objects."

Duration of the second part: one hour and a half. Ossowiecki is exhausted by his efforts.

***

Sadly for psychical research, Geley was killed in an airplane crash while on his way from Warsaw, carrying with him some undeveloped photographic plates used in a very imaginative experiment. An obituary of Geley written by Richet appeared in the July-August issue of the *Revue Métapsychique* 1924, and the outcome of this experiment was reported by the new editor, Dr. Eugène Osty. Though the evaluation of the results had to wait until the following year, the target reading of the undeveloped plate was made by Ossowiecki a week before the experiment with the fish scales, which was the last one carried out by Geley.

Report by Geley

I had brought three photographic plates 13/18, exposed but not developed. Each one was enclosed in a black paper packet. Each packet had been put into a large sealed envelope.

The whole thing had been made up by M. Jack, photographer, 62 Avenue Bosquet, Paris, on my instructions. I was entirely ignorant of the contents. Using invisible ink, I made some irregular marks on the back of the external envelope, so that I should know if any attempt were made to open the flap. Any such attempt would for one thing have been absurd, since the undeveloped plate would have kept its secret, and for another the plate would have been fogged if it had been exposed to light.

At 1700 hours on 4th July I take one of the three plates at random and I give it to Ossowiecki. (We were angling for crayfish, seated on the grass.) Ossowiecki takes the plate and concentrates. After 10 minutes:

"This, this is a photo taken indoors, not outside. There are two people in the room. A girl comes in, takes something and leaves the room. She is blonde or auburn, small.

"I see it. It is the photograph of a woman; but not a nude; it's the photograph of a portrait or sculpture ... I have the impression of something quietly situated.

"The man who took this is very nervous; rather dark. He has a little clipped moustache; rather a lot of hair.

"The photograph was taken between 1 and 3 o'clock. There are a lot of pictures or portraits in the room. I see something like a group of sculptures ... in marble or in bronze ... it's dark."

(Very long pause. Some idle chat.) Ossowiecki takes up his theme again:

"I see these two gentlemen again. The road is not very busy. It's on the third floor or thereabouts. One of the men is in a hurry. He leaves suddenly after the photo has been taken. The second one arranges the plate in the black packet. I think it's the second one who has done everything. The first one is pale, tired.

"The woman is the dominant feature in the group."

***

The circumstances of Dr. Geley's tragic death have reduced the value of the assessment of this ingenious experiment. Mme. Geley, on the occasion of her sad journey to Warsaw, found the three plates that her husband had carried with him reduced to fragments, but all three remained enclosed in their sealed black envelopes. One of these plates was reduced to powder, so Mme. Geley threw it away, not thinking at that time about the evaluation of the experiment.

In October 1924, Mme. Geley asked M. Jack, the photographer, and Dr. Osty to come to the Institut Métapsychique. She showed the envelopes that she had brought back with her to M. Jack, who recognized them as two of the unexposed plates given by him to Dr. Geley in June 1924, and that the seals on the envelopes were still intact.

After Mme. Geley read the report written by Dr. Geley, M. Jack remarked that M. Ossowiecki's words corresponded very well with a photograph taken by him, but that under these conditions he had no way of judging whether the plate put by Dr. Geley into the hands of M. Ossowiecki was indeed the one that went with his descriptions.

Here are the descriptions given by M. Ossowiecki and the observations of M. Jack.

> O: It's a photo made inside, not out of doors.
> J: Correct.
> O: There are two people in the room.
> J: Correct.

O: A girl came in and went out after taking something.

J: Yes, my daughter.

O: She is blonde or auburn, small.

J: Yes, but medium built.

O: I see, it's the photograph of a woman ... but not a nude. It's the photograph of a portrait or of a sculpture. I have the impression of something [sic] seated quietly.

J: I have photographed the photograph and here it is:

O: The gentleman who took this is very nervous [or wiry, sinewy], rather dark ... and he has a little clipped moustache, quite a lot of hair.

J: Correct, except for the hair, which is only average.

O: The photograph was taken between 1 and 3 o'clock.

J: Correct.

O: There are a lot of pictures or portraits in the room. I see something like a group of sculptures, in marble or in bronze—it is dark colored.

Photograph of a woman

J: This group exists, but on the first floor, in my apartment and not in the studio where the reproduction was made.

O: The road is not a very busy one. I see these two gentlemen again. Numerous photographic prints.

J: Avenue Bosquet [Grove/Thicket/Spinney Avenue]. My operator and myself.

O: It is on the third floor or thereabouts. One of the gentlemen is in a hurry. He leaves immediately after the photograph has been taken.

J: No, it's on the ground floor. Perhaps. The operator.

O: The first one is pale, tired. The second one arranges the plate in its black packaging.

I have the impression that it is the second one who has done everything.

J: Yes, me. Yes, the operator. I carried out everything with the operator.

Signed J. JACK   62, Avenue Bosquet, Paris

***

It is a great pity that no one obtained a description of the other two plates, but perhaps Mme. Geley could be forgiven for assuming that the photograph so clearly described by Ossowiecki did indeed relate to the correct target, and that the other photographs would have been manifestly different in character. The attendant circumstances and personnel are described as fluently as the target itself, though it is possible in this case that he may have had some prior acquaintance with the photographer and his entourage.

The experiments devised by Geley give much food for thought, and his premature death was a great loss to research. Dr. Eugène Osty, also a physician, succeeded Geley as Director of the IMI as well as taking over editorship of the RM. He continued to publish reports by other contributors, though his only personal experiment with Ossowiecki (also using undeveloped photographic plates) did not succeed, and has to be recorded as one of Ossowiecki's failures.

Geley does not, however, pass out of sight, as he and Osty were also concerned in two experiments carried out with co-operation from London based researchers.

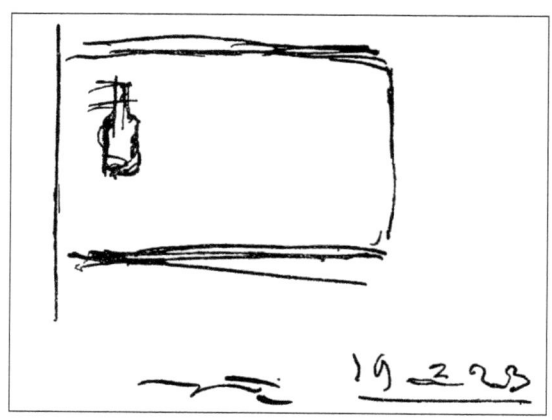

Ossowiecki's drawing of a bottle

Cooperation from London

It is a matter of great regret for the English speaking world that the Ossowiecki phenomenon could not be investigated in depth by English researchers. In our time, when English has become the international language and when London and Paris are a few comfortable hours apart, it is easy to forget that in the 1920s French rather than English was the language educated people were expected to be able to speak, and getting to London necessarily involved crossing the channel by boat.

The eminence of the Society for Psychical Research was however such that the French researchers turned to English researchers for co-operation in the setting of targets by people not directly connected with those conducting the experiments in question. The first of these took place in a very public setting, and was acclaimed with an enthusiasm matched by the language of Geley in a headline of the sort not often seen in a scientific publications.

Experiment 6—Warsaw Conference September 1923
A SENSATIONAL EXPERIMENT WITH M. STEFAN OSSOWIECKI AT THE WARSAW CONFERENCE*

(*Revue Métapsychique* 1923, No.5)

The Society for Psychical Research, with a view to carrying out a crucial experiment with M. Ossowiecki, had prepared a document, the responsible officer being Mr. [Eric] Dingwall, its delegate at the Warsaw conference.

Mr. Dingwall is known to be a renowned conjurer and at the same time a distinguished psychical researcher. He took the principal role in devising the target material. In order to avoid, if possible, thought-reading, he did not want to take part in the actual experiment, so he entrusted the sealed packet to Dr. von Schrenck-Notzing, who brought it with him to a meeting with M. [René] Sudre and me at M. Ossowiecki's house. At M. Ossowiecki's request, and while we took our tea, the experiment started immediately.

The French original mistakenly gives Vienna as the venue of the conference. In fact it took place in Warsaw, 29 August–5 September 1923. This has been corrected in the translation.

In addition to the target document from the SPR, Dr. Schrenck-Notzing had brought with him two other letters prepared in advance, given to him by two conference delegates. These had been packaged and sealed with wax at the Hotel de l'Europe after dinner that same evening.

M. Ossowiecki took the three letters, felt and fingered them, and chose the envelope from the SPR, which was gray in color. The two others were in white envelopes. (The significance of these small details will become clear).

Ossowiecki concentrates, clutching the envelope convulsively, and walking up and down, but not so that we lose sight of him. He speaks in short phrases, with long pauses, and I note down his words as he speaks them.

"I am aware of the restaurant ... at l'hôtel de l'Europe.... It's not you (Schrenck-Notzing) who wrote this.... It's another man, and I can describe him. The letter I am holding (the document from the SPR) has several envelopes.

"It's a letter, but not really a letter.

"I see something greenish, in cardboard.

"It is the other letters (the ones with white envelopes) that come from l'hôtel de l'Europe. I see a foreigner, 34 to 35 years of age. He doesn't say much. He is rather plump. You had a talk with him.

'The letter I am holding was prepared for me. I don't understand. I see something red ... something red ... some colors.

"I don't know why I see a little bottle. I see an office and some carved wood, large and rather dark. It's your office (to Schrenck-Notzing). (There follows a detailed and precise description of Schrenck-Notzing's office.)

"In this envelope there is a drawing by someone who's not much of an artist. There's something red with this bottle.

"There must be a third envelope that's red.

"There is a square drawn in the corner of the paper.

"The bottle is very badly drawn.

"I see! I see!"

At that moment Ossowiecki takes the pen and makes the drawing shown (see p. 62):

"Before 1923 something is written.

"There is also something written on the back, which I can't read.

"I see the two men who wrote the letters in white envelopes. One is the plump man I mentioned earlier. The other looks like the conference secretary" (M. Vett).

Dr. von Schrenck-Notzing speaks up to say that these statements are correct; one of the "white" letters comes from M. Neumann, distinguished practitioner from Baden-Baden; the other comes from M. Vett. Both of them are staying at hotel de l'Europe.

Ossowiecki continues:

"Before the year is a date or a town ... it's the writing of a woman rather than that of a man."

Dr. von Schrenck-Notzing asks, "In what language?"

Ossowiecki replies, "In French," and adds "The bottle is leaning slightly. It does not have a stopper. It has been made with several fine lines. The package is made up like this: first a gray envelope, on the outside; second a darker envelope, greenish in color; third a red envelope. Then a sheet of white paper, folded in two, with a drawing on the inside."

Despite our impatience we decide to keep the envelope intact and hand it to Mr. Dingwall unopened, which Dr. von Schrenck-Notzing did that same evening.

Two days later, following his presentation on his experiments with Willi Schneider, Dr. von Schrenck-Notzing announced that he was going to tell the

Dingwall's drawing of a bottle

assembly about the experiment carried out with Ossowiecki and check the outcome. I then read out the written record of the clairvoyant's utterances reported above, and made a copy on the blackboard of the drawing made by Ossowiecki.

Mr. Dingwall showed the package intact with its seal in place. He explained the precautions he had taken in order to be certain that the package had not been opened. He said that it contained a sheet of paper folded in half placed in the first envelope; this first envelope was itself in a second envelope, and the second was in a third, gray, outer envelope, this one sealed.

As well as that, the package had been perforated in four places by a very fine needle, so that the holes would not have corresponded and let light through if the envelopes had been opened. Mr. Dingwall added that these precautions could be relied on with absolute certainty, and he certified that the package had not been opened.

People waited impatiently. The great hall of the university was crowded and silent. Ossowiecki himself, rather pale and nervous, was in quite an emotional state.

Slowly and calmly Mr. Dingwall, using a knife, carefully cut open the first envelope. He took out the second one, a greenish black; then, in like manner, from this second envelope extracted a third envelope, a red one. Applause.

Then he cut open the red envelope and pulled out a piece of paper folded in half. He displayed its contents and copied it onto the blackboard beside the Ossowiecki drawing. They corresponded absolutely.

On the back of the drawing was the following sentence (in French), which the clairvoyant had said that he could not read:

"Les vignobles du Rhin, de la Moselle et de la Bourgogne donnent un vin excellent."
[The vineyards of the Rhine, of the Moselle and of Burgundy make excellent wine.]

The date was incomplete in Ossowiecki's drawing. The original had: *"22 Aug. 1923."* But Ossowiecki had said

"Before 1923 there is something that I can't read, a date or a town."

The whole assembly, everyone on their feet and with eyes fixed on Ossowiecki, burst into applause and gave him a standing ovation. Dr. von Schrenck-Notzing exclaimed "Thank you, thank you, in the name of science!"

Such was this splendid and decisive experiment. It completes our numerous examinations of M. Ossowiecki's amazing faculty.

P.S.—This is the report of Mr. Dingwall about the precautions taken for the experiment.

The sealed envelope

I prepared the sealed packet on the afternoon of 22nd August 1923. No one else was present during the procedure and no one was told what I had written or drawn on the sheet of paper that it contained.

The paper measured about 17.5 cm by 11 cm. I wrote at the top of the paper, before placing it in the first envelope the words: *"Les vignobles du Rhin, de la Moselle et de la Bourgogne donnent un vin excellent."*

On the lower part of the page I made a very primitive sketch, intended to convey the idea of a bottle without drawing the exact image. I enclosed it with three lines, the fourth being formed by the left side of the paper. I then wrote in the lower right corner: Aug. 22 1923. The sheet was then folded, the writing on the back, and placed in an envelope made of opaque red paper measuring about 11.5 cm. by 9 cm. The paper was placed so that the writing was on the top side of the envelope and the sketch was on the opening flap side.

This red envelope was not closed but was inserted into a black, opaque envelope, the flap side going in first. There was no room for play between the envelopes. This second envelope, also not sealed, was then inserted, the flap side first, into a gray colored envelope, and this was stuck down, then sealed (with wax) on the end of the flap.

Four holes were made, in the four corners of the package, which was put away until the departure for Warsaw. There, the document remained locked in my suitcase or carried in my jacket pocket, squeezed between the pages of my passport. So it was kept up to the moment when I gave it to Baron von Schrenck-Notzing for the experiment.

***

In his own account of the experiment, published in the *Journal of the Society for Psychical Research* of May 1924, after ruling out any possibility of access to the contents of the envelope by normal means, Dingwall concludes, "The supernormal character of the incident seems to me quite clear and decisive" (p. 263).

At the time, Dr. Eric Dingwall was Research Officer for the Society for Psychical Research, and it is correctly stated that he was a skilled conjurer. There came a time when he fell out with the SPR (in connection with his investigation of the American medium Margery) and his appointment was not renewed.

Though he remained an active SPR member he would often, especially in his advanced years, be heard to declare that despite some bold endorsement made in earlier times he had never witnessed a paranormal incident. Asked how he reconciled this utterance with his unequivocal assurance that the envelope used in this experiment could not have been tampered with he said that he could not be sure what was done with it while it was in the hands of Schrenck-Notzing.

Professor Dr. Baron A. von Schrenck-Notzing, a gynecologist, may possibly on certain occasions have been imposed on by fraudulent mediums, but there is absolutely no reason to impute bad faith to him.

It was put to Dingwall that even supposing Schrenck-Notzing to have been dishonest, Dingwall himself had asserted at the time with total certainty that the pinholes were undisturbed and that the envelope had not been opened. Asked to explain how he could now deny his contemporary statement Dingwall made no attempt to answer this question, or any others concerning his retraction of earlier statements. The term "retrocognitive dissonance" has been used to describe people who after some years deny earlier affirmations of confidence in paranormal events attested to by them, but this describes those who genuinely fall into a state of dissonance; people who knew Dingwall well said that in fact he harbored no doubts about the reality of paranormal activity.

Experiment 7—The Besterman Report, 1933

The second experiment in which the target was set by an English researcher took place some years later, the researcher in question being Dr. Theodore Besterman. His choice of target was more process orientated than was Dingwall's, in that he sought answers to two questions, firstly, whether the medium, despite not knowing any English, perceived the meaning associated with the drawing of a bottle of ink with the words "Swan Ink" written on it; i.e., would he show any apprehension of the black swan trademark associated with those words, or would he show any apprehension of "swan" or "bird." Secondly, Besterman folded the paper so that one of these words was folded over on itself, while the other was not; a psychic operating by clairvoyance might be expected to have clearer sight of the unfolded word, on the principle that if you hold up to the light a paper on which a word is written and then folded over on itself, you would normally have great difficulty in deciphering the word. We shall see what happened.

This report is taken from the Proceedings of the Society for Psychical Research [XLI, Part 132, pp. 345–351].

An Experiment in "Clairvoyance" with M. Stefan Ossowiecki by Theodore Besterman

During the course of a visit to Warsaw in the spring of 1933, in company with Dr. Osty, I made the acquaintance of M. Ossowiecki, well known as an amateur clairvoyant who has obtained striking successes. It was not at the time possible for me to arrange an experiment with M. Ossowiecki, as he was busy with one prepared by Dr. Osty. M. Ossowiecki kindly promised, however, that he would attempt to "read" the contents of a sealed envelope if I cared to send him one on my return to England. Immediately on my return to London I accordingly, on 17th May, sent M. Ossowiecki a sealed envelope. Receiving no reply I caused inquiries to be made and finally, in July, I heard from M. Ossowiecki that the envelope I had sent him had been regarded as suspicious by the censorship, and had been opened by them. M. Ossowiecki suggested that I should prepare another envelope and send it to M. Gravier, the President of the *Polskie Towarzystwo Badań Psychicznych*, before which he would then carry out the experiment. This I did, dispatching the second sealed envelope on 14 July to Madame Wodzińska, for passing on to M. Gravier, as I did not know the latter's address. There the matter rested so far as I knew until the end of September, when, knowing that Lord Charles Hope was going to Warsaw, with Miss A. Reutiner and Mr. John Evelyn, both Members of the Society, I asked him to make an effort to get the experiment carried out. This he accordingly did, with the kind help of M. Gravier. Actually, however, as I afterwards learned, there had already been two preliminary and fairly successful sittings.

But before dealing with these preliminary sittings, I will describe the sealed packet, which, with its contents, was prepared at, and dispatched from, my desk in the Society's rooms. Figure 1 [see p. 67] is a photograph of the paper I had prepared. When folded it measured 93 mm by a trifle over 107 mm. It was placed in a reddish orange "Ensign" light-tight envelope (that is, not transparent to white light), measuring 94 mm by 119 mm. This envelope was in turn enclosed in a black "Ensign" light-tight envelope, measuring 106 mm by 130 mm. This black envelope was finally enclosed in a large Manila envelope doubled in two and thus measuring 114 mm by 152 mm. Each of these envelopes was closed in a special way and bore private and invisible marks. The outer doubled envelope was in addition sealed with surgical tape arranged in a special way and signed by me. This packet was then further enclosed in a stout outer envelope and sent to Mme. Wodzińska, who remitted it direct to M. Gravier. A statement from her to

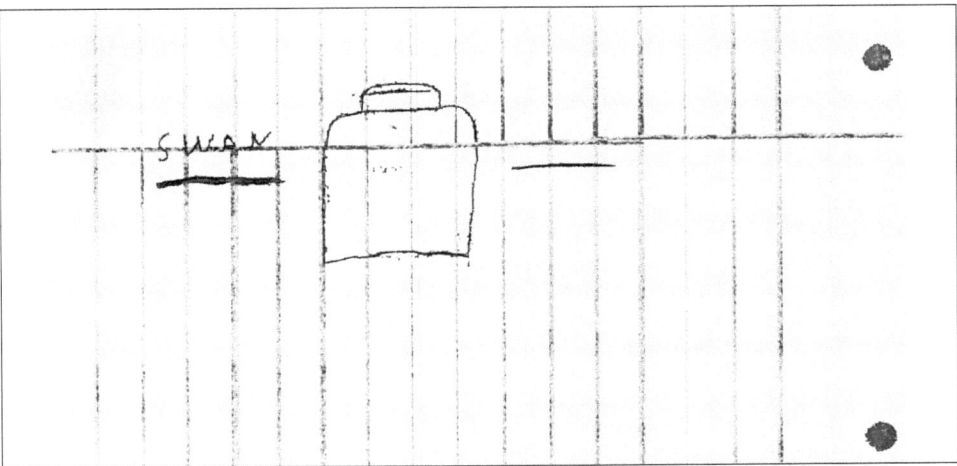

Fig.1 Reduced photograph of the original drawing; the actual size of the paper is 219mm x 139 mm. The line under "SWAN" is blue, and that under "INK" [obscured] is red.

that effect follows in Appendix Ai. M. Gravier retained the packet in his possession until the beginning of the sitting described below. A statement from M. Gravier follows in Appendix Aii.

I will now give an account of the two preliminary sittings, in the form of a statement by M. Gravier, who writes:

"After receiving your sealed envelope the contents of which were to be detected by M. Ossowiecki, he and I had two sittings on 8 and 9 August 1933.

"During these meetings the following was said.

"On 8 August M.O.: Sees Mr. Besterman,—he sees that it is between 6 and 8 o'clock in the evening and that Mr. Besterman cuts a picture from an illustrated English paper. Picture of the size of 6 x 7 centimeters. He sees four envelopes one in the other.

"This meeting took place in my house."

The following day, 9 August, meeting at M.O.'s, who says:

"It is not an illustration cut from a paper.

"It is a drawing made on a big piece of paper, this drawing is 5 x 6 centimeters.

"There are three envelopes—one exterior, the next black, the third colored—it is neither yellow, nor blue, nor red, I think that it is rose, but I do not see very well.

"Besides the drawing there is something written:

"It represents something like a goblet, closed with a cork, and there is something written, not on the goblet, but around it—I see a W—I see a capital I,—I also see an S and something red and something blue. That makes me confuse it with the letters."

Since then M.O. was unwilling to give any further sitting, saying that he had thought it over and could not agree to continue if the envelope was not afterwards opened before him.

When Mlle. Reutiner, Lord Charles Hope and Mr. Evelyn came we decided that they would take the responsibility of opening the envelope on your behalf and that it should be opened immediately after [the sitting].

You know the rest.—

[Signed] A. Gravier

[Literal translation.]

On 29th September 1933 M. Ossowiecki invited a number of friends to his flat for the purpose of witnessing his attempt to "read" the contents of the envelope. Lord Charles Hope writes: "*Soon after M. Gravier's arrival at M. Ossowiecki's flat he handed the envelope over to me and I kept it in my pocket. I watched the envelope the whole time during the experiment and myself opened it at the finish of M. Ossowiecki's 'reading' of the contents. The lighting of the room during the 'reading' was dim, the only light actually in the room being from two large candles near the clairvoyant, and electric light in the adjoining room.*"

During the course of the experiment M. Gravier made a record, in French, of what was said and done by M. Ossowiecki. I now give a literal translation of this record, only inserting inverted commas where necessary and reference figures within square brackets.

Warsaw, 29 September 1933.

Sitting at M. Ossowiecki's

Lord Charles Hope hands to Mr. O. a letter sent to M. Gravier from London by Mr. Besterman, to be "read" by M. O.

Numerous persons [present]—we begin at 6 o'clock in the afternoon.

The piano is played.

[1] O. says: "I am already in England—in London—[2] it is a very big house, [3] in the center of L.—Not altogether in the center, but on the right side—[4] a gray house, [5] three or four floors. [6] He lives at the bottom. [7] I see Mr. Besterman dressed in black."

[Notes by Th.B.]

[1] *Yes, but M. Ossowiecki knows that the Society's Rooms are in London.* [2] *Moderately large.* [3] *In the West Central District.* [4] *No, the house is in brick and stucco.* [5] *It has a basement and four floors.* [6] *I do not live at the S.P.R.* [7] *No.*

O: [8] In the next room (a cote) a gentleman in black—he goes away.

B: [8] *Possibly, as the adjoining room is open to members.*

O: [9] A lady dressed in white sweater returns into the room.

B: [9] *Possibly, see* [8].

O: [10] There are a lot of books about in the room.

B: [10] *Yes, it is part of the Library.*

O: [11] He approaches the table—not that in his room—but in the room adjoining. [12] It is a little salon. –

B: [11] *Yes, but in my own room, not that adjoining,* [12] *which is also part of the Library.*

O: [13] I see a black envelope, [14] and some black paper on the table.

B: [13] *Yes.* [14] *No.*

O: [15] Ditto a red envelope—no, rose (rosatre).

B: [15] *Yes, but actually a reddish orange. The outer envelope sent to M. Ossowiecki on 17 May similarly contained black and orange envelopes; it must be assumed that this was known to M. Ossowiecki.*

O: [16] He intends to cut out a drawing from one of the English papers—something like an advertisement.

B: [16] *No; but the envelope mentioned in* [15] *contained an illustrated advertisement cut from a newspaper. This no doubt was also known to M. Ossowiecki.*

O: [17] It was between 4 and 5 o'clock.

B: [17] *Yes.*

O: [18] I see him again, he had changed his mind.

B: [18] *No.*

O: [19] He takes a piece of white paper and cuts it—[20] he has pencils of three colors, blue, red, black. [21] He takes the black pencil, [22] it is a drawing.

B: [19] *No.* [20] *Yes, though the drawing was done in ink, not in pencil.* [21] *See* [20]. [22] *Yes.*

O: He draws [23] and then he writes [24] in English,— unfortunately I do not know the language. I see some letters—[25] it is just 4 o'clock. [26] He is now alone.

B: [23] *Yes.* [24] *Yes.* [25] *It was about 4.30.* [26] *I was alone throughout.*

O: [27] In the second room there is this gentleman and this lady.

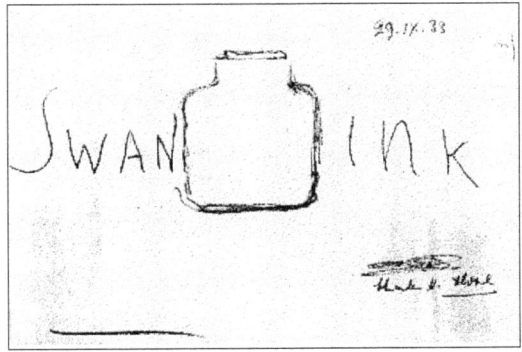

Photograph of Ossowiecki's final drawing. The actual size of the paper is 220 mm by 142 mm.

B: [27] *See* [8] *and* [9].
O: What is he drawing? Give me the pencil.

Ossowiecki takes the pencil. He draws. Ossowiecki draws a rectangle—above it is a small rectangle. [Here follows a sketch of M. Ossowiecki's drawing.* In his sketch M. Gravier indicates that M. Ossowiecki said, in regard to the lines at each side of the lower rectangle (28), "There is something written," and of the single line lower down and to the left, (29) "Something red."]

B: [28] *Yes.* [29] *No, this line is blue, it is the opposite one which is red.*

O: He has drawn—[30] he puts into a yellow red (orange) envelope—[31] he gums it —

B: [30] *Yes, but see* [15]. [31] *Yes, though actually I used paste.*

O: [32] He puts into a black envelope.

B: [32] *Yes.*

O: [33] The gentleman comes into the room.

B: [33] *No.*

O: [34] He gums the black envelope all around.

B: [34] *No, only at both ends.*

O: [35] The drawing is a bottle—no—it is like that. [Here M. Gravier gives a sketch of M. Ossowiecki's,* indicating that of the lower left line M. Ossowiecki said, (36) "A rose line."]

B: [35] *Yes.* [36] *No, see* [29].

O: I see—[37] there are two words—[38] each letter is big and each letter is by itself—[24] it is English, there is [39] (on the left) S W A (each letter written apart) and also a fourth letter which I do not understand—an N, but I am not sure.

B: [37] *Yes.* [38] *Yes.* [39] *Yes; all four letters are correct and in the right order.*

O: [40] Then there is (on the right) I N

B: [40] *Yes; both letters are correct and in the right order, though the word is incomplete.*

O: No, the drawing is a little bit different. (O. again begins to draw.) [Here M. Gravier gives a sketch of M. Ossowiecki's final figure, marking the line in the left hand bottom corner A—B.] Yes, that's right—I see very well now—table, office, envelope, black, rose. (It is 6.25).

O: [41] There is something red at A.B.—I cannot understand. I have already finished. 6.26

*Not reproduced here.

B: [41] *No; see* [29].

It was after this that Lord Charles Hope opened the envelopes, taking care of course not to destroy the sealing of the outer and inner envelopes. The above account was signed by M.A. Gravier, Miss Alice Reutiner, Lord Charles M. Hope, Mr. John Evelyn, Prince J. Woroniecki, and seven others.

On 3rd October 1933 Lord Charles Hope handed to me, in London, the original of the above account, M. Ossowiecki's drawings, and the opened envelopes. I minutely examined the envelopes and found that, with the exception of considerable wear and tear on the outer envelope, they were all intact. The private marks which I had made and which would have been inevitably disturbed on any attempt to open the envelopes, were all in order. I have no hesitation in saying that none of the three envelopes was opened [surreptitiously]. I am also satisfied that no effort was made, an effort which would not in any case have been successful (because, among other reasons, of the special folding of the paper), to render the contents transparent by chemical means. The same is true of X-ray and similar methods. It will thus be seen that M. Ossowiecki's clairvoyant reading (as it may for convenience be called, though other supernormal theories are not excluded) was almost completely successful. It would of course have been more satisfactory if the envelope "read" had been the one I had with me in Warsaw, or, failing that, the first packet I sent. Still, the main point is clearly that the packet should not have been tampered with; and of that I am satisfied. Cordial thanks are due not only to M. Ossowiecki himself for his brilliant performance, but also to M. Gravier and to Mme. Wodzińska for their invaluable help.

A point of theoretical interest is this: the subject of the test was deliberately of such a kind (e.g. "Swan") as to be capable of being symbolically "perceived"; also the drawing was so disposed that the folding of the paper completely destroyed the form of the bottle and of one word, leaving the other word intact. None of these things affected M. Ossowiecki's "reading," which is almost an enlarged facsimile, except that in his second drawing there are lines that might be taken to indicate the folding.

APPENDIX A—Statements

i. In accordance with your wish I certify having received your sealed envelope and having remitted it intact to M.A. Gravier.

[Signed] Marie Wodzińska
[10 October 1933]

ii. The envelope was preserved intact by me until the sitting held in the presence of Lord Charles Hope, Mr. Evelyn and Mlle. Reutiner.

[Signed] A. Gravier
10 October 1933

Reports by Various Other Researchers

Prosper Szmurło, editor of *Zagadnienia Metapsychiczne*, was respected by Geley to the point where his reports were published mostly in the RM as well as in the Polish society's own publication. Some of the most imaginative procedures were devised by Szmurło, who seems also to have taken pains to impose strict control conditions.

Experiment series 8 — March 1923 (identifying contents of a package)

EXPERIMENT 1

Szmurło starts by explaining that this is the written report on a presentation made at the Warsaw conference on 2 September 1923. He adds that he wanted his experiment to exclude telepathy.

> To avoid this contingency the Committee of the Society decided to prepare several objects all provided by one person, from which we should submit only one to the clairvoyant. In this case the action of telepathy would be made more difficult, the person in question not knowing which target has been used for the experiment. In this case the mind-to-mind action would focus not on the target document but on the one its owner happened to think about most at the time.
>
> With this purpose in mind we addressed ourselves to someone who was not a member of our society: Mr. Marjan Wawrzeniecki. MW is a distinguished painter who also works in the fields of archaeology and anthropology. We asked him to be good enough to let us have some items that could be used in an experiment, and to tell no one about this. MW does not know M. Ossowiecki. The members of our society also agreed to keep the experimental project secret right up to the time it was to be carried out.
>
> MW was to place some articles, each one separately in boxes of equal size, wrapping them first in cotton wool, to prevent any noise that might indicate the nature of those items. In each box there would also be a label bearing a number. In some sealed envelopes marked with corresponding numbers, would be placed a description of the articles. To lighten his task I personally sent him four square boxes of equal size, 9.5 × 9.5 × 2cm, and a packet of cotton wool.
>
> On 14th February 1923 MW sent us the four boxes tied up crosswise, the loose ends sealed with his own seal (we had absolutely no idea of their contents) and four envelopes, also sealed, marked with numbers 1, 2, 3 and 4. All these objects were kept by me, under lock and key.
>
> On 28th February we approached M. Ossowiecki, asking if he would grant us a session. On 10th March we received an answer telling us that M. Ossowiecki would receive us as his guests at the hotel de l'Europe on 12th March at 8 p.m. MW was not informed of this.
>
> On the agreed day I went to the hôtel de l'Europe together with the Vice-President of our society, the late General T, physician and head of the health division of the Ministry of War (he died on 4th July). We found M. and Mme. Ossowiecki, M. MN, Envoy Extraordinary and Cabinet Minister from Latvia, together with his wife.
>
> M. Ossowiecki took one of the boxes that had earlier been chosen at random by me, wrapped in several layers of paper, tied and sealed with my seal, and he sat on the sofa, beside me. From time to time M. Ossowiecki joined in the general conversation, which was interrupted several times by the telephone.
>
> Every word spoken by M. Ossowiecki was taken down carefully by me. They were as follows.
>
> "It is a black box. It used to contain a dozen photographic plates. One of the plates was broken. They were taken out of the box by a slim woman, who loves music. The box was found somewhere in the area of Chmielna street, in Warsaw, but it comes from abroad, from Germany, or so it seems to me. On the lid there is a label which has something on it in Egyptian style. I see a factory ... a place ... a lot of young girls working around these boxes. There are stacks of them.

There are no plates in the box now, it contains something that has no connection with them ... a gray object ... in glass ... no, in porcelain. I see fire ... it's not an object, but a fragment, a small part. Oh, it's so old! Hundreds, hundreds of years old—it's a fragment of a prehistoric urn ... broken.... I see it, it looks like this" (here M. Ossowiecki described the shape by gestures).

"It was found by someone digging in the ground—yes—I see sand, people turning the earth with spades. Ah! There is something else in the box—something white. I don't understand the connection between this object and the pharmacy—I see her in the pharmacy—here in Warsaw, Marszałkowska street—it's a lady buying that stuff." Here M. Ossowiecki stopped, saying that he felt tired.

Including intervals and conversation, the session lasted about 50 minutes. Before opening the box M. Ossowiecki drew for us with a pen the shape of the object that was in the box. Then we untied the cords, removed the wrappings and before our eyes appeared a black box in which, some months ago, I received some photographic slides from Szalay's, which is situated in Chmielna Street, Warsaw. They were delivered to me by one of the shop assistants, a slim lady who, as we verified later, was very fond of music. The box contained a dozen transparencies 8.5 x 8.5 cm in size.

We were not able to ascertain later who had taken the slides afterwards, nor if one of them had been broken. The plates came from the Ernemann factory at Dresden (in Germany). The label showed a woman's head looking rather like the head of Isis between Egyptian style columns. Inside the box we found a fragment of an urn wrapped in cotton wool and a label bearing the number 2. After opening the envelope marked with the same number we read the following description, signed by M.W.: "Fragment of a prehistoric urn, found by M. Wawrzeniecki in 1904 near Warsaw."

The cotton wool in the box that I sent to M.W had been bought by my wife in a pharmacy situated in Marszałkowska Street, Warsaw. So M. Ossowiecki's description was perfectly accurate and matched the true facts.

I consider this experiment to be one of the most interesting and instructive of its kind, because we are able to observe the whole process of the phenomenon of "psychometry." The "psychometrist" starts by describing the exterior of the box and seems gradually to move into the interior until he reaches the object itself. Neither General T nor I had expected that M. Ossowiecki would tell us anything about the box: we thought he would go straight to a description of the object that it enclosed. This factor was therefore quite unexpected, and any conscious suggestion on our part must be excluded.

Our session also gives the lie to the widely held view that M. Ossowiecki can see only material that is handwritten and cannot say anything about printed matter, though it is true that most experiments up to now have been done with writing. But one can affirm that M Ossowiecki's faculties are universal. The drawing he made for us of part of the broken urn before the box was opened looked just like the article itself.

Further, MW was quite astonished when he learnt the result of the experiment, and he was sorry that we had not picked another box containing an object that interested him much more. This is another indication against telepathy, for an interest of that sort fixed on another article could have confused the clairvoyant.

[RM 1923 No. 6]

***

The next experiment is one of those unplanned, impromptu drawing tests, con-

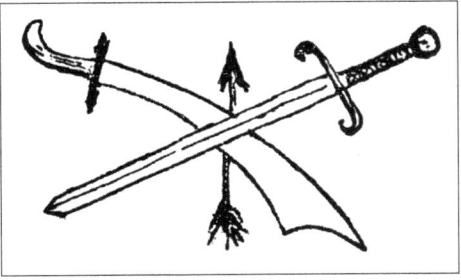 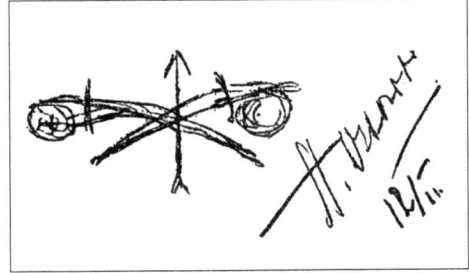

Left: **Drawing by Szmurło.** *Right:* **Drawing by Ossowiecki.**

ducted under quite good conditions, in that the target was prepared in another room. It cannot count as among the most probative, since Szmurło could not resist being present when Ossowiecki made his drawing, but as we have seen from several of the tests carried out in Paris, the presence of the target-maker does not seem to help Ossowiecki at all. When the drawing is complex, with several unrelated themes, cueing can reasonably be excluded in practical terms.

EXPERIMENT 2

After a short interval during which we had tea M. Ossowiecki suggested doing another experiment, this time with a drawing. I took a pencil, a piece of paper (M. Nuksa's visiting card), an opaque envelope and a book to serve as a desk top, and I left the room, closing the double door behind me. I stood there a moment, considering what to draw, then I moved a few steps to my right, where I saw a bench across the corridor. I sat down on it and, balancing the book on the arm of the banquette I made the drawing shown above.

When I had finished I put the card in the envelope, sealed it and gave it to M. Ossowiecki. He took it, and holding it behind his back, he said almost immediately:

"You have certainly drawn something very complicated, something with a cutting edge; I see: They are two sabers, two crossed foils. There's something else in the middle, you drew it last—ah! I see now, it's an arrow, and it has its head pointing upwards. I shall try to draw it, though I am not very good at drawing."

So saying M. Ossowiecki sat at the table and made the drawing shown above, starting from the same point and making the same pencil strokes as I did, a point that he made himself.

Even if telepathy is possible in this case, it is nevertheless much more difficult to accept in many other experiments that have been carried out in the past. There were effectively three target objects, not just one, as is usually the case, and M. Ossowiecki had to divine their relative positions. Taking into consideration M. Ossowiecki's faculty of psychometry, which has been proved many times, it is fair to say that in this case too we were in the presence of a psychometry demonstration, and not telepathy

What makes it even more interesting to me is that M. Ossowiecki told me precisely, and in detail, everything that I had done when I went out of the room; he told how I had stood there for a moment or two, then turned right, sat on the banquette; in which direction I turned my head and how I had rested my book on the banquette, etc.—all as if he had been there with me and had seen what had happened. Furthermore, he had told all these details to the people who were with him in the room before my return. So that would be clairvoyance! M. Ossowiecki really seems to possess all the supernormal faculties!

The records of the experiment, signed by all those who were present, are held at the Psychophysical Society of Warsaw. I should like to end this report by expressing profound gratitude to M. l'ingénieur Stefan Ossowiecki whose generosity has made it possible for us to accomplish these interesting experiments. If his kindness to our Society is not exhausted, I hope to carry out with him an experiment that I have devised which, I think, has not yet been done. I shall not fail to report the outcome to the IMI.

PROSPER DE SZMURLO   [RM 1923 No. 6]

Experiment 9 — May 1924
(Szmurło — undeveloped photograph)

The next report in the RM appears under the heading of a Report by Osty, its editor, but it is in fact a report by Szmurło, using a carefully devised protocol, on 15 May 1924. It was preceded by a rather informal test devised by Charles Richet, Jr., son of his more famous father.

> To avoid all possibility of telepathy, we decided:
> (1) To have some photographs made, not by just one, but by two or more individuals, each of them giving us not just one, but two plates already exposed but not developed.
> (2) These individuals would tell no one, and above all not tell us, what they had taken.
> (3) The only people who would attend the session with Ossowiecki would be those who had not played any part in the taking of the photographs and knew nothing about them.
> (4) The photographers would bring us the plates enclosed in sealed envelopes. The plates would be code-marked and the envelopes would also contain a detailed description of the way the photograph had been made.
>
> We got in touch with some people who had their own photographic equipment, and who were members of our society: Mr. JB, Vice-Director of the Agricultural Bank, and Mr. GP, naturalist and chemist. We asked these gentlemen to send us their plates and a description of how the photographs were taken all in sealed envelopes.
>
> GP made up four envelopes with plates, two of which were his own, and two were obtained from JB, all wrapped in red and black paper in exactly the same way. He tied the packages with tape, and applied seals, put them in a cardboard box and brought them to me. I immediately put them under lock and key and kept them at my house until the day of the experiment.
>
> After many attempts I finally succeeded, early one morning, in bearding the elusive Mr. S. Ossowiecki, elusive because of his many engagements. He was still in bed, but agreed with great cordiality to give his time to the experiment that I asked of him in my name and in the name of our Society.
>
> On the day in question, 15th May 1924, at 6 p.m., I went to the illustrious psychometrist's house accompanied by members of our Society, M.S. Rzewuski and Dr. SD, and taking with me, as well as the plates and the envelopes, everything needed to develop the plates. After a short wait, our engineer friend M. Ossowiecki arrived. He had come from a meeting with his nephew Mr. OM. He told us he was feeling extremely tired and out of sorts, however, not wanting to disappoint us, he said he was ready to carry out the experiment. He warned us,

The Formal Experiments

however, that he doubted if he would succeed at such an unusual experiment, something quite new for him, and in any case he was suffering from stress and depression, the effects of working too hard.

I did not take all this too seriously, and not wanting to put the experiment off for another day I offered M. Ossowiecki the box with the four plates, wrapped in their red and black envelopes.

By then it was 7.14 p.m. M. Ossowiecki took by chance the first plate he came to, and put the box with the remaining plates on the table. SR and SD took a pencil and prepared to write down the psychometrist's words.

M. Ossowiecki was seated on the ottoman, pressing the plate between his hands while talking to us. At times he would be silent and seemed to concentrate. After six minutes he started to speak, with pauses. This is a résumé of what he said:

"This is a photographic print, taken in an apartment. This is a difficult task: I have warned you that I don't see things that are printed or drawn mechanically, and photography is mechanical. Yes! One thing is for sure, this photograph was taken in an enclosed place. I see a nicely furnished room ... a lot of ornamental objects ... framed portraits. I don't understand what this has to do with a chateau. At the moment when this photograph was taken I see three people ... a woman and two men. I don't see it clearly. I see as if through a fog. I see a tall man, slim, with a long, thin face. The second is rather small, stocky, with a round face ... and I think he has a beard. One seems very strong, the other rather delicate, much weaker. One is in military uniform. I don't understand what the chateau signifies and what it has to do with everything I am seeing ... but I see it all the time. The room is very beautiful ... portraits ... a desk ... no, it's bigger, more robust. I see a sculpture on it. I am seeing badly ... the chateau again! My head is spinning. What a pity that all these plates were kept together. That's why my head is spinning."

Then, without letting go of the plate in his hand, M. Ossowiecki puts his other hand on the box containing the three other plates, and continues:

"It's strange, now I see lots and lots of trees, and it's as if ghosts or men are in among the trees: a lot of heads ... one of the heads is dark. (At this point I think suddenly that one of these photographs was taken in a cemetery, and at the same time SD thinks of the spirit photographs of Conan Doyle.) I see a man with a small moustache, very pale ... it's as if he is sickly. I see things that are contradictory.... I can't do any more.... I'm not in a fit state."

We stop the experiment at 7.42 p. m. The sitting has lasted 28 minutes. Those present, including the psychometrist himself, are enormously interested, and want to see the result as soon as possible. They all insist that I develop the plates at once. We close the shutters, make room on the table and turn on the red light. I unwrap the plates from their papers and plunge them into the developer. Everyone leans over the bowl, but the red light is too weak for an image to be seen and all we see is two light strips enclosing a gray space. We turn on the white light and then we are all able to see the photograph of a painting, which was taken in a room. The painting shows an oriental landscape with the frontage of a chateau or a mosque.

I tear open the envelope containing an account of the circumstances in which the photograph was taken, and we find the report of JB: the photograph was taken by him, in his apartment. It is of an original painting by the painter Lachenko, who painted an oriental landscape with a chateau or a mosque.

Wanting to know if the other details given by the psychometrist corresponded to reality, I telephoned JB next day, and asked if there had been witnesses present when he took the photograph. I asked him to describe these people, their appearance, their dress, the furnishings in the room where the photograph was taken, but without telling him anything of what M. Ossowiecki had said.

I received the following written reply: During the taking of the photograph JB was assisted by his younger brother, an officer in uniform, tall, slim, with a long, thin face. JB himself is smaller but stockier than his brother. Neither of them has a beard. While they were engaged on the photography, their mother came into the room several times. The walls of this room are covered with a lot of pictures by known artists. The furniture is mahogany, covered with silk material. Among the pictures are a lot of sketches and a portrait of Napoleon. They are all framed. On the desk is a stag in bronze and a statuette of a warrior.

The description of M. Ossowiecki's vision corresponds with reality, except for some details such as the man with a beard and the age of the woman, which one might explain by M. Ossowiecki's fatigue, which caused him to see things through a fog.

I must add that none of us had ever been to JB's home, and we went there without M. Ossowiecki, when we were able to confirm for ourselves that the description given in JB's letter was perfectly accurate.

The pale and sickly man with a little moustache, seen by M. Ossowiecki, was GP, who took two photographs and enveloped them. The portrayal of him was precise.

We asked M. Ossowiecki to give us a reading of the three other plates. Unfortunately he was too exhausted to do this. We contented ourselves with reading the three written accounts contained in the envelopes. On one plate there was the photograph of JB's brother, and officer; on the second, the photograph of a family picture showing Notre-Dame d'Ostra Brama; on the third, the photograph of L.S., a chemistry student. On the report relating to this third photograph there was written:

"The day before being photographed, L.S. had come back from Posen, where he had just attended the funeral of his aunt in the town cemetery."

The scene described by M. Ossowiecki: a place with a lot of trees and a lot of people, could be a sighting of the funeral in the Posen cemetery. All the plates, letters and envelopes are to be found in the archives of the Polish Psychophysical Society.

[RM 1925 No. 6]

***

Szmurło's report is followed by a lengthy note by Osty, in which he takes issue with Szmurło's conviction that the conditions of the experiment excluded the operation of telepathy, putting forward his own theory that once an article that has been in the presence of a person is placed in the hand of a psychometrist a telepathic link is set up between the two persons.

As part of his argument Osty compares the accurate description of the tall officer and the small, stocky man with the relatively vague description of the photograph. If all four plates had been judged against Ossowiecki's mentation (a method frequently used when testing people of marginal psychic ability) we cannot be sure that they would not have preferred Notre Dame d'Ostra Brama.

We now turn to the reports of Eugène Osty, who describes four experiments carried out during his stay in Warsaw, of which the last must rank among the most spectacular.

 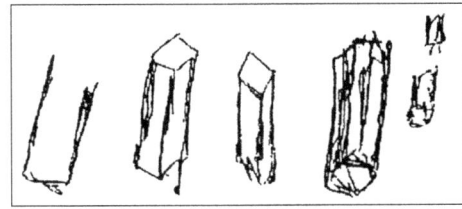

Left: Drawing by Mongel. *Right:* Drawing by Ossowiecki.

Experiment series 10—1934 (Osty in Warsaw)

EXPERIMENT 1

The first experiment is unusual in that it shows a total failure to describe the subject of an undeveloped photographic plate. Ossowiecki had visions of the portrait of a lady, whereas the developed plate showed the statuette of a medieval pilgrim. A lesser psychic might have taken comfort for having recognized the portrayal of a human being, but for Ossowiecki this was a failure, though not unexpected. He had issued a warning:

> You are asking for something extremely difficult. I have done it successfully several times. I am not certain about always succeeding. For me it is something quite different from taking cognizance of writing, or a drawing, or of a person and an event or touching an object. To please you, I shall try.

This failure contrasts with the successful test carried out with the Polish society.

EXPERIMENT 2

The second experiment was one of those spontaneous events so typical of Ossowiecki, when he felt some special rapport with someone he had just met and asked him to go outside the room and write or draw something. This happened during the interval at a sitting for physical phenomena* and others present were the hostess, Mme. Wodzińska, and Theodore Besterman, the member of the Society for Psychical Research who had provided the Swan Ink target in 1933.

"M. Mongel did as he was asked. A moment later he handed to Ossowiecki an envelope which the clairvoyant, seated beside me, took and kneaded between nervous fingers, his eyes turned elsewhere, like one who is waiting for a memory to come to the surface. Less than a minute passed, and then:

"I see," he said, "what you have written. It is not words, it's a drawing. I shall reproduce it for you."

> The envelope was opened. Inside was Mr. Mongel's visiting card, on which there were drawings symbolizing the recent loss of a dear one: a cross, a coffin and tears [see above].

Ossowiecki was an active member of the Polish Society for Psychical Research, and the "sitting for physical phenomena" referred to would probably involve an investigation into one of a number of physical mediums active in Poland at the time. The effects produced (paranormally or otherwise) might range from movement of objects to materialised phantom forms.

Left: Drawing by Ossowiecki. *Right:* Target drawing.

By Ossowiecki's standards the preceding experiment was only a partial success, in that he picked up nothing about the cross (unlike the experiment with Chauvet) and the coffin representation came over in stages and never reached a state of precision. The confusion between the coffin and the tears is interesting, and what stands out is the total failure to capture the idea behind tears, a gravestone and a coffin.

The other two experiments reported by Osty were devised, carried out and reported by M. Dulché, a French railway engineer attached to the Advisory Council of the Franco-Polish Railways. Osty had made his acquaintance on a previous visit to Warsaw, and Dulché took considerable pains to set up some rigorous experiments.

Experiment 3

Dulché obtained from a friend living in Paris four envelopes containing material unknown to him. The envelopes were opaque and sealed, and the target papers inside the envelopes were folded and wrapped.

> I. One of the sealed envelopes is given to M. Ossowiecki by M. Dulché, Mlle Abramowicz being present at the sitting.
> The time is 21.15. M. Ossowiecki fingers the envelope and says very quickly:
> There is a star (at the same time he makes the drawing shown above) a star stuck on to a rectangular sheet of pink paper. There is something written at the bottom, in pencil, but I can't read it.
> M. Ossowiecki declaring that there was no more he could say about it, the

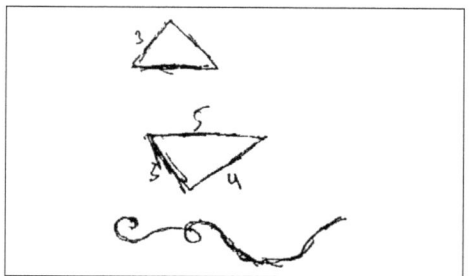 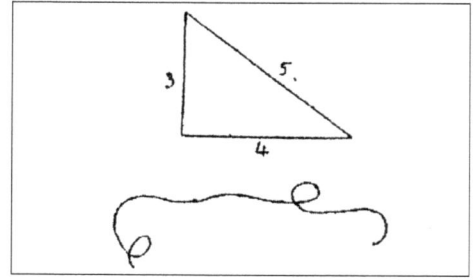

Left: Drawing by Ossowiecki. *Right:* Target drawing.

envelope is taken back by M. Dulché and opened by him. He takes out something wrapped in gray paper, which he unfolds and in it he finds a piece of paper folded over bearing the images shown [see p. 78 top right].

M. Ossowiecki has drawn a star with four points instead of 6 [sic, though there are actually 5]. The star was not stuck, but drawn directly onto the paper. The written phrase underneath had been made by a transfer from a blue chemical paper.

EXPERIMENT 4

At 20.40 a second envelope, similar to the first one, is given to M. Ossowiecki. He kneads it for a moment and soon afterwards says:

"It is another drawing. There is something written in French. I am there, in Paris, I can see it. There are some letters written, difficult to read. There are two triangles; no, there is only one triangle, then another drawing: a rope. The author wanted to draw two triangles, but he made only one. Then there are three digits, 3, 4, 5. It's done on grayish pinkish paper. The numbers are by their sides. A figure 3 on one side, 4 on another side, and 5 up above, outside the drawing. Under the triangle there is a cord.

"Again I see two triangles. I can't understand it. I should like to know if there is one triangle or two. I don't know why I see sometimes one triangle, sometimes two. There is only one triangle. I shall draw what I see."

M. Ossowiecki then made the following drawing [see p. 78 bottom left]:

The envelope is then taken back by M. Dulché, who examines it, then opens it. He takes out an opaque wad of gray wrapping paper, and from it he takes a folded paper bearing the drawings shown [see p. 78 bottom right]:

> A little while later, in Paris, M. Dulché learns from M. Valentin Thomas that the knotted rope represented for him, when he drew it, the rope used in earlier times by surveyors to form right angles on the ground, the set distance between knots allowing them to make a right angled triangle.
>
> It may be surmised that M. Ossowiecki's visions, which presented themselves sometimes as two triangles and sometimes as only one, and which caused him so much hesitation, were motivated by the idea of one actual and another potential triangle. One may also be permitted to speculate that in this case, as in many others, M. Ossowiecki was also confused by two successive visions of a triangle, the first presenting itself in his consciousness as a triangle with a single figure beside it, the second showing the complete drawing.

[RM 1934 No. 1]

The railway engineer must be credited with one of the best designed experiments, and his collaborator certainly produced a fruitful target drawing. The "potential triangle" may, unusually, suggest the telepathic reception of an idea from the mind of M. Thomas, especially as Ossowiecki did not put knots into his drawing. However, the broken up line of his cord may suggest that his subconscious clairvoyance of the rope was clearer than the image he was able to bring up into his conscious mind, and the 12 divisions may have linked up with the 3, 4 and 5 so that the potential triangle was an idea gnawing at him just below the threshold of consciousness.

While the clarity of his clairvoyance enabled him to see a right angled triangle, complete with numbered sides, the evanescence of his vision makes the reproduction of drawings something like an exercise in memory, and we see that he has oriented his triangle about 45 degrees anti-clockwise, and though the rope captures the spirit of the target's loop and curl, its curves are quite different.

The last Ossowiecki experiment related in the *Revue Métapsychique* is unique in that it deals with material supplied by a donor who was dead by the time the experiment was carried out, though this had not been planned by the donor, survival research not being on the agenda of these investigators. The report was supplied by Prosper Szmurło.

Experiment 11—January 1935
(The Jonky case—cognition of things unknown to anyone living; related by Szmurło)

PARANORMAL COGNITION OF THINGS UNKNOWN TO ANYONE LIVING

An account of experiments carried out by the Polish Psychophysical Society
An experiment under exceptional conditions
I have had the opportunity of dealing with an article the contents of which were unknown to any living person; this came about as follows.

In October 1925, i.e. six years ago, while I was in Vilna, I was invited to meetings of a society for psychical research, no longer in existence. The meetings took place in the apartment of the society's secretary, Mlle Barbara Czengery. Ten or twelve persons would meet there and hold discussions. Among them was M. Deniose Jonky: an elderly man, with gray beard and very lively eyes. He seemed to be in his mid-sixties. Despite his age he was full of vitality. Judging by the discussion he seemed to be widely read and *au fait* with psychical phenomena, though with a tendency towards spiritualism and the occult, on which subjects he had decided personal opinions.

During the last meeting he asked me to go with him into another room, then discreetly gave me a small package well wrapped, asking me:

"As you know M. Ossowiecki well, would you ask him to do an experimental reading?"

"I doubt whether he will want to do it," I replied, "because he is very busy. Lots of people he knows very well make similar requests to him almost daily. I shall have many encounters with him before I shall be able to find a favorable moment for the experiment. In any case, he will ask to have immediate verification of the test. Perhaps, if you want the experiment done in the name of your society, it would make it easier for the test to go ahead?"

"Not at all," he said, "it is an experiment for me, it is absolutely personal, and no one must know anything about it. After the reading you can open the package; I think the results will be interesting for you. Please let me know at once when the test has taken place. I am prepared to wait a long time."

"Very well," I said, "I shall do my best." And I put the package in my pocket.

I have never seen M. Jonky since that day.

On my return to Warsaw I unwrapped the package, removing the exterior envelope. I found inside a package 7cm × 4.2cm × 4 cm, of cylindrical shape, covered with cloth and cross-tied with cord sealed with wax at the ends and the crossing points.

The package weighed 59½ grams. Shaking it one could hear the movement of some objects like small stones.

I put the little package in my desk where it stayed for several years, untouched, seen by no one. Anxious to keep my promise, I asked M. Ossowiecki, at times during the first two years, if he would do the experiment. He could not find the time, and it was put off for later.

In short, not wanting to pester M. Ossowiecki, in the end I left the little packet in my drawer, forgotten.

After a number of years I learned, from someone who came from Vilna, that M. Jonky had died. This was confirmed later in correspondence.

I realized then that I was in possession of an article of exceptional value, one which allowed me to verify the independence of clairvoyance from telepathy, the contents of the little package being unknown to anyone living.

If one believes the literature on the subject, a similar experiment has never been attempted before, certainly not on a large scale. There have certainly been analogous experiments, the object of which has been to verify "post mortem survival." These consisted of sentences written by people and closed in envelopes before their death, material that was unknown to anyone else. Sentences or other written material left in secure places were to be read at séances by mediums (to whom nothing was disclosed) after the death of the writer. As far as I am aware no such experiment has succeeded.

There follow two pages in which Szmurło explains that before engaging the services of Ossowiecki, who expressed great interest in the proposal, he wanted first to obtain readings from as many clairvoyants as possible. He also sent the package to Osty, who arranged for two sittings in Paris. The whole enterprise took 14 months, and readings were taken from a total of 17 clairvoyants during 22 sittings.

He devotes a further page to relating what he has learned about Jonky, an engineer by profession, whose age Szmurło seems somewhat to have misjudged. Jonky was 77 when he handed over the package and 79 when he died in May 1927. It seems that he was a frequent attendee at séances, and was also a powerful hypnotist.

Séance with M. Ossowiecki

On 20th January 1935 we carried out the experiment with Stefan Ossowiecki.

I went to his house with the secretary of our society, M. S. Rzewuski, bringing the little package with us. M. Rzewuski took a careful note of what Ossowiecki said.

He gave his readings over three sessions.

On 22nd April 1934, in an interview when only the two of us were present, he gave a very short sitting, and he said almost nothing, feeling indisposed.

On 13th January 1935 a sitting took place in the presence of M. R. Chłobowski, Mlle M. Chyr, M. Z. Dreyszer, General Kątkowski, the painter S. Niesiołowski, Mme. Ossowiecka, M. S. Rzewuski and myself.

On 20th January 1935 the last sitting finally took place in the presence of Prof. Alphonse Gravier, M. Giżycki, Dr. C. Kaliński, General Kątkowski, M. O. Missuna and Mme. H. Rzewuska.

The reading made by Ossowiecki was as follows. Pauses between phrases are indicated by dots.

"There is a light colored box, factory made. Various objects have been put inside it. Samples of soil ... earthy substances ... but not from Poland, it comes from far away ... from the East ... it's as if something has been cut in stone or metal."

At this point the clairvoyant paid attention to the paper wrapped round the packet.

"Oh! Here is a wax seal. The wrapping, the paper, the box get in the way.

"It has a very curious history, very complicated. I see the owner of this object. He is no longer alive. He has been dead a long time, tragically. He had done well for himself, he had a house ... but the tide of success ebbed away.

"He was an old man, with a gray beard, and he had a wife.

"He was a man of great spiritual worth, of wide culture, highly educated, especially knowledgeable with regard to the paranormal ... he used to arrange séances, and experiments, he read and wrote a lot, he traveled a lot.

"The package has been sent to someone who looked very much like M. Gravier. It was in his apartment, the package stayed there, I see it down there in the bookcase.

"There are some pieces of something in there, several things ... two ... three ... they are of mineral origin ... stone ... metal ... stone ... metal ... gray color ... brown ... like lime stones. There are also some metal clips. There is a connection with volcanic mineral. It was once in the hands of a girl. She was to give them to someone ... it's something like a family souvenir.

"There is something here that pulls me away to other worlds ... towards another planet. Now I am seeing a huge planet, immense, a distant world quite unconnected with ours.

"It is rushing headlong through outer space. It collides with another body. There is a catastrophic cosmic event.

"Something breaks away, breaks up, shatters into small pieces. They rush on, they fall to earth in various places. Yes, yes, they are pieces of meteorite.

"This experiment was devised specially for me. Perhaps there are two experiments, because I feel drawn in two different directions.

"This old gentleman also prepared the pieces of sugar. On one side he had a box with minerals ... some with sugar ... others with meteorites. Up till now I felt the meteorites very distinctly, but there was also the sugar. Just then someone came and brought him some tea. I see him drink it with the sugar between his lips. [This is the Russian way of drinking tea.] It is at this moment that the idea came to him ... unfortunately this cannot be verified.

"I can't tell you any more."

I must add that Ossowiecki had earlier described M. Jonky's appearance at the second sitting. After that sitting the idea had come to me to see if Ossowiecki would recognize M. Jonky among a group of photographs. I had already had a photograph of him since July 1934. I got together, with some pains, in concert with Mr. R, twelve photographs of gentlemen with beards. Together with the photograph of M. Jonky there were 15 portraits.

After the last sitting with Ossowiecki, after he had finished speaking, the 15 photographs were placed on a table by Dr. K, who was seeing them for the first time and did not know which was a representation of M. Jonky. Ossowiecki was asked to pick out the photo of M. Jonky. The persons who knew all stayed in another room. Ossowiecki, together with the others who stayed with him, grouped themselves around the photographs.

He immediately eliminated 12 of the photographs. Then he took in his hands the three remaining ones, among which there was also one of a young man without a beard, and, after a moment of concentration, picked out the photograph of M. Jonky. As to the young clean-shaven man, he claimed, correctly, that he had committed suicide. It was in the hope of eliciting a spontaneous statement from him that this photograph had been placed among the others.

[The package was not opened immediately, but was reserved for a meeting at which many eminent members were present, who were given an account of Ossowiecki's reading.]

The opening of the package
I come now to the opening of the package.

I see first of all a pale pink of rosy white cardboard box, closed up and fastened with metal threads. On this box is written in blue pencil the following note: "Corner of Subocz Road" (this is a road in Vilna).

After pulling back one side of the box, a green label was displayed with the words printed on it: [in translation] "Eugène Matula, pharmaceutical products manufacturer, limited company registered at Kraków." I spread the contents of the box on the table. Three pieces of light brown stone fall on the table, which seem to indicate the presence of some iron oxide. A subsequent analysis establishes that the stone is limestone. There are also some smaller fragments, debris that has broken off from these pieces.

So this part of the clairvoyance was successful. Ossowiecki saw and described the limestone and defined the color and even the mineral composition of the rock.

We took the investigation further; we found inside the box yet another tiny box, hidden deep inside the package. It was a little wooden matchbox. This box had stuck on top of it a dark blue paper inscribed in blue pencil "The Tower."

It was probably a fragment from the tower of Vilna Castle. After opening the matchbox we found inside five little fragments of the same stone as before, as well as a very small container wrapped in a piece of newspaper. Under this I found folded several times a small piece of paper on which was written in black pencil "AEROLITH," which is another word for meteorite.

Once more Ossowiecki had seen true. One can say that this is a triumph of clairvoyance.

Under the piece of paper there were two receipt stamps, one for one million marks and the other for fifty thousand. There were still 18 rounded fragments, dark gray, sticky and misshapen, looking like gunshot. Trial with a magnet showed later that this was iron which, in its original state, is found only in meteorites and in certain telluric rocks. When I examined the paper wrapped round the meteorites, I found on the reverse side, written in pencil, three mysterious words the meaning of which escapes us:

NETO IDATE POKOYMO

No one present could say what they meant, nor in what language they were written. Certainly the author of this inscription meant it to have some significance, as it was placed among the objects to be clairvoyantly detected.

Could Ossowiecki have been wrong in stating that there could also have been sugar in the package, for we have not found any, as well as in saying that the old gentleman died tragically, which is contrary to what we know to be the reality?

After emptying the contents of the package, and examining the objects inside it, we put off until later the examination and description of the wrappings. This was so as not to hold up the reading of the statements made by the other clairvoyants whose readings were still sealed up in their respective envelopes.

Some days later, 31st January 1935, the council of the society met again. Once more we examined the objects from the package and also the wrappings. In the fragment of newspaper that served as wrapping, where we found the date of July 1923, there were some items about the stock exchange prices, an article on agriculture, a party political announcement, a long article about reclaiming shares sent out and some small advertisements.

We also took out the part of the cardboard box which had not been examined at all and, we found on it a printed label reading: "MALT SUGAR." Right inside the box we found traces of sugar still stuck to it. An assay with our tongues convinced us that it was indeed sugar. So the incomparable Ossowiecki was not mistaken in talking about the sugar we could not find.

Further on again, on a small fragment of torn newspaper that had been wrapped around the meteorites, we found mention of an airplane catastrophe: "The mechanism sparking ... violently falling towards ... wings torn off ... another plane coming to the rescue ... debris all over the ground."

So we see that here it is a question of a catastrophe that probably ended with the death or injury of the airmen. We think that we now have the explanation of Ossowiecki's statements, in that other subjects pointed to a tragic end and an unfortunate accident, which events he mistakenly related to the person of M. Jonky.

[RM 1936 No. 1]

3

Informal Experiments and "Fieldwork"

Background and Sources

So far the cases reported are those that were investigated by dedicated researchers, most of them scientists, and published in reputable journals. These researchers have become familiar figures, and though not all their experiments were equally rigorous it has to be on the strength of these reports that confidence in Ossowiecki's paranormal cognition will be most soundly based. But below the base is a considerable store of supporting testimony, some of it from researchers who had only sporadic encounters, some of it from witnesses well qualified and respected in other fields, and some from ordinary members of the public who became involved in the story of Ossowiecki only because they were seeking a solution to their problems.

There is always something detrimental that can be urged against every sort of witness, and against researchers such as Geley and Osty, both physicians who made psychical research their main occupation, it could be said that they had so much intellectual and emotional capital locked up in *la Métapsychique* that they needed to get positive results; the same arguments could be extended to Richet and Schrenck-Notzing even though they maintained distinguished professional careers outside their paranormal investigations. But the more researchers who have to be 'branded' as too involved to be capable of reporting fairly and honestly on their psychical studies the more strained does this argument become, and the strength to be derived from numbers becomes apparent.

So also does the importance of the "others," the less notable, dedicated or experienced "friends and strangers" who describe their occasional encounters in terms that are strikingly consistent with reports made by the researchers, with the added value that in what may have been more relaxed conditions the Ossowiecki repertoire is seen to be even more extensive than has appeared hitherto.

It is in fact the abundance of both quality and quantity, and his willingness to be tested by all and sundry, that gives the Ossowiecki material its special value. In practical terms there is always room for actual or potential doubt in much the same way that imperfection is built into any system of evaluation. The froth that fills the space between practical and perfect conviction can be reduced by an ever-increasing weight of evidence, and the further testimony adduced in this section is directed to that end.

The selection of reports which follow comes from a number of sources. Most of those originating from before 1933 appeared in Ossowiecki's autobiography, *The World of My Soul and Visions of the Future,* which was published early in that year, with a review and extensive excerpts appearing shortly after in the respected national daily *Illustrated Daily Courier.* Surprisingly, the book contains little biographical information, but consists mainly of accounts of "experiments" (the term used by Ossowiecki to refer to all categories of cases) largely either already published elsewhere (*Revue Métapsychique, Zagadnienia Metapsychiczne [Metapsychical Issues], Ilustrowany Kuryer Codzienny [Illustrated Daily Courier]*) or quoted from contemporaneous notes of experimenters or witnesses. Sources other than the autobiography were consulted wherever this was possible, but in a number of cases Ossowiecki's book is the only source open to us. Psychical research in Ossowiecki's time suffered from severe financial constraints, much as it does today. *Zagadnienia Metapsychiczne* ceased publication in 1929 for lack of funding; the prestigious "metapsychical" supplement to the *Illustrated Daily Courier* appeared only fortnightly. The less highbrow publications were as unreliable then as they are now when dealing with the subject of the "paranormal." There thus existed a substantial body of unpublished reports held in various archives which, had they survived, would have been available to researchers today. As things stand, one is forced either to ignore a substantial body of reports published in *The World of my Soul,* or to introduce some criteria for judging their veracity.

It is important to note that, where independent records are available, they correspond to the accounts given in Ossowiecki's volume. He also makes it very clear in each of his accounts whether he is quoting from reports (often signed by more than one witness) or relying on his memory. The variety of styles and quality of reporting, often lost in the process of translation and abbreviation, is clearly perceptible in the original and distinguishable from the author's own writing. Apart from being the subject of so many experiments himself, Ossowiecki was also engaged in numerous psychic investigations as a researcher for the Psychophysical Society. He was very much aware of the importance of reliable corroborating evidence, as his painstaking gathering of witnesses' letters and signatures shows; it is unfortunate that he did not foresee the fate awaiting his and his Society's archives.

If one accepts that the accounts in his autobiography are given in good faith, it is still the case that Ossowiecki's absentmindedness and forgetfulness do not make him the perfect witness. For this reason, the only reports presented in this selection are those provided by first-hand witnesses. A record of the known cases in which Ossowiecki was involved is given in Appendix II.

Additional information about Ossowiecki comes from letters sent to his widow after the war by people whom he had helped at that time and from Jerzy Jacyna, journalist and relation of Jan Jacyna, whose reminiscences, *Facts and Legend about Ossowiecki,* were published in a Polish national weekly in 1970/71. These were instrumental in producing yet another batch of letters, some of which offered a fresh insight into several aspects of the Ossowiecki phenomenon. It should be emphasized that the sources used here are not the only ones available (see Bibliography), but the ones regarded as the most reliable.

The cases that follow fall into four overlapping categories:

1. the less formal "experiments," which confirm and sometimes extend the range of psychometric abilities demonstrated in the formal experiments;
2. the real-life cases where Ossowiecki's abilities are put to practical use;
3. four war-time cases reported after 1945;
4. phenomena beyond the range catered for by most of the experiments.

Demonstrations of Clairvoyance

Cognition of various targets is the principal feature of this selection of cases, though other elements are often present as well. The experiments are presented chronologically.

Experiment 12—1922

Report by Geley. Source: *Revue Métapsychique* No. 4, 1922.

> Marshal Piłsudski [Polish head of state] was good enough to recount this to us, authorizing publication in the *Revue Métapsychique*. We shall reproduce his report of the experiment, just as he gave it to us, together with a photograph of the document written by the President and also of the opaque envelope, sealed with the seal of the Minister of War, in which it was placed [p. 88].
> In this statement I certify that the enclosed document, denoting chess moves written down by the President, Marshal Piłsudski, moves known only to him, put in an envelope by the Marshal in person, sealed under the seal of the Minister of War, General Sosnkowski,* was read by M. Stefan Ossowiecki in 15–20 minutes.
> C2—C4——————C5—C7
> Present were: Mme. Jacyna, wife of General Jacyna, M. Ossowiecki's sister, Mme. Neuman, Princess Michel Woroniecki, General Sosnkowski, Minister of War, General Jacyna, aide de camp to the President, Lieutenant Saszkiewicz, aide de camp to General Jacyna, and the undersigned.
> Once the reading had been done by M. Ossowiecki, I telephoned to the Belvedere [presidential residence], in the presence of the persons named below. I received confirmation by telephone of the contents of the written material, confirmation given personally by the President, who was greatly interested in this experiment. The Marshal told me that M. Ossowiecki had not made any mistake. The next day the envelope was unsealed by the President, at the Belvedere.
> I must add that when M. Ossowiecki took the sealed envelope in his hand, before saying what it contained, and not knowing who had written it, he asserted to those attending the session that the note inside was written by the President.
> At the same time, M. Ossowiecki drew a plan of the President's apartment at

---

*General Sosnkowski was Piłsudski's second in command; during the Second World War he became commander-in-chief of the Polish army after the death of General Sikorski.

the Belvedere, a place where he had never been, and went on to a description of the furnishings and their arrangement, and even described the table Marshal Piłsudski had used to rest the paper on when making his note.

This experiment took place at 39 Ujazdow Street, in General Jacyna's apartment. Warsaw, 1920. Signed: Lieutenant C. Świrski, aide de camp and personal secretary to the President.

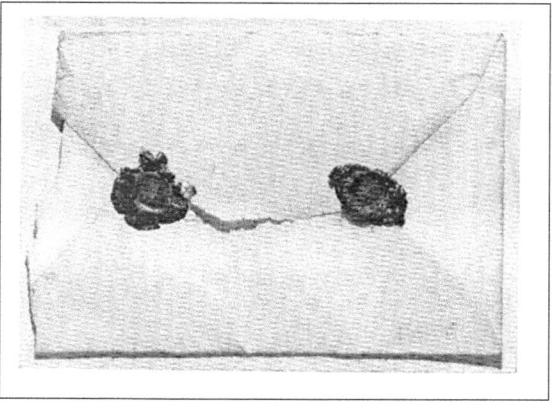

Photograph of envelope sealed by the Minister of War.

Experiment 13—25 May 1923 (Sokołowski)

Report by Dr. T.E. Sokołowski, a very active psychical researcher, and signed by two witnesses. Source: Ossowiecki, 1933, pp. 225–6.

Messrs. Chamski and Szajkiewicz have just met Ossowiecki for the first time. Mr. Chamski gives Ossowiecki his nickel watch (with a single case) and asks what is underneath the watch case. Ossowiecki talks about unconnected matters for about 15 minutes, looks at the watch he is still holding, and in the end says he sees nothing.

Dr. S. suggests that perhaps O is tired by the previous experiment and that the experiment should be stopped. However, at the last moment Ossowiecki withdraws his hand with the watch just before handing it back to Chamski, holds it for a moment over the table and says:

"No, definitely there is nothing there. On the inner case there is an engraving of a kind of circle and a number, but apart from that there is nothing."

Chamski says that he recently had a new glass put in the watch but that he forbade the watchmaker to open the case, under which there was a lock of hair. The lock of hair thus must be under the case. Mr. Ch. opens the case with difficulty, but there is no hair there; however, there is a circle and a number on the inner case.

Experiment series 14—May 1924 (Ponikowski)

Report by Mr. Z. Przybyszewski. Source: Ossowiecki, 1933, pp. 227–233. One of the witnesses is Professor Ponikowski,* whose reputation for scientific objectivity and public prominence, both at the time of the experiment and the publication

---

Antoni Ponikowski (1878–1949) had a very distinguished career in science, business, education, politics and social reform. He served as a government minister (1917–18), prime minister (1921–22) and senator, professor and chancellor of Warsaw Polytechnic. He was also active in underground education and the resistance movement during the Second World War.

of Ossowiecki's book, make this experiment particularly valuable. *Experiment 1* is also one of the few experiments reported in enough detail to examine the process of mentation, recording the misses as well as the hits, particularly in regard to the originator of the target.

Experiment 1

On 11th May 1924 a series of experiments took place in Warsaw at the apartment of Prof. Antoni Ponikowski in Aleje Ujazdowskie. Also present were Mr. & Mrs. Przybyszewski.

Mr. Z. Przybyszewski took notes.

The session concerned a number of points established beforehand, relating to a variety of financial matters, the death of a close person, a missing person or missing objects. These items were collected earlier by Mr. Przybyszewski. However, since Mr. & Mrs. Ponikowski, the hosts, were witnessing Ossowiecki's clairvoyance for the first time, they were asked to start the session, without being told as to what kind of experiment it was supposed to be.

Mr. Ponikowski went to one of the further rooms, where he wrote a few words in pencil on a visiting card and sealed the card in an envelope. Mr. Ponikowski was the only person there, and nobody else knew what was on the card. Mr. Ponikowski returned to the room where everyone was gathered and handed the envelope to Ossowiecki. Ossowiecki asked Mrs. Ponikowski to sew the envelope through. Not content with that, Ossowiecki himself sewed through the envelope in 12 other places, pricking through the text. Below I quote Ossowiecki's words:

"This is not a drawing, I find that easier. I don't know why I am in Poznań. No, in Warsaw. Aleja Róż ... I am, I am, wait, a woman, no, a priest.

"A woman in a black dress with a purple belt.

"She stops before the porch of No.6. The Potulickis live there, the Grzybowskis, the Załęskis, second floor on the right."

A moment's silence.

"This is a bishop, a pleasant face. His name is Adolf. He was here recently. You (he turns to Mr. & Mrs. Ponikowski) saw him. Why did you (turning to Mr. Ponikowski) think of writing his name? Isn't he in Poznań? Not tall. Age 42–43. He represents some organization. Dalbor ... no, 6 or 7 letters. I can see him clearly—I don't know him. The little cap (bishop's calotte) is purple, a purple belt, age 43–44. You wrote down his name: Adolf. He is not a military bishop. No, you wrote more, name, surname, house number."

Pause.

"He has something to do with scientific organizations, in libraries, in archives. The name seems Samogitian ... Lithuanian ... unclear. Something like a Lithuanian name. As if Dokurek (do-ku-rek). No, not clear.

"I can see him, he lives there, he has one room in that apartment."

Mr. Ossowiecki put down the envelope, still explaining that he is sure the surname was not written clearly.

Those present open the envelope. In the envelope there is Prof. Ponikowski's visiting card, and on the reverse written in pencil:

"Bp. Adolf Szelążek, Aleja Róż 6." The surname of the bishop indeed not written clearly.

In order to open the letter after the experiment it was necessary to cut the thread with which it had been sewn through.

The facts were as follows: bp. Szelążek used to visit the office of the Religious Department of the Ministry of Education, opposite the apartment of Mr. & Mrs. Ponikowski.

The bishop then lived at Aleja Róż No. 6 and had a large library in his apartment.

Experiment 2

On the same day, i.e., 11th May 1924, another experiment took place. It concerned two letters: one was in an open envelope with a Russian postage stamp; the other, sealed, was handed over by Mr. Michał Ślósarski.

At 10 p.m. Mr. Ossowiecki started to speak:

"This takes me to Szkolna Street No. 6–8, in the period 1915, 1916. Was he in the army?"

A long pause.

"This second letter keeps getting tangled" (he picks up the other letter). "I blame you."

A two minute pause. The second letter, sealed, has been put down.

Without holding it, Ossowiecki says:

"Get writing: Witold ... [a long pause] Ślósarski ... during the years, at the beginning of the war, year 1914–15, reserve standard-bearer of the Orenburg regiment. I see barracks in the Vilnius area. Some name keeps getting tangled close to him: Gunrach, Gundelach, Witold ... Stanisław ... no, Stanisławowich (the son of Stanisław), he wrote to Ślósarski, to his brother, his last letter before dying, to Szkolna Street 8. Soon after that he went into battle. I see a small town, small houses, little trees in front of them, women in white at his side ... nurses. He died after an illness."

A long pause.

"Ślósarski, a technologist, has a technology office. The brother wrote to him to reassure mother. The letter was short. He died wounded in an attack. I see what he looks like: dark blond, has a mother and a sister. He was killed in 1915, he wrote the letter from the hospital.

"He died in terrible agony, close to Orsza."

The letter was in fact from the brother of Mr. Ślósarski, and was reassuring in tone. Ślósarski was a co-owner of a private firm and lived at Szkolna Street No.8 in Warsaw. He can confirm the facts with his signatures, although he was not present, as his brother really had been wounded and died in hospital.

Experiment 3

This experiment, like the two previous ones, took place also on 11th May 1924.

Almost immediately, while still talking about Ślósarski, Mr. Ossowiecki put his hand on the second letter, supplied by Mr. Przybyszewski and concerning Mr. Albrecht.

"Now I will talk about this.

"This is a genius, a wise man, and could have gone far if he had not died prematurely.

"There is some close tie between him and your sister." He turned to Mrs. Przybyszewski.

One should add that Mr. Ossowiecki was not warned by Mr. Przybyszewski that the letter concerned his brother-in-law.

"He left one child, but not here.

"He died at the age of forty. Nobody close was present at his death."

All this information about the death of Mr. Albrecht coincides with the information received later from Russia, from the colleagues and subordinates of the deceased, as well as with the more intimate details supplied to the family by a trustworthy person, the chairman of the State Prosecuting Office in Vilnius, Mr. Adolf Kopeć. According to those, Albrecht was executed (shot) when General Yudenich was approaching Petersburg.

***

Experiment 15—July 1924 (Charpentier)

Reported by G. Charpentier, a League of Nations delegate visiting Warsaw. Source: *Revue Métapsychique* 1925, No.2. This is one of several instances of what appears to be cognition of an unrealized intention.

At the invitation of Commandant de Mazerat together with M. Ossowiecki, whom I did not know, we lunched together the three of us at the Hotel de l'Europe, Warsaw.

The conversation turned to the phenomena of clairvoyance demonstrated by M. Ossowiecki, who suddenly said to me:

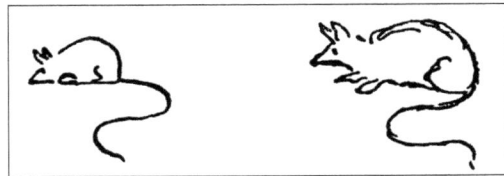

Drawings by Charpentier, left, and by Ossowiecki

"You don't look very convinced, and if you like, we can do a little experiment by way of demonstration. You go out of the room, conceal yourself anywhere you like, then make some sort of drawing on a card, put it in an envelope and bring it back to me: I shall tell you just what you drew."

I left the restaurant and installed myself at the far end of the hotel cloak room, in a corner well tucked away, some 20 meters away from our table, with two thick walls between us.

When I came back, M. Ossowiecki and the Commandant de Mazerat were still having lunch and conversing. I gave the envelope to M. Ossowiecki, who held it in his left hand under the table, and almost immediately said:

"It's quite a small drawing. There is a long tail, quite curly ... it's a mouse. I'll draw it for you." And asking the Commandant for paper and pencil he made the following sketch [reproduced above], apparently not knowing much about drawing.

After opening the envelope to compare the two drawings, he added:

"You settled down at the far end of the hotel cloak room, I followed you; you didn't sit down, you knelt on a stool, drawing on a little table; you thought at first of drawing something round." (My intention was in fact to draw a sleeping cat curled in a ball, head between paws.) "You had fun drawing the mouse's tail and you also took some trouble over the paws."

The envelope was then opened to show the drawing that I had made.

The resemblance is really very curious in its imitation of the general outlines and above all the tail, as well as the evident intention of M. Ossowiecki to take some care over the drawing of the paws, as I had also done.

All told, I must admit that, point by point, M. Ossowiecki related everything that I had done and thought during my absence from the restaurant; his entire recital was correct in every detail.

Moreover, the Commandant de Mazerat confirmed to me that M. Ossowiecki had continued to have his lunch and converse normally while awaiting my return.

G. CHARPENTIER League of Nations Delegate at Warsaw

Experiment 16—November 1924 (Osty—Santoliquido)

Reported by Osty. Source: *Revue Métapsychique* 1925, No. 2

M. Ossowiecki, briefly in Paris, was at the Institut Métapsychique on the evening of 3rd November [1924]. During the course of the conversation with Prof. Santoliquido* and myself [Osty] he said to the Professor:

Dr. Rocco Santoliquido was a scientist, university professor, International Red Cross representative at the League of Nations and the first President of the Institut Métapsychique International.

"Take a card from your wallet, make a drawing on it. Enclose it in an envelope and call me when it is ready. I shall tell you what you have drawn."

The Professor, left alone in the salon, all doors closed, M. Ossowiecki goes into an adjoining room and stays there under my surveillance, his back turned to the door that separates him from the salon.

Some moments pass. M. Santoliquido calls M. Ossowiecki and puts into his hand a gum-sealed envelope, an opaque kind from the Institute. M. Ossowiecki immediately puts his hands behind his back, fingering the envelope with nervous energy, but not looking at it for a moment. After a few seconds he says:

"You didn't make a drawing as I asked you. You wrote a word. It's in Italian."

A few seconds more passed.

"You wrote Fran … Francesco. I want to write it down, just the way I see it."

And he wrote this: [first version not reproduced here].

"It's not exactly like that," he said at once, and did this: [signatures reproduced together below].

"Yes, that's better," he exclaimed.

At this moment M. Santoliquido takes the envelope from M. Ossowiecki's hands, and confirms that it is almost a perfect match. He opens it himself. And here is a photograph.

Writing by Ossowiecki, left, and by Santoliquido

***

Experiment 17—October 1925 (Sokołowski—Cobo Martinez)

Report by Dr. T.E. Sokołowski. Sources: Ossowiecki, 1933, pp. 169–176; *Kuryer Poranny* [Warsaw daily *The Morning Courier*] 30 October 1925; *Zagadnienia Metapsychiczne,* December 1925. The sudden announcement that the experiment will be performed is consistent with Ossowiecki's behavior on other occasions: when he feels confident, and among friends he will take the risk on the spur of the moment. It is the only fully public experiment undertaken by Ossowiecki, and presumably the atmosphere of the meeting was congenial enough for him to perform as he would among friends.

The experiment took place on 29th October 1925.

A sealed letter, written in Spanish, was sent from Spain by Dr. T. Cobo Martinez to Dr. Sokołowski for a clairvoyant test with Ossowiecki. This took place after a lecture by a Russian speaker, attended by over a hundred people, after Ossowiecki offered to perform the test there and then. The clairvoyant sat at a table surrounded by a committee including the speaker, psychical researchers and journalists, who signed the written record. As usual, Ossowiecki gave a very full description of persons, places and circumstances surrounding the creation of the drawing:

"A letter from Spain ... I see a yellow-white house, two story, entrance through a small garden, and on the right a lot of greenery, stone stairs around, entrance on the right hand side. The house of a man of modest means. Then a moment in the study, when he is writing this letter, not a letter. A small dark-haired man, an open forehead, very lively, dressed in black, six o'clock, a hall next door. His wife passes, he is upset by a terrible tragedy, he has lived through the loss of a child, a girl. His wife expects another. A boy has been born already, they wanted a girl. Masses of books around, leather seats, not new. When he was writing this letter, a man entered, they talked. Next to the study a narrow vestibule, from there a tiny hall, glass verandah towards the garden, lots of flowers and greenery.

"A strange child next to them. The wife is 32, dark hair, pointed nose, dressed in black, something black hanging from the neck—these are dice.

"The master, the doctor, he has scissors on the table; he is cutting up paper, holding papers. It is not a letter, only something written down. A man of science, studies a lot, has a number of degrees, has encyclopedic knowledge.

"He has approached the table and he begins to write, he is bent. He is cutting bits of green paper, the seal ready on the table. I see what and how he draws.

"He wanted to draw a circle within a square, then a face, and he finished with a point." (Ossowiecki draws.) He gets up, lights a cigarette and comes back to the table, he picks up a pencil or a pen and writes a question, draws an enormous T. Here he writes something, two questions, questions about the paranormal. He asks me if I believe in telepathy. "At the top it is written in French. There is someone else in the room, an older man. The question: 'Croyez-vous à la télépathie?' The second—do I believe in life after death? The apartment has four, six rooms."

When the envelope was cut open, inside was found a sheet of white paper, folded in two, covered by three rectangular sheets, two of which were green. The drawings and the sentences written on the white sheet correspond in the smallest detail to the drawing by Ossowiecki [p. 94].

The documents were sent to Martinez, who wrote back to the Metapsychical Institute and to Ossowiecki, who cites from the letter to himself:

"Everything that you saw, apart from a leather armchair, is totally accurate."

***

Experiment 18—May 1928 (Barrington-Emerson)

Reported by Professor Barrington-Emerson. Source: *Revue Métapsychique* 1929, No. 1.

A professor of engineering, in a letter dated May 1928, written from the transatlantic liner *Berengaria*, relates his personal experiences.

The purpose of this letter is to give you my opinion on the experiment I did with you in my room at the Hotel de l'Europe....

We met in my room. During the first part of the sitting there were seven of us present. For the second part there were just M. de Drzewiecki and myself.

They started with a typical drawing experiment, with the usual result....

Here is the document reproducing my drawings and yours.

When the other persons present had left, except for M. de Drzewiecki and

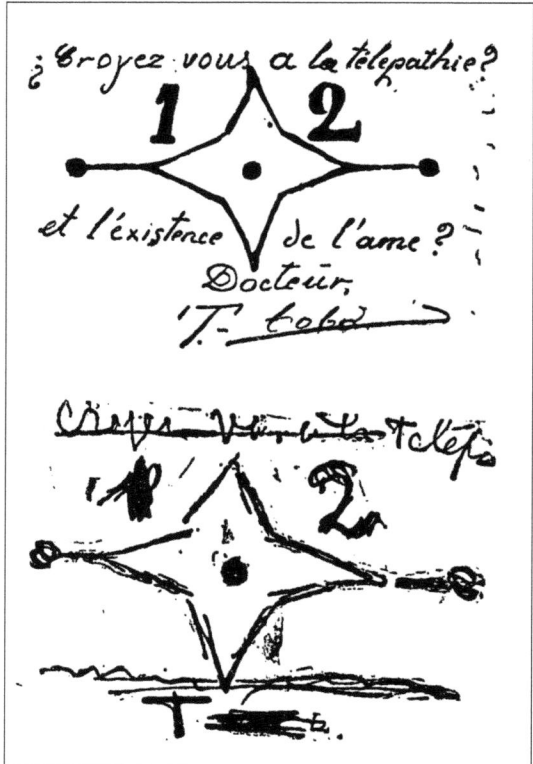

myself, you told me my life history, with extraordinary accuracy.

You said that I was married young, that I had lost two children when they were quite young: a boy and a girl. [Correct.]

That I started my career in the discipline I had studied at university, and then I had taken a completely different direction.

That I lived in a house surrounded by a garden outside the center of New York, with a fine view across a stretch of water. [Correct.]

You described the furnishings of several rooms, but your description of the location of the pieces of furniture was confused.

You said that I have a son who is an aeronautical engineer and three daughters of whom two are married; you described the character of

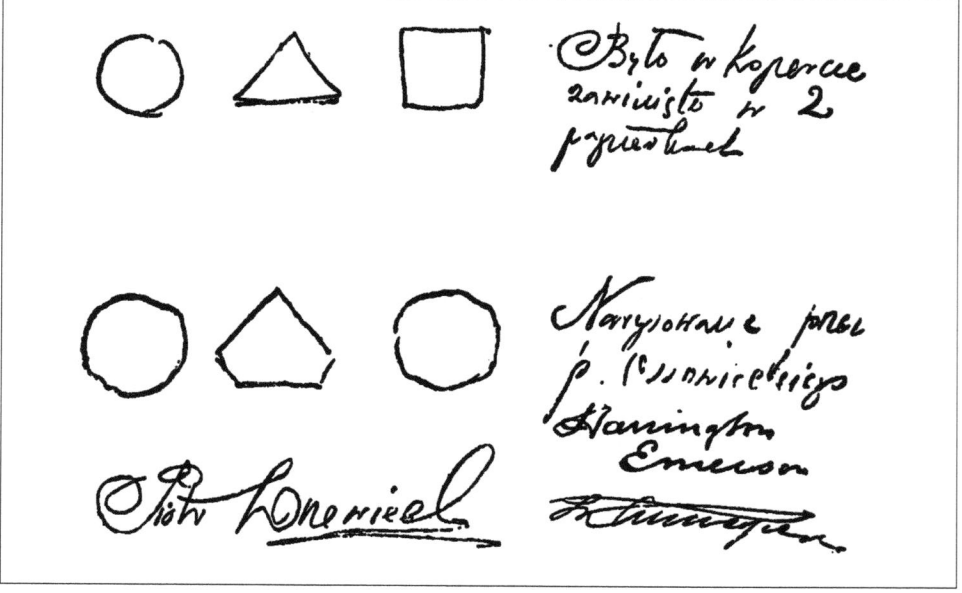

Top: Drawings by Martinez, top, and by Ossowiecki. *Bottom:* Drawings by Barrington-Emerson, top, and by Ossowiecki.

my wife and said that I had taken her to a place very far from New York, but that after a short time I had sent her back. [All that is correct.]

You talked correctly about my estrangement from my brother with whom I had for a long time been on very close terms.

All in all, your statements were as exact and precise as your representations of the geometric figures, though some details were a little vague. It is clear that you were able to read my thoughts with exactness and clarity.

It was a great pleasure to make your acquaintance and to have the best demonstration that anyone has given me in the whole of my life.

    Prof. BARRINGTON-EMERSON
    of New York

Experiment 19—reported 1928 (Tugan-Baranowski)

Reported by N. Tugan-Baranowski, a Russian scientist. Source: *Revue Métapsychique* 1929, No. 1.

Though I had only a few encounters with M. Ossowiecki, there were some occasions on which I was present at some demonstrations of his faculty for reading the contents of a sealed envelope or of other opaque materials.

1. The first time, in 1920, was at his house when, after a conversation on various subjects, I asked him to let me witness one of his experiments in reading a concealed target.

Moving to one side of the room, I wrote 102, then folded my visiting card and sealed it up in an envelope and gave it to him.

Ossowiecki took the envelope and held it behind his back, and said at once that there was a number on the card with three figures. Then he named the second figure 0, and the first 1 and finally the third 2, remarking at the same time that this last figure was difficult to decipher. Well, it turned out, after the envelope was opened, that the ink had made a blot on this figure.

2. One day, at the house of some friends, while I was seated at a fair distance from M. Ossowiecki, I wrote on a piece of paper his family name; then I put the note in a thick envelope.

M. Ossowiecki placed it on the table and put his hand on it. After two minutes he said:

"On this paper there is a word with 10 letters. You were thinking about me." And a few moments later he added: "It's my name."

3. At the house of the same friends, M. Hoori, the representative of the Swiss Red Cross, had brought an envelope with him and asked M. Ossowiecki to read its contents. The clairvoyant had to hold it quite a long time in his hands, and then said:

"I see a sort of office ... a counter ... but, you have put money in this ... one pound sterling."

Indeed, inside two thick sealed envelopes there was a £1 note.

4. In my apartment, I gave M. Ossowiecki a wallet, which I had taken out of a drawer. M. Ossowiecki, holding it cupped in his hands in front of me, asked me if I made drawings, because in the wallet there was a pen and ink drawing of a bearded man. I replied that I did not draw at all and that there was no drawing in the wallet. But, having opened it up and examined the papers in it, I found, drawn by me on the back of a piece of paper, a sketch (very badly drawn) of a bearded man.

I observed several other similar incidents. In only one case did M. Ossowiecki make a mistake. Someone had written "NON." He said "A number with three figures, with a zero in the middle."

I must add that if I had not personally observed this faculty of M. Ossowiecki I should not be so convinced that it surpasses everything that hitherto I had regarded as possible.
N. TUGAN-BARANOVSKI
Former Senator and Professor at the Institute of Civil Engineering at St. Petersburg.
Warsaw, 10th July 1928

Experiment 20–1931 (Szpotański)

Reported by: Stanisław Szpotański. Sources: Ossowiecki, 1933, pp. 112–3; article titled "Clairvoyance," *Świat* [The World] magazine, 16 May 1931 (unconfirmed).

> Ossowiecki speaks first:
> "Now I should like to test myself. Draw something for me." I leave the room. I draw an isosceles triangle on my visiting card and in the middle of it I put a cross. I put the card into a thick, lined envelope. I seal the envelope. There is no way that the drawing can be seen. Anyway, Ossowiecki does not look at the envelope. He takes it in his hand and puts his hands behind him. After a moment he says "A geometrical figure." At the same time I keep saying to him in my mind: "Circle, circle, circle!"
> He takes the pencil and on the envelope he draws an isosceles triangle, after which he thinks for a moment: "There is something in the middle, like a star." And he draws a cross.

***

Experiment 21—May 1931 (Francisco Madrid)

Reported by Francisco Madrid. Source: Ossowiecki, 1933, pp. 188–192.

On 3 June 1932 Ossowiecki received a very long letter in French from Francisco Madrid, attaché at the Chilean Consulate. It describes a clairvoyant reading given in May of the previous year, when Ossowiecki felt in the mood to display his talents to a Norwegian lady, Unni Langard, who was visiting Warsaw. She put a letter into his hands and awaited results. Francisco Madrid's account has been condensed to about a quarter of its length.

> You were talking without a break for over an hour ... about Oslo, where I had lived for six years, until the end of 1930.
> "Oh yes, I see your husband, tall, slim etc." and you sketched his portrait in amazing detail, so that Mrs. L. kept nervously confirming: "Yes—yes—that is true; what? Oh my god!" There were details of his hairstyle, and with your finger you drew the shape of Mr. Langard's nose. Then you said, "I see him at the moment of writing this letter. He is at the office. But what house is that—so large? I see wide stone stairs, wide halls, many paintings. This is a museum." Mr. Langaard, who is an art critic in Norway, has an important position at the National Gallery in Oslo, where he has his office. [Ossowiecki then described her own home and furnishings].
> "In the same house," you continued, "lives your mother-in-law. I see her, she is tall, plump and wears a wig."

The clairvoyant handed the letter back, but after some conversation he asked to have it back as he had never been to Norway and wanted to see Oslo.

Ossowiecki then gave a running commentary of his clairvoyant tour around Oslo.

Experiment 22—November 1931 (Konrad Strauss)

Reported by Konrad Strauss. Source: Ossowiecki, 1933, pp. 204–6.

Ossowiecki cites a long letter from the German art historian Konrad Strauss, describing a session carried out in Warsaw in November 1931. The account has been shortened by nearly a half.

> I was introduced to you by Count Wielopolski (Mr. Ossowiecki did not know me personally and had not heard of me before). At our table ... [also] ... sat Mr. Górzyński, who listened to our conversation.... Mr. Ossowiecki took my hand, and I put before him the photographs of my parents, but face down.
>
> "You live in Berlin, but have not lived there long. You were born in a town not far from Berlin, between Berlin and Warsaw." This was true, as I was born in Frankfurt am Oder.
>
> "Your parents, who are alive, still live in that town. You are now the only son, but you used to have a brother who died quite a long time ago" (then correcting himself) "he was killed in the war by a shot in the head." (True.) "From your mother's side you have French blood in you. Your father is still very lively and active. However, for some time now he has been ill with diabetes, the sugar level in the body is between 2 and 4%" (true, the doctor recommended treatment at the bathing resort of Preschdorf).
>
> "I see very clearly your apartment in Berlin. The entrance is through the back." (True.) "Above the settee I can see a dark oil landscape." (True, this is a Dutch landscape.)
>
> I can confirm that out of 100 facts 95% were absolutely correct.

Experiments 23 and 24—18 May 1932

Reported by Stefan Rzewuski, the experimenter. Source: Ossowiecki, 1933, pp. 129–33. The autobiography claims that they had already appeared in the *Ilustrowany Kuryer Codzienny*, but it has proved impossible so far to trace the relevant issue (abridged version).

> *Experiment 23*
>
> I prepared two series of sheets, 30 in each, identical in each series as to size and paper quality. The sheets for use in the experiment were to be chosen from both series at random. Before going to Ossowiecki's apartment I wrote in ink on each sheet an equation consisting of three numbers, in the form of one of the four arithmetical operations, e.g. 3−8=5, 12−9=7, 4x2=10, 0:5=6 etc. The resultants of the equations, as will be shown later, in principle had to be wrong, as I wrote them in with the left side of the equations covered.
>
> Nobody knew about the intended experiments, even Ossowiecki himself, whom I visited on quite a different matter.... After arriving I told him only that the intended experiment was a modification of those conducted so far and that the only target was to read the contents of a sheet placed in a sealed envelope.... I took out, without looking and at random, one sheet and, holding it with my hand folded around it, placed it in a separate envelope taken out of a pack which I brought with me ... folded in four ... the numbers overlapped....
>
> Ossowiecki took the envelope and, sitting down, held it in his left hand, either

behind him, or leaning his hand against his leg, all the time looking ahead of him.... After two and a half minutes from the moment I handed him the envelope Ossowiecki started to talk haltingly:

"I see some numbers. I see ... a seven, two zeros—no, that's an eight. It is not written by a mathematician: this is strange, it is not a mathematician."

At this moment he took from me the paper on which I was making notes and wrote, or rather drew enormous figures: 7 × 8 = 6. The whole experiment lasted 4½ minutes. Removing the sealed envelope from his hands, I opened it and, unfolding the sheet which I took out with my own hands, I found, written in my own hand: 7 × 8 = 6, and my initials in the right place. Ossowiecki agreed to carry out another experiment.

Experiment 24

Holding the envelope, Ossowiecki, probably still influenced by the previous experiment, says:

"I have a 7 in my thoughts ... it's so difficult to say immediately. Yes, I have a 7. I now see a 5. I see a 3. 5, 3 there is also a 1. 1 and 8."

Here Ossowiecki takes the paper from me, saying, "I shall do the writing now." And he writes: 5 × 3 = 18.

This experiment also lasted 4½ minutes. Ossowiecki, interested in the result, opened the envelope himself with me looking on, and took out the sheet on which—unfolding it gradually—together we checked the numbers one after the other, together with the multiplication sign. On the sheet, marked with my initials, I had written 5 × 3 = 18.

***

Experiments 25 & 26—23rd November 1932

Experiment 25

Reported by Stanisław Szpotański. Source: Ossowiecki, 1933, pp. 250–252.

At 10 pm in the apartment of Mrs. Zofia Świda at Bracka Street 3, Mr. Stanisław Szpotański handed to Mr. Stefan Ossowiecki an envelope sealed with a special glue, in which there was a letter, wrapped in a double sheet of paper. This was done in the presence of the hostess and Mrs. Irena Skibińska, Baroness Maria Luder and Mr. Leon Skibiński. The envelope had been sealed a few weeks beforehand by Mr. Szpotański in the presence of witnesses.

Mr. Ossowiecki, with the envelope in his hand, after a while stated that he sees in it a postcard which is a reproduction of a painting by a foreign painter. On the postcard he could see the figure of Adam Mickiewicz [famous nineteenth-century poet], standing. Apart from Mickiewicz there was another figure of a man there, an enormous man on a white horse. On the left hand side, at the top, there was a large white cross, radiating to all sides.

According to Ossowiecki there was no address on the other side of the postcard.

The whole picture was against a black background, only the figure on the horse was light, bright, and pointed with his hand to the radiating cross. Mr. Ossowiecki stated that he did not recognize the second figure.

He told those present that the postcard had been sent to Mr. Szpotański by a man from another town. The surroundings of the person sending the postcard were remarkable, very interesting. Mr. Ossowiecki emphasized a number of times that there was a large cross on the left at the top, as well as some details, such as: a cross, a white horse and the place where Mickiewicz was standing. He drew the figure on the horse on a piece of paper.

After the sealed envelope was opened, we found in it a postcard wrapped and sealed in a number of sheets of paper. The postcard corresponded in detail to Mr. Ossowiecki's description. Mr. Szpotański stated that the postcard had been sent to him a few weeks ago from another town. One side of the postcard shows a black and white reproduction of the well-known painting by Fossombrone called "A. Towiański" [nineteenth-century Polish mystic]. The painting shows Towiański on a white horse, with his hand pointing upwards to a large white cross on the left, radiating to all sides. Immediately behind the horse, on the left, stands Adam Mickiewicz. On the reverse of the postcard there was a four-line verse in small print, concerning Mickiewicz (this had been mentioned by Mr. Ossowiecki), and a few words directed to Mr. Szpotański (which Mr. Ossowiecki did not mention). There was indeed no address on the postcard, as it had been sent in an envelope. As far as the remarkable "surroundings" of the sender are concerned, one should note that the handwritten signatures were put down by a group of Towiański's followers. This report has been written on the basis of notes made by Stanisław Szpotański. Mr. Ossowiecki's notes and the postcards are attached. The experiment was witnessed by: [five signatures follow] [p. 101].

Experiment 26—23rd November 1932

Immediately after this experiment, Mrs. Irena Skibińska gave Mr. Ossowiecki a sealed envelope. Mr. Ossowiecki said, after a moment's concentration:
"I see a sentence, written in French." He picked up a sheet and wrote:
"Le Roi de Rome 1811–1832."
Mr. Ossowiecki wrote exactly what was there and, amazingly, not only was the content identical, but the handwriting also: small, feminine.

Experiment 27—undated

Reported, exceptionally, by Ossowiecki himself, but translating from German notes on an experiment provided by Professor Kallenberg from Sweden. Source: Ossowiecki, 1933, pp. 162–3.

Ossowiecki starts by saying how willing he always was to carry out tests for scientists who came from abroad, as did Prof. Kallenberg, from Sweden. He came prepared with sealed envelopes, and Ossowiecki took the heavier one.
"I transported myself to some balcony and I saw two persons. Prof. Kallenberg did not know what was in the envelope I was holding, as it had been prepared in Stockholm by some scientist. He did this to avoid telepathy. The professor started noting down my words, which were as follows.
"There is a photograph here, taken from a photograph; a young girl with long blond hair is standing by a window, wearing a white dress. This is happening on a verandah. Behind her there are some flowers standing, and by her is sitting a young man with a smiling face, one leg crossed over the other....
"I was mistaken only on one point: the young man sitting down was the doctor himself, who in reality was elderly—everything else was totally accurate" [p. 100].

***

Experiment 28—November 1937

Reported by Marian Wojdyłło. Source: *Illustrated Daily Courier*, 30th November 1937.

This account was published in full on 30th November 1937. Its author, Marian Wojdyłło, describes an elaborate experiment carried out in the open air while Ossowiecki was on holiday in Marienbad. A special committee under Dr. Robert Fulda, from Nice, was formed to "ensure that there were objective controls and that the experiment had scientific value."

The designated author of the target drew with a pencil a geometric figure (a pentagonal solid) and, without showing it to anybody, sealed it in an envelope which was then sewn through by one of the ladies, so that there would be traces if it were opened. This envelope was deposited with a member of the committee. Ossowiecki was to draw a picture of what was inside the envelope. A few minutes after being handed the envelope O. said that the task was complicated, that the drawing was a solid or a stone. The experiment took place in the open air. There were more than 20 witnesses; journalists were also present.

When Ossowiecki was surrounded by people, he took from the author of the target three objects which the author habitually used: a fountain pen, a handkerchief and a glove, and sat down by the Kreuzbrunn spring, while the author with the members of the committee went to Rudolfsquelle, 900 m away. At a given signal the author started drawing in the sand with his cane the same picture

Photograph of woman and Professor Kallenberg

Informal Experiments and "Fieldwork"

Postcard (see page 98, Experiment 25)

which was in the envelope. The drawing was ready in a few minutes, and at the same time Ossowiecki reproduced it in the sand by Kreuzbrunn in the presence of all the witnesses. However, before the judges came to them and opened the envelope for checking, the author of the target was approached unexpectedly by a skeptic (a Latvian industrialist) who asked for his own drawing (a shape like a wide "W" with added lines at the top) to be added. The author did this, and the skeptic went to watch Ossowiecki, who drew an elliptical shape and said, "I see a swastika in it." Then he changed the shape with his cane in the sand, and said, "No, it is not a swastika, it is a double "V," and drew a "W."

There were scenes of indescribable enthusiasm, with the skeptic being particularly affected. It should be added that the skeptic intended originally to draw a swastika within an ellipsis, but realizing that there were Germans present changed his mind at the last moment.

The judges decided that the drawings made by Ossowiecki corresponded exactly to the drawing in the envelope and the one drawn in the sand by the author of the report, and the same applied to the additional task provided by the Latvian businessman. The full report was deposited with the editorial office.

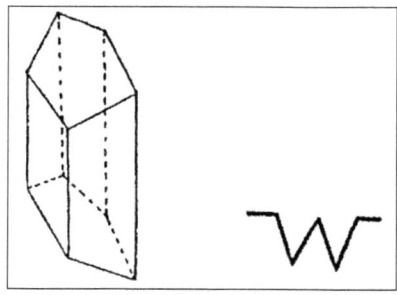

Target drawing

The author adds that he himself was quite skeptical about the claims made for the experiments with Ossowiecki, but the events he witnessed convinced him of their reality.

***

Experiments 29 and 30—undated

Reported by Professor Artur Chojecki. Source: Ossowiecki, 1933, pp. 233–234. It has been confirmed by independent sources that Professor Artur Chojecki was one of a group of academics from Warsaw University who devised a variety of tests and experimented with Ossowiecki on a regular basis.

Experiment 29

The accounts given here of this and the following experiment are attributed to "Prof. Artur Chojecki of Warsaw University."

In order to exclude the possibility of telepathy, I decided to get Mr. Ossowiecki to "read" a text which I did not know myself, nor would I know from whom it came. I thus asked six people in the office where I used to work—the Ministry of Foreign Affairs—to write down a short sentence and put the piece of paper with the writing into an envelope. I put the six envelopes I received into other envelopes, sealed them and took them to Mr. Ossowiecki. The envelopes were identical. Mr. Ossowiecki chose one of them and pressed it in his hand, then he kept putting it to his forehead, and after about a quarter of an hour he said: "This talks about silver and gold, it's a proverb." We opened the envelope and found the sentence: "Speech is silver, silence is golden." Mr. O. added, "This sentence was written by a young, lively single girl; she wrote it standing, leaning on a desk." (I checked the veracity of this information the next day. Mr. O was mistaken only in calling the person in question "Miss," as she was divorced.)

Experiment 30

Immediately after the experiment described above, Mr. O. suggested: "Write something down yourself now. I feel it will be even better." I then wrote down the first line of Dante's Divine Comedy: *Nel mezzo del cammin di nostra vita*. Mr. Ossowiecki took the sheet of paper with my hand and held it for a while, then said, "This is written in Italian. I am very fond of that language. To start with it talks about some 'Nelli' and it ends with the words 'Nostra vita.'" "This is enough for me," I answered. We ended the experiment with this.

***

Experiment 31—undated

Reported by Wilhelm Neumann. Source: Ossowiecki, 1933, pp. 354–7. The account of this experiment, carried out by Wilhelm Neumann jointly with William Mackenzie, appears in Ossowiecki's autobiography with the information that it is taken from *Über das Hellsehen und den Hellseher Stefan Ossowiecki* [Clairvoyance and the Clairvoyant Stefan Ossowiecki]. It has not been possible to trace the original publication. The account has been reduced in length by the omission of introductory detail and a digression on telepathy.

> I ... simply drew a heart, such as you find on cards (ace of hearts) and put the card in an envelope, which I sealed and put in another envelope, which I also sealed, and sewed through the whole with a thread. It would have been impossible to open it by invisible means. The paper of both envelopes was totally opaque.
>
> I handed the envelope to the clairvoyant. He did not look at it at all. He held it for a while at his side, then behind his back. All those present [eight people] watched him carefully. The room was brightly lit. After five minutes he said, "You wrote this with friendly thoughts about me." Then there was a short silence. "Have you got a pencil?" and he quickly drew an ace of hearts on the outer envelope....
>
> I drew the ace of hearts—accidentally—asymmetrically: the left half was slightly bigger and had a more square shape, while the right was smaller and rounded. In Mr. Ossowiecki's reproduction even these minor details were taken into account. One could suspect coincidence if this precision were not a constantly repeating phenomenon. Mr. Ossowiecki did the same when he reproduced the almost unnoticeable features of the drawing of the bottle (slight leaning to the right and the absence of a cork) and other objects.

"Fieldwork"

The cases reported here differ from the other voluminous anecdotal evidence relating to Ossowiecki only in having been recorded in detail close to the time of the event.

Missing Property

CASE 1: THE MISSING BROOCH—
JUNE 1922 (ALINE DE GLASS)

Reported by Mrs. Aline de Glass, Source: Revue Métapsychique 1922 No. 4.

Mrs. Aline de Glass, the wife of a former High Court Judge, wrote her own account describing how Ossowiecki retrieved a lost brooch, and Geley published it under her signature. The language in the *Revue Métapsychique* has been toned down, with talk of miracles and some exclamation marks deleted, but the story is the same.

> On Monday 6th June [1922] I lost a brooch in the street. On the same day in the afternoon I visited the wife of General Krieger, Mr. Ossowiecki's mother. I was accompanied by my brother, Mr. Bondy, an engineer, who was an eyewitness to what I am going to relate.
>
> [Ossowiecki suddenly came in, and Mrs. de Glass asked him if he could say anything about the lost brooch. At first he described another brooch of hers, one that was kept in the same box. Ossowiecki then asked to hold something that had been in contact with the lost brooch, and Mrs. de Glass indicated a place on her dress.]
>
> Mr. Ossowiecki put his hand on the bodice of my dress where I showed him and after a few seconds he said:
>
> "Oh yes, I see it clearly" (and he described it minutely).
>
> "I see, I now see—you lost it somewhere a long way from here" (it is true, I was then four kilometers away). "A small, shabbily dressed, dark-haired man with a tiny, trimmed black moustache is bending down to pick it up."
>
> The next evening my brother came to me shouting from the moment he entered, "A miracle, a true miracle! Your brooch has been found."
>
> Mr. Ossowiecki told us simply what happened, "The next day I met that gentleman. A small, dark-haired man with a tiny trimmed moustache—I recognized him immediately. I talked to him, and in the evening I received the brooch from him, which I now return to you."

In the *Revue Métapsychique* version the telling detail is included that Ossowiecki encountered the man with the trimmed moustache in his bank the next morning. One is bound to ask what brought these two people together.

CASE 2: THE MISSING BRACELET—
SEPTEMBER 1923 (KIMACZYŃSKI)

Reported by Jan Alfons Kimaczyński. Source: Ossowiecki, 1933, pp. 255–6.

> On 15th September 1923 in Warsaw at 30 Sienna Street, at 5 p.m., there took place a séance with Mr. Stefan Ossowiecki. [He names others present, including his mother, the hostess, and identifies himself as note taker.] The aim of the séance was to discover what happened to a lost bracelet and, if possible, to get it back. Mr. Ossowiecki was given a small box in which the lost bracelet used to be kept.
>
> After concentrating for a few minutes Mr. Ossowiecki took Mrs. Moniuszko by the hands, and at the same moment those present noticed a strange change in his expression. Until then it was lively and cheerful, but suddenly he seemed to exude total inner calm. When he started speaking, sentence after sentence, cer-

tain of what he was seeing, he gave us the impression of being somewhere far away in his spirit, even though his physical presence was with us. The facts were forthcoming very quickly, as Mr. Ossowiecki began to journey to where Mrs. Moniuszko came from.

He described in detail the purpose of her journey to Warsaw and the state of her health. He said that she did not live in Warsaw but some 3–4 hours away by train; that her property lies several kilometers from the railway station. Her husband, a judge, in spite of the late hour, is at present attending a court case not far away, using a local line. Further on he remarked that, when traveling to the property, one has to turn off the main road into an unmade road and that very close to the house there is a large stone which gets in the way and that she is intending to use it as a tombstone for her mother's grave.

All this was true, and those who knew the place and the family lifestyle were astounded by the wealth of accurate detail. Mr. Ossowiecki asked for paper and pencil and after a moment drew the whole building and the orchard surrounding it on the left and the right. After a moment those present had the impression that Mr. Ossowiecki was climbing the stairs and entering the verandah. Having drawn the shape of the windows, remarking that in the corners of the verandah he could see peacock feathers, and entering the other rooms, he stopped by a small medicine cabinet. He mentioned that, on the day she left, Mrs. Moniuszko gave some drops in ether to a "very sickly woman" (the wife of the manager of the property), which was also true.

He then started talking about the people he could see around the property at that moment. He saw the small children of the owners, playing. He gave their sex and age, which he confirmed a moment later on the photographs handed to him; he also saw a small boy who brought a letter and he said that the house was very noisy because of an unexpected arrival of guests. He described in detail the external appearance and personality of each person in the house.

On his way to the intended target he entered the corridor, remarking that it was dark and saying who inhabited the rooms leading off it. As a further detail he mentioned seeing a little servant girl (whose name was Steph) arguing with the old nanny wearing a beige blouse, and a dress of the same color, with warm slippers on her feet. At the end of the corridor he saw a door the glass of which was covered in opaque colored paper. These doors led to a room where Mr. and Mrs. Moniuszko spend a lot of their time, although it is not their bedroom (it was indeed Mrs. Moniuszko's boudoir) as the bedroom was beyond the next door.

At that moment, with a confident gesture, as if he entered the room and reached for the box (which had been given to him at the beginning of the séance) lying on the settee next to us, his face clearing and in a full voice he said: "I see the bracelet; it is a thick gold chain, traditional work. It is hanging on the lilac bush in front of the bedroom window. It slipped out of a pocket and fell out unnoticed when the servant was shaking things out. Search carefully there and you will find the bracelet."

The séance ended. It had lasted 25 minutes, and everything Mr. Ossowiecki saw at that time and related to us in such detail exceeded our wildest expectations. It even changed the mind of such a confirmed skeptic as General Listowski (now deceased).

The report is accompanied by a copy of a letter from the note-taker, stating that the following events described by Ossowiecki were confirmed on checking: (1) guests did arrive at the time indicated; (2) there was an argument between Steph and nanny, and the colors of the clothes were described correctly; (3) a little boy (son of the district secretary) did arrive with a letter at the time indicated; (4) the bracelet was found among the thick leaves of the lilac bush growing outside the bedroom window.

CASE 3: THE STOLEN DOCUMENTS—1927 (GRAVIER)

Reported by Alfons Gravier. Sources: *Revue Métapsychique* 1927, No. 4; this account forms part of a long article by Osty.

> A theft was committed recently at the Central Savings Bank, Warsaw: it consisted of the disappearance of an important collection of high-value share certificates that a client had left on deposit.
>
> Three women employees who were responsible for the deposit were presumed guilty as soon as the disappearance became known. [Ossowiecki, moved by their plight, agreed to help them.] His great reputation as a clairvoyant immediately secured the assistance of the police authorities at the bank.
>
> He went to the building and was shown the place where the stolen share certificates had been. He ran his hand over the surface of the safe where the certificates had been kept and then said:
>
> "I am there at the scene of a crime. A man comes into this room. He starts to sort through the documents kept here. He leaves some behind. He puts others into a briefcase. Then he leaves the building without being stopped. It's an hour after closing time. He himself must be an employee, because no one is surprised that he is there. I see this man so clearly that if I encounter him I shall be able to recognize him."
>
> Ossowiecki suggested going round the office with the authorities, as he thought he would be able to pick out the guilty man.
>
> The next day, without attracting any attention, and acting as if he were simply on a visit, Ossowiecki went all round the offices. There came a time when he found himself confronted with the man he had seen in his vision. Discreetly he signaled to the police authorities who accompanied him.
>
> An immediate search was made of the man's lodgings. There they found the stolen share certificates. The thief was arrested. The vindicated women were reinstated in their employment.

***

CASE 4: THE THWARTED SABOTEUR—1930 (PINTOWSKI)

Reported by F. Pintowski. Source: letter to Ossowiecki's widow dated 3 June 1952; Jacyna 18/4/71

> During the autumn of 1930 we had to cope in the Wedel factory [well-known manufacturer of high-class confectionery] with a malicious contamination of chocolate pulps by bits of metal, extremely difficult to trace on account of their minute dimensions. We were very concerned with small pieces of metal, flattened by the milling and mixing machines, frequently appearing in finished chocolate products.
>
> All our efforts to trace the malicious worker ... were of no avail.... Mr. Jan Wedel, the owner and manager of the factory walked around distressed and nonplussed, until someone ... proposed to consult Engineer Ossowiecki. The latter, whom Mr. Wedel did not know personally ... invited us to bring one of the dis-

covered bits of metal. Mr. Wedel ... handed him a part of a nail, 5cm long and 3–4mm broad, flattened by the milling machines and found in a bar of chocolate.

Engineer Ossowiecki gripped the piece of metal and held it in his hand, requesting us to engage in talk and pay no attention to him. He fell into deep meditation and after a minute or two began to speak, seemingly to himself:

"I see, standing in a large hall, a machine with shining parts resembling steel rollers, or something like that. Near by a door and behind it a staircase. A worker comes down it. He doesn't work on the machine, he works elsewhere. He takes a piece of metal out of his pocket, a small nail, drops it into the machine and goes back up the staircase."

Our conversation now turned on how to reveal the offender. Eng. Ossowiecki proposed a walk around the works and Mr. Wedel readily agreed. On the agreed date and hour Eng. Ossowiecki arrived and piloted by Mr. Wedel strode around as if this were his habitual daily walk. He never faltered in choosing a way to reach the sabotaged production department. On his way he showed us the staircase the worker was supposed to have come down in order to reach the mysterious machine and drop the nails into the chocolate pulp. It was a secondary staircase, rarely used and invariably locked. It never entered the mind of Mr. Wedel to point the stairs out to the engineer, though they ran from the upper storeys directly down into the mixing hall....

We did not use these stairs ourselves; Eng. Ossowiecki only showed us where the worker came from to get down to the mixing machines. It proved to be the soft sweets department. We went there up another staircase, agreeing that Eng. Ossowiecki would engage the employees in leisurely talk and designate the culprit by questioning him on the length of his professional career.

He chatted with them and, at length, conversing with a young confectioner's assistant set him the predetermined question. Then, after a while, he took us both aside and begged Mr. Wedel not to discharge the man, as he would desist for good from his harmful activities. On Mr. Wedel showing perplexity Ossowiecki explained that he had clearly felt "a withdrawal" of the worker from his hostile designs against the factory. He assumed that the man must have felt the concentration of the engineer's thought on his person and had become inwardly alarmed.

Mr. Wedel gave his promise, but looked dismayed and apprehensive. Such a promise incurred the risk of further 'stuffed' chocolate coming into the market. However the engineer's prediction proved true and there were no further accidents with nails or other objects.

CASE 5: THE MISSING CASH BOOKS—1932
(CHMIELEŃSKI)

Reported by A. Chmieleński. Source: Ossowiecki, 1933, pp. 118–121.

Ossowiecki's concern for the reformation of an amateur thief is also shown in this summary of a letter from the Chairman (A. Chmieleński) and two other members of the Civil Engineering Society of the Students of Warsaw Polytechnic, dated 14 March 1932.

Description of the finding of the financial records of the Treasury of the Civil Engineering Society by Stefan Ossowiecki.

On 13th January 1932 the financial records ... disappeared. Mr. Ossowiecki received me very graciously and promised to help, but asked me for letters by persons who either had something to do with the above-mentioned documents or whom we suspected of theft. I thus got hold of the letters by the former Treasurer, the former Chairman and the book-keeper, and went with them to Mr. Ossowiecki. He handled each letter in turn, and described in detail the appearance and personality of each of these persons.... He then gave a general description of the Society's premises ... three bookshelf units ... four tables in a row, but they are not ordinary tables, having special flaps that cover a kind of small cupboard at the back of the table. This detail, and also some others relating to the bookshelves I only checked ... afterwards.

He then explained that the documents are in one of these tables, in an unlocked drawer on the left-hand side. At this point he stopped in his explanations and declared, with surprise, that he could see the documents in the drawer.

I then explained that these were the new cash books he must be seeing.

Mr. Ossowiecki then said that he was certain that the stolen documents had not been taken outside the main building of the Polytechnic, and advised us to look behind the bookshelf units in our office. As Mr. Ossowiecki foretold, we found the two cash books behind the units, but the receipt book was missing and the last pages of both books had been torn out.

Mr. Ossowiecki explained that they had been concealed in pockets and disposed of in the toilet. Mr. Ossowiecki, when asked about the reason for destroying the documents and who was responsible, would not give a clear answer, supposing, however, that it was an act of revenge, and he would not reveal the perpetrator, not wanting to ruin his life.

Ossowiecki adds his own comment: "I met twice with the student who was responsible for the theft. I wanted to make him stop and realize that this act could have serious consequences for his future."

***

CASE 6: THIEF FOUND BUT NOT UNMASKED—1936
(LOTH)

Reported by Felicjan Loth. Source: *Stolica* [The Capital, a weekly] 1977, No. 33 (1548).

The following is a greatly shortened summary of Loth's reminiscences.

It was 1936. I was a third year medical student and supplemented my income by doing injections for the patients of senior doctors I knew.... One day I was instructed to carry out a series of 24 injections for Mr. Ossowiecki, who lived at Polna. He was then about 50. At first I knew nothing about my patient, but after a while I found out that this man was well known in Warsaw and throughout the country for his clairvoyant gift....

Towards the end of the series of injections Ossowiecki suggested a demonstration—this involved Loth writing something at the desk, while O. sat in an armchair in the corner. Loth wrote a page-long letter to a friend, with suggestions as to how they would spend the holidays together. Ossowiecki then asked Loth to put the letter in an envelope and give it to him. He put the envelope on his knee, covered it with his hand, and after a little while told Loth almost word for word what was in the letter.

At a later date Felicjan Loth was witness to the following events:

Loth's father was a professor of anatomy at Warsaw University; his secretary locked the departmental salaries in the drawer of her desk in the library over the weekend. On Monday the money was gone, though there was no sign of a break-in. Loth's father asked Ossowiecki for help; Ossowiecki told him to come round, bringing the empty money box with him. Ossowiecki saw a tall, thin, blond man with a gaunt face, wearing a gray overall, open the drawer. The description fitted the caretaker, who, when tackled, returned the money immediately.

The second incident involved Felicjan Loth directly.

On Loth's mother's name day there were many guests, and next day his sister found that a sum of money was missing from the drawer of her desk. His mother was distraught at the thought that they had a thief within their immediate circle. His father was away, and Felicjan Loth asked Ossowiecki to help.

Ossowiecki held the box from which the money had been taken and described in accurate detail the appearance of the house, his mother, her clothes, the scene of guests arriving. But he refused to tell Loth who took the money; he said he thought the person would return it and explain.

He would not budge in spite of Loth's insistence that his mother had to know. The person who took the money did return it to Loth, explaining that (s)he had no idea why (s)he did not simply ask for a loan, and Loth never told his mother the identity of the thief.

Missing persons

CASE 1: SEEING A MURDER—1924 (SZPYRKÓWNA)

Reported by Maria Szpyrkówna. Source: Jerzy Jacyna, *Fakty i Legendy*, 4/4/71.

The source of this story, cited by Jerzy Jacyna, is Maria Szpyrkówna, secretary of the Psychophysical Society. It is one of several accounts in which Ossowiecki gives a vivid description of a violent crime.

> In 1924 Ossowiecki was asked for help by a Rabbi whose 14 year old daughter, Rebecca, had failed to come home after attending school in a neighboring town.
>
> "I see clearly.... The little brunette with the briefcase is hurrying home. There is somebody behind her, following silently in the dark. A terrible man. He is carrying a suitcase, and in that suitcase he has a rope, an axe, an iron wrench ... not in the suitcase, in his pocket ... he hastens his step to catch up with the girl, he sighs and moans. He asks politely if she could carry his suitcase for a little while, he says he is very tired and ill, he limps. He is in a hurry to catch the train, but he cannot walk any faster with the suitcase....
>
> "She takes the suitcase from him. They walk together, the girl in front, the man limping behind. They enter a small wood; seems to be next to a cemetery.
>
> "What I see now is terrible. The man approaches the child silently, reaches into the pocket of his coat, takes out the iron, hits the girl on the head from behind. The child falls in the grass unconscious. This is dreadful. He throws himself on his victim tears her dress, drags her into the bushes.... He rapes her. I cannot watch any more."
>
> We later found out that the description given by Ossowiecki to the Rabbi's representatives of the murder scene and the place where the girl was buried was accurate. He had also said that the burial place would be easy to identify, as a piece of the victim's red skirt was sticking out from under the earth. He also gave a detailed description of the murderer, and said that he got on the train and went south.... The murderer was caught shortly afterwards.

This account is third hand, in that Ossowiecki recounted in the presence of Szpyrkówna a vision he had already described to the victim's relatives.

CASE 2: A MISSING FATHER—1928 (MISSUNA)

Reported by Olgierd Missuna. Source: Ossowiecki, 1933, pp. 137–140.

Olgierd Missuna asked Ossowiecki to give some (clairvoyant) news to Miss Irena Szarska about her father, of whom she had had no news for some time. The sitting took place on 21 November 1928 in the presence of two named witnesses in addition to Missuna. Ossowiecki started by taking and holding Miss Szarska's ring. The report has been shortened by nearly a half.

> It must be emphasized that Mr. Ossowiecki was introduced to Miss Szarska only that day and that he had never seen her or heard of her before.
> "This ring," he said, "comes from very far away, as if China or Japan.... You received it long ago, from your father. I can see him, he is alive. I see him in uniform. He has no hair on his head. He is clean shaven. I see a scar on his face, perhaps from a bullet." Ossowiecki pointed to his right cheek. "He also has a smaller scar by his nose. He is very far away—at sea. Somewhere between America and Asia. At the moment he is on board a ship. He has a boil on his neck. There is a kerchief round his neck. The ship is carrying tea in chests wrapped in some kind of woven stuff. I can see writing on the side of the ship, this is the name. I can clearly see five letters, one above the other. This is Chinese writing. Your father ... wants to come to Poland and take you to China. He will come in about a month's time. He is on his way...."
> I will add that the father of Miss Irena Szarska is in fact a captain in the Chinese fleet, that in January 1929 he did arrive in Warsaw and confirmed the truth of the details given by Mr. Ossowiecki. I have seen Captain Szarski myself. Ossowiecki described his appearance with total accuracy, including the scars. Captain Szarski was indeed carrying a shipment of tea on a merchant ship. In February 1929 Captain Szarski left with his daughter for Shanghai, where he still remains.
> Warsaw 17th January 1930   Vice-Prosecutor O. Missuna

CASE 3: A MISSING SON—1930 (GODEJSKI)

Reported by G. Godejski. Source: Ossowiecki, 1933, pp. 140–42.

Ossowiecki was asked to help a friend's mother by "seeing" if her son by her first marriage, Ryszard, was alive and well. Ossowiecki quotes the letter from his friend and also the letter received later from the Polish Consul in Paris confirming that the missing man was currently employed on board the French ship *Rousillon*.

> In February 1930 ... I was approached by Mr. Godejski, who asked me to see him and his mother. They asked me to ... tell them whether her son was alive.... Mrs. Milewska ... has had no communication from him for a number of years. I ... took the letter from Ryszard Korwin-Milewski in my hands. After a few minutes I was with him, at sea.... At once I could tell them with joy that her son was alive. He was on board a French ship, in the middle of the ocean, in good health and full of energy. I told them that she would receive news of him very soon.... After a few weeks I received a letter from Mr. G. Godejski.
> *"Dear Mr. Ossowiecki,*
> *"When, at the beginning of February, my mother turned to you.... You told her that you could see him alive, as a sailor, on board a big ship on an ocean, and that we should soon receive news of him. A few days later we received an official answer to the inquiry directed at the end of last year to the Polish Consulate in Paris through the kind serv-*

ices of Prof. Mościcki. I enclose a copy of the letter, which, amazingly, confirmed all the details you mentioned.
"Yours sincerely"
[The letter from the Consul was dated 12th February.]

CASE 4: A MISSING BARRISTER—1931 (BACHRACH)

Reported by Mr. Bachrach, [a well-known and reputable detective]. Source: Ossowiecki, 1933, pp. 152–57.

Ossowiecki cites here a very long and circumstantial report. The following account has been shortened by about a half.

> In the winter of 1931 ... I was ... asked to come immediately to S. Street on an urgent matter.... In the apartment of the well-known barrister, Mr. X, I met his wife and daughter, who were desperate. As I found out, X had left the house on the morning of the previous day, in a state of high nervous tension, and had not returned.... On hearing that the missing man was also an acquaintance of Mr. Stefan Ossowiecki, famous throughout Poland and abroad, who had already helped me a number of times and in whose powers I firmly believe, I decided to ask him for help. Taking the missing barrister's pajamas, we went with the deputy investigating judge to Polna Street, to Ossowiecki's apartment.
>
> Ossowiecki did not allow me to say what the matter was and, taking the pajamas, after a brief period of concentration, started as follows:
>
> "The missing man left the house yesterday morning; he had a few coins on him. He went to visit some acquaintances near Marszałkowska Street and wanted to borrow money. He left them in a highly excited state. For a few hours he wandered aimlessly around town. In the afternoon he went to one of the side streets of Nowy Świat. There is an old house there; on the second floor at the back there lives a woman of about 40, tall, blonde. She is a woman with a past. He went to see her. Off the hall, opposite the main door, there is a little room with a settee. The missing man sat in that room with the woman, the owner of the apartment. He received some money from her and left her apartment after a few hours. About 11 p. m. I see him in the bar opposite the Main Station; he is eating frankfurters and he has a glass of beer in front of him. About midnight he went out onto the platform—his hat pulled down over his forehead and the collar of his coat up.
>
> "He got onto a long distance train. He is sitting in a third class compartment. In this compartment there is a priest and two ladies. I see him on the train, but he did not travel to the end station, he got off along the route. He got off at a station where there is a long railway bridge. It is dark, he is fighting a battle with himself. He wants to kill himself. He has not got the courage. He is walking beside the bridge, he throws himself into the water; he is lying on the ground, but he is still alive—he will live."

Bachrach confirms that X really did visit relations and ask for a loan, which he did not get. Bachrach also traced the blonde woman of 40, who did indeed live on the second floor of an old house; she confirmed that X had come and borrowed some money from her. The detective also took the train toward Gdańsk, where there was a casino thought to be frequented by X, and got off the train at Grudziądz, where there was a long railway bridge.

Most fortunately, Mr. Ossowiecki's prophecy was also totally accurate. I found the barrister in Grudziądz; he had already been moved to Hotel Polski in the Market Square. It turned out that Mr. X really did want to commit suicide ... at last he threw himself into the river but fortunately so that on falling he got caught on the ice, fainted and came to himself only after a long time. He was taken to a hotel and put into bed with frostbitten legs. That was where I found him.

***

CASE 5: A MISSING RELATIVE—1932 (MOHUCZY)

Reported by M. Mohuczy. Source: Ossowiecki, 1933, pp. 116–17.

On 5 February 1932 a Mr. M. Mohuczy asked Ossowiecki for news of a missing relative. Ossowiecki used his recent letters as a psychometric link.

> I saw him lying on a hospital bed, in white clothing. He looked very ill—yellow skin, mouth open, a big tooth sticking out on the left side. I told his relatives that he was alive, that he keeps thinking about returning home as soon as the illness passes. I also added that he had written asking them to send money for the journey and to pay off debts. After only a few days, on 10th February, I received a letter from Mr. Mohuczy.
>
> *"Dear Mr. Ossowiecki—In February I and my cousin Mr. Piotr Szawernowski asked you to find out what happened to his brother, Wlodzimierz, who left for the Belgian Congo in Africa and disappeared.... We have now in fact received a letter. Mr. S [the missing man] did suffer from a serious illness but is alive, although still very weak. He was in hospital and the doctors have recommended that he returns to Europe. The detail about a big tooth sticking out on the right side is absolutely accurate."*

Remote viewing by request

CASE 1: A VISIT TO RIGA—NOVEMBER 1931 (LUDER)

Reported by Maria Luder, (witnesses Zofia Świda and Dr. Stanisław Górzyński). Source: Ossowiecki, 1933, pp. 114–16. The accuracy of this account was confirmed by Zofia Świda, Ossowiecki's widow, in an interview with Jerzy Jacyna (38/70).

Ossowiecki was asked by Baroness Luder to transport himself to Riga to report on the state of her mother's health. Ossowiecki was ready to make his report within five minutes, and he cites Baroness Luder's report, which is also signed by two other witnesses.

> On 9th November 1931 in Warsaw Mr. Stefan Ossowiecki, an engineer, who was with us in a restaurant, used his supernatural gift of clairvoyance to transport himself to Riga in Latvia ... to visit the apartment of Mr. and Mrs. Bluhmen ... at Muhlenstr. No. 58, which he had never visited.
>
> He described it in great detail as if he were there. There was no detail that he missed: the location and the external appearance of the house as it used to be years ago and as it is now, the plan of the apartment, the rooms, and even the smallest objects there. Apart from this Stefan Ossowiecki described in detail the people living there, complete strangers to him; he did not even omit the old servant who usually wears slippers, or the faithful dog.
>
> Among other things he said that Mrs. Bluhmen suffers from kidney trouble and, not feeling well that evening, she got up from supper earlier and went to

bed; also that Mr. Bluhmen was visited by a gentleman with a bad leg, who was lame. The only detail which Mrs. Luder denied was O's statement that above the bed in her room there hangs an embroidered rug.

Since these last three facts could not be checked at once, after writing to Riga it was revealed that (1) on the night of 9th November Mrs. Bluhmen felt ill in the evening and got up from supper to lie down; (2) a lame gentleman did visit Mr. Bluhmen that afternoon; (3) after Mrs. Luder left her room was occupied by a teacher, a Frenchwoman, who hung the rug above the bed, of which Mrs. Luder was unaware. We confirm the truth of this report with our signatures.

CASE 2: A SICK MAN IN HEIDELBERG

Reported by Prof. Witold Doroszewski.* Source: Jerzy Jacyna: *Fakty i Legendy* 9/5/71.

I spent the academic year 1936/37 in the USA, where I opened a Polish Language Department at Wisconsin University. I returned to Warsaw in September 1937 (it will shortly become apparent why I mention this fact). At the beginning of February 1938 Prof. Jan Łukasiewicz of Warsaw University telephoned me and told me that next Friday a number of Warsaw University professors would be meeting at 7 p.m. at the apartment of Ossowiecki, and that he is letting me know because he knows that I am interested in this matter.

On that same Friday, at 10 a.m., a friend of mine, a teacher from the Górski School, Władysław Koneczny, was to undergo an operation. He had a serious lung disease and the doctors decided that he could only be saved by an operation which at that time could not be performed in Poland. The patient was thus sent to a hospital in Rohrbach near Heidelberg.

On the morning of that Friday I met Mrs. E.B.... She promised to bring me some objects belonging to Mr. Koneczny and asked me to ask Ossowiecki what the chances were of the operation being successful. She brought me a soap dish and a comb (she had a key to the Konecznys' apartment which the patient's wife, Dr. Halina Koneczna, later a professor at Warsaw University, left with her).

At seven I entered the apartment of Mr. Ossowiecki.... Among others, those present included Prof. Łukaszewicz, Prof. Krokiewicz, Prof. Kamielski. I asked the host to give me a little of his time, as I had a question. He politely pointed me to a settee, and sat next to me watching me attentively. I handed him the soap dish and the comb and asked whether he could tell me anything about the fate of the owner of these objects.

By a strange coincidence, only a few days previously, while looking for another text, I found a kind of report of my conversation with Ossowiecki on that occasion. Someone sat down on a chair next to me and took notes, while I wrote down part of the answers immediately after the end of the conversation. This is the text of Ossowiecki's answers, which I now copy from the notes taken then.

"This is not your property, nor anything from your house. Somebody gave this to you, a woman, so that you could bring it and give it to me. There is something the matter with that man—an illness—some uncertainty in relation to (?). The unfortunate thing is that this is a thing he used very little, and so it has little connection with that man—this is very difficult." (It turned out later that in fact Mr. Koneczny had not been using this soap dish and comb for some years.)

"I see that room," continued Ossowiecki. "It is quite modest, but I do not see

---

*Professor Witold Doroszewski, of Warsaw University, asked that his letter should be treated as documentary evidence. Doroszewski was one of the most prominent Polish language specialists.

that man. He has nothing to do with that apartment, he is a long way away from here and has been very ill recently. I am getting lost in my search, I do not know if he is alive. This is somewhere outside Poland, perhaps in Soviet Russia? He is from that area. I see water, oceans, but not that man. Many years have passed, this happened a long time ago.... No, this is not in Russia, it's a different country." (The source of association with what was then called Soviet Russia and the ocean might have been myself, as I spent a long time in Russia, and a few months before February 1938 I crossed the Atlantic by ship, returning to Poland.)

Meanwhile Ossowiecki carried on, "He was married—this is the wife's sister, in the family home. I cannot see that man, there is no contact. There are three people living there, in the place where this comes from. This is a memento of him, he has left."

Then Ossowiecki asked me to formulate my question more clearly. I said:

"I want you to tell me the condition of somebody who was operated on at 10 a.m. this morning."

Ossowiecki answered: "It was a diaphragm operation. No, it was a lung operation. But he had been operated on before." (It later turned out that Mr. Koneczny did have an operation for his diaphragm at some earlier time, which I did not know about.)

"This second operation will end in tragedy. He will not live long. This man is already on his way to the world beyond. He is not an old man, 50–48 years old." (The patient was then in his forties.) Ossowiecki continued: "More than average height—and now he is lying down. He has such long fingers." (That was true.) At that moment Ossowiecki, with his fingers held down, smoothed his hair with his right hand. This gesture was very characteristic of Mr. Koneczny, and made quite an impression on me.

"There was a moment ... when they were totally against the operation. Even today they did not want to. And he is married. Has one or two children." (Incorrect! Mr. & Mrs. Koneczny did not have children. Mrs. Koneczny lost a baby prematurely once.) I quote Ossowiecki's next words:

"I do not see her with him. Ah! No, she is there. She is quite stout. This is on the second floor, stone stairs, long corridors." (I thought then that this would be natural in a hospital). Meanwhile Ossowiecki continued, "He has such glassy eyes. And as if going a little gray. Oh dear, he looks so ill! His last, penultimate operation, that was four years ago, he was operated on by a stout man, quite small, with glasses. He will not make it through this illness. One lung totally empty. But they were still trying to do something. They collected some money. Because this operation, they don't do that here at all, that is why they sent him.... Yes, about 800 zlotys" (Polish currency), "write this down. This is such a misfortune, that he has to go to Menton. Such despair, such heavy atmosphere. There is a gentleman there, young, pleasant." (This was Dr. Skorupka, whom we sent to help the sick man's wife in the strange town). "They live somewhere over there," continued Ossowiecki. "Narutowicz Square."

(Mr. & Mrs. Koneczny lived at Klonowa Street [very near Ossowiecki's apartment; Narutowicz Square is about 2 miles to the east]. Mr. Koneczny died on the 18th or 19th February 1938. We had a collection to cover the cost of bringing the body back to Warsaw: the cost was 800 marks. Not zlotys, marks, but the sum was the same as that mentioned by Ossowiecki).

Ossowiecki had nothing of a poseur about him. He seemed to be more of a friendly bon vivant.

***

Wartime Accounts

Three out of the following four accounts are abbreviated translations of letters written after the war by people who had been helped by Ossowiecki. The fourth (Case 2) comes from a biography of General Stefan Grot-Rowecki, head of the Home Army (Poland's main resistance movement during the Second World War). It is one of the very rare accounts reporting Ossowiecki's failure. The reports are presented in chronological order.

CASE 1: REPORT OF MARIA BOŁTUĆ—24 SEPTEMBER 1939

Source: Letter to Zofia Ossowiecka dated 24 June 1947, Alexander Imich archives; Jacyna, Jerzy 3/1/71, Boruń & Boruń-Jagodzińska, 1990, pp. 98–99. It describes a visit made by Mrs. Bołtuć to Ossowiecki on 24 September 1939, a time of great stress in wartime Poland, when she was desperately anxious about her husband, General Mikołaj Bołtuć.

> I took my husband's cap and photograph with me. The engineer closeted himself with me in a small room and unheeding of his own peril (everybody was fleeing to the cellars) quietly attained a state of deep concentration. Presently he started to relate.
> My husband was walking with a large detachment, he saw officers beside him. He described it vividly and with great detail [so] that I recognized Major Kunc, Captain Kwiatkowski and others. He saw my husband receiving a wound in the neck and falling into a ditch, trying to rise while blood spurted from the wound.
> He told me my husband greatly needed assistance and bade me go through the Żoliborz district promptly, along the high road to a small bridge with white houses in the foreground and seek him there. To my father he confided that my husband's condition was very grave, nay, hopeless.
> On the 25th.... I received ... a safe-conduct. Equipped with ... the instructions of Engineer Ossowiecki I departed on my quest.
> I did not, alas, find my husband alive. He had, as described by Ossowiecki, been wounded in the neck and had swiftly died of hemorrhage.
> On the neighboring graves I deciphered the names of the officers whom Ossowiecki had seen near my husband in his vision.

***

CASE 2: REPORT OF IRENA ROWECKA-MIELCZARSKA— OCTOBER 1939

Source: Irena Rowecka-Mielczarska, 1985, pp. 218-1–219. It should be noted that her account of the sitting is not firsthand.

> Colonel (then) Stefan Rowecki was commanding the Home Army (the resistance movement directed by the government-in-exile in London) and was in Warsaw. His family pretended that he disappeared during the campaign of September 1939 and they had no news of him. In fact he had false identity papers as a fictitious member of the family, but for obvious reasons very few people were allowed into the secret.
> Irena Rowecka moved to her uncle's apartment in the center of Warsaw in September 1939, fearing German attack. Ossowiecki's brother-in-law had his office on the ground floor of the same apartment block. During the heavy bom-

bardments in September Ossowiecki and his wife stayed at her brother's office with the rest of the family.

On hearing that Rowecki was missing, Ossowiecki offered to hold a séance, but needed an object belonging to the Colonel. Rowecki gave his daughter his watch, joking about wondering whose "magnetic forces" would be stronger. The daughter could not be present at the séance, but was told later that O. could not concentrate for a long time and saw nothing. Then in the end he saw the colonel wandering in a wilderness, across some sands.

CASE 3: REPORT OF JERZY OLEWIŃSKI— SEPTEMBER 1940

Sources: Letter to Zofia Ossowiecka from Jerzy Olewiński dated 27 August 1946, Alexander Imich archives; Jacyna, Jerzy, 1/3/71; Boruń & Boruń-Jagodzińska, 1990, pp. 99–100.

My brother, Ensign Janusz Olewiński, was killed during a cavalry charge in the locality of Palmiry near Warsaw, on 22nd September 1939.... After being exhumed from the battlefield his body was put into a collective grave of about 700 Polish cavalry soldiers in the parochial cemetery of Kiełpin, district of Łomianki near Warsaw. I intended to transfer his remains to our family vault in Radom ... and tried therefore to locate the approximate place where his body lay in the over 200m long grave.... The task seemed hopeless. I therefore contacted and visited, together with my mother, Engineer Stefan Ossowiecki to whom I brought a photograph and a letter written by my brother.

After examining both, Mr. Ossowiecki drew a detailed sketch of the cemetery and grave, marking the spot where my brother lay. He further defined the cause of my brother's death, a heavy wound on the right side of the abdomen and groin. He also stated that he had died unattended after an hour in great pain. The sketch contained details of which we were unaware (for example, the belfry).

On our entreaties, Mr. Ossowiecki attended the exhumation in September 1940. Before the digging began we left him alone, at his request. After walking up and down the burial ground several times, Mr. Ossowiecki stopped and said that was the spot where my brother lay (it corresponded to the one marked on the sketch) and that the corpses lay in great disorder in several layers.

Upon this the workers began the digging, supervised by Mr. Ossowiecki. After setting several bodies aside he told us the next one would be the one of my brother and asked for it to be taken out of the grave. After it had been washed, my mother, sister and I recognized the body by the stature, military rank, personal garments and gold crowned tooth. The doctor attending the exhumation found the wound to the right part of the abdomen and groin. The clenched fingers proved that my brother had died in great pain.

CASE 4: REPORT BY DR. TADEUSZ GLIWIC —APRIL 1943

Source: Boruń: & Boruń-Jagodzińska, 1990, pp. 38–39. This account was sent to Boruń by Dr. Tadeusz Gliwic and concerns the circumstances surrounding the death of his father, Professor Hipolit Gliwic.*

Professor Hipolit Gliwic (1878–1943), economist, former minister for industry and trade, and deputy leader of the Senate.

My meeting with Ossowiecki took place in circumstances of personal tragedy. My father, who during the occupation worked with the government-in-exile, was arrested by the Gestapo on 9th April 1943 around noon, and taken to Aleja Szucha, where, probably during the night 9–10th April, he took poison, whose action turned out to be very much delayed. However, about 10 am on 10th April he was unexpectedly released. He got home about noon and very soon after lost consciousness. He died in the evening on 10th April, in the clinic Omega.

A meeting with Ossowiecki was arranged by Prof. Wolfke—a friend of my father and a fellow conspirator. The purpose was to obtain information about the interrogations. Ossowiecki took up an object which belonged to my father, and started talking. He described the cell in which father was kept, the position in which father sat writing the secret message (which we received later via a Polish policeman). O. also said that my father was arrested as a result of an untrue denunciation, the matter got cleared up, and the Germans knew nothing about father's real activities. That is why he was released. O. then described father's return home from Aleja Szucha to Lekarska 10, the time of day and how father looked when he was trying to get inside the house.

This description was then fully confirmed by statements from people who helped him on his tragic journey whom I succeeded in contacting. I reached them on the basis of fragmentary statements made by my father to my mother before he lost consciousness.

After father died, the underground leadership instituted an investigation into the reasons for his arrest and the circumstances of his death. The investigation was conducted by Kazimierz Moczarski on behalf of the Chief Command of the Home Army. This led to the discovery and execution of the denunciator, thus confirming O's statement about a denunciation having been made.

***

We now come to a miscellany of cases which are difficult to classify. They point to a possible range of abilities not fully explored by the main body of the experiments, and for this reason are reported under tentative headings, indicated by the question marks.

Telepathy?

Case 1: Piłsudski—undated

Source: Ossowiecki, 1933, pp. 108–9; also Piłsudska, 1989, pp. 215–216.

At the appointed time the Marshal [Piłsudski, the head of state] arrived. He suggested we conduct a mutual experiment in this way: exactly at midnight we were both to concentrate as hard as possible, each in his house. In that state of deep concentration during the first eight minutes I was to say a sentence wanting the Marshal to hear it—then there was to be a 10 minute break, and then I was to concentrate on trying to hear the words sent by the Marshal.

In accordance with the agreement, before 12 o'clock I lay down with a notebook and a pencil. Just at the moment when I began to see the Marshal telepathically my wife came unexpectedly into the room. Not having been warned about anything, she shrugged her shoulders and said loudly "There you are, awake again, again some experiment? Isn't it a waste of electricity?" Then in order to say something, I said without thinking: "I don't know why my left hand is aching so badly." I quote my wife's answer, because these words were also heard by the Marshal: "If we stay on in this damp hole we shall both become ill."

At that time we lived on the ground floor at Piękna 5 and there really was some damp there.

I was really upset, because the above conversation took up the time assigned by the Marshal to the experiment. I assumed that the experiment was unsuccessful. The next morning Col. Wieniawa-Długoszowski visited me and asked me to go to Kanonia Street, to the apartment of Minister Patek, where I was to meet the Marshal. I went there at the appointed time. The Marshal received me politely and said: "Yes, yes, I did hear, the left hand aches very badly, and the answer of another person and the word 'hole.'"

Out-of-Body Experiences?

Case 1: Leszczyńska—undated

Source: Ossowiecki, 1933, pp. 240–42. In this case Ossowiecki's own report from the autobiography is used as the source. There are only two known accounts of this type of experience in his life, and therefore an exception has been made to the principle of quoting only witnessed reports. The events must have taken place during one of Geley's early visits, as Ossowiecki mentions in his account the address he occupied before Piękna 5 (Trębacka 11).

Geley is named as the instigator and invigilator of a highly dramatic, and in Ossowiecki's own words, "dangerous experiment" in out-of-body projection. There is no independent account by Geley, who may have thought it not rigorous enough in its conditions to be reported in the *Revue Métapsychique*.

> This is traveling in the astral space without losing contact with the physical body. I carried out seven experiments of this kind in Poland, and I shall describe two of them.
>
> The first one took place in the presence of Prof. Geley, who talked me into undertaking this kind of experiment.... I chose Miss Leszczyńska, an actress of the Polish Theatre, by now Mrs. Jackowska. I invited myself to her apartment for an evening, and observed it intensely, trying to absorb as far as possible the surrounding atmosphere. I must note that I did not warn Miss L. that I intended to experiment with her. Between 10 and 11 p. m. I returned home, where Prof. Geley and Mrs. W. were waiting for me. On the table I noticed the syringe with camphor which, I must admit, did not create a pleasant impression on me. At that time I lived at 11 Trębacka Street, Miss L. at 34 Smolna Street.
>
> I sat down comfortably in a deep armchair and started putting suggestions into my consciousness, holding a crystal ball before my eyes. At that moment I was trying very hard to re-create the interior of Miss L's apartment, and its owner. I put so much effort into it that I totally lost awareness of myself and at that moment I was in Miss L's room.
>
> Miss L. started shouting "Ossowiecki, Ossowiecki, Ossowiecki!" As far as I remember she shouted three times, jumped up from sleep, came to and turned on the light. This lasted a good few moments.
>
> My whole body seemed to be floating in the air; I was not aware of my hands or my legs. I could not say a word, and I became frightened of dying when I thought about how am I to get back and whether I shall get back. I saw Miss L. and her room quite clearly, more clearly than one would in reality.
>
> After a moment I slowly began to awake. Geley was already holding the syringe with the camphor, as my heart was beginning to stop. At last I came to and told him about all I saw and experienced. In the morning we telephoned

Miss L. Geley invited her and myself to a restaurant for 12 noon. She was greatly impressed by the phenomenon.

She related in detail what had happened, and this fully coincided with the report I gave to Geley directly after the experiment. We immediately went to Miss L's apartment, where I pointed out the wall through which I had entered and where I had stood, which was also correct. This experiment cost me two weeks' illness.

CASE 2: BYSZEWSKI—1921

Source: Ossowiecki, 1933, pp. 242–3. Report by Stanisław Byszewski dated 22 October 1932.

In the winter of 1921 in company with others I often encountered Mr. Stefan Ossowiecki, whom I have actually known almost since childhood.

At one of the public functions we spent some time with him, and my wife had the opportunity to discuss clairvoyance with him at some length—a subject she found interesting.

After returning home I was woken up in the night by the sudden screams of my wife, who announced that she had woken up a moment ago, feeling someone's presence in the room, and stated that she saw Mr. Ossowiecki there.

We should not have paid any attention to this dream hallucination if it had not been for the fact that the next day Mr. Ossowiecki, meeting us in Hotel Europejski, said "I paid you a visit last night." He then described in detail all our apartment, the bedroom, the furniture, the lamp and other small items, and I must emphasize that he had never visited us before. I confirm the authenticity of this inexplicable event with my signature.

***

Premonition/Precognition?

CASE 1: KOZIEŁŁ 1923

Source: Ossowiecki, 1933, pp. 231–240. Report confirmed by Zenon Koziełł, Warsaw District Court Judge and two other witnesses.

Though described as an experiment, this is a long account by Ossowiecki of how he had a waking clairvoyant vision in which he saw some men in danger of drowning, and took spectacular steps to save them.

It happened in 1923, at the end of June. Working in my study and feeling a little tired, I leaned comfortably in my armchair and traveled with the "eyes of my soul," turning my "sight" into space. Looking at the Vistula I noticed suddenly, close to the Poniatowski bridge, on the Praga district side, some men drowning. [It would have been impossible to see any of these sights from Ossowiecki's apartment.] I knew clearly that I am seeing something which is still to happen. It was an impression as if the changeable currents of the Vistula carried off a number of people, who were desperately fighting against the vortex.

Wanting to prevent this terrible accident at any cost, I immediately rushed out of the house, took a horse-cab ... and drove to the banks of the Vistula. Here, without wasting a moment, I jumped into a boat and told them to take me in the direction of the bathers, from whom I was separated by a considerable distance.

When I was close to them I told the boatman to take the boat among the bathers, who by now were drowning—their contorted faces showing that these were their last efforts. The boatman would not approach them, afraid that they would overturn the boat and pull us into the river. Only a generous tip made him turn the boat towards the drowning men. With some effort I managed to save three, as it turned out all soldiers of the 30th regiment. I pulled them into the boat using my strength, as they were already very weak [the fourth man drowned].

[Witness report:]
In 1923, on a hot day at the end of June, about 5–6 p. m., we were sitting on the shore of the Vistula, on the right side of the Poniatowski bridge. On the other, the Praga side, a group of men—as we later found, soldiers—were bathing. We could hear their cheerful shouts across the river. Suddenly we saw a stout man approach the river with quick and nervous steps, and we recognized Mr. Stefan Ossowiecki, whom we knew by sight. We had the impression that Mr. Ossowiecki was in a great hurry, because as soon as he arrived on the shore by a horse-cab he jumped into the nearest boat (the bridge had not then been rebuilt) and sailed immediately for the other shore, towards the bathing soldiers. At that same moment we noticed some commotion among the bathers and it became clear that some of them got into deep waters and were beginning to drown. Just at that time Ossowiecki got there and with the help of the boatman saved the lives of three of the people, the fourth unfortunately drowned. Myself, my wife and Count Antoni Jundziłł witnessed this event.

When a while later we met Mr. Ossowiecki and I reminded him about his part in the saving of the drowning men he told us he had had a vision, that he found himself on the shore of the Vistula and got into the boat under some internal compulsion that made him drop his work and rush immediately to the river to help the drowning men.

CASE 2: JAROSZEWICZ/SMIRNOV—1927

Source: Ossowiecki, 1933, pp. 243–44. Report confirmed by A. Jaroszewicz.

The trouble with most cases of prediction is that the outcome has to be awaited for an unknown time, but in this case Ossowiecki cites a confirmatory report from an independent source. The sitter was "the famous tenor" D. Smirnov.

After one of his concerts Mr. A. Jaroszewicz gave a dinner in his honor. The mood was very festive. During dinner Smirnov asked me to tell him what would happen to him in the near future. After concentrating for a few minutes, being in a very good mood, I easily transported myself into his world and told him, "You will divorce your wife. You will be invited for a number of concerts to America, where you will meet a woman, a Russian, with whom you will fall in love and whom you will marry shortly after. Her name will be Lydia."

Smirnov denied this vigorously, saying that this was impossible, since he had no intention of going to America and getting married again. Two years later, in 1929, he visited Warsaw again. My prophecy turned out to have been accurate.... Here is a short report by Mr. [Antoni] Jaroszewicz:

"I confirm that everything Mr. Ossowiecki has written about Smirnov and the prophecy according to which the singer would divorce his wife and marry again, this time a Russian called Lydia whom he would meet in America, came true exactly."

CASE 3: JERZY JACYNA—1932

Source: Jacyna, Jerzy, 18/4/71.

This case of prediction was not recognized as such until a corresponding event took place. The case is summarized as follows:

> Some time in 1932, Jerzy Jacyna was bitten by wild bees during a walk in the forest with his father. He had a terribly swollen head and face, and was saved only by jumping into some water. In spite of the seriousness of his condition, it had its funny side as his appearance was a source of amusement. He then remembered what happened two weeks previously at the apartment of Ossowiecki's sister. It was after lunch, during a lazy siesta time, when Ossowiecki suddenly said,
> "Wait a moment! Don't move! Why is your head so big? And your face is enormous—is it some sort of swelling?"
> Everyone looked at Jacyna, but there was nothing wrong. Ossowiecki continued:
> "It's all right, it will be fine, it seems like laughter through tears. I don't understand—some flowers, water and this head—I must be hallucinating."

***

CASE 4: JERZY JACYNA—1939

Source: Jacyna, Jerzy, 10/1/71. The first part of the dramatized account has been translated, the main body summarized.

> After Christmas of 1939 I was visiting Wiktoria Jacyna in her apartment in Filtrowa Street. O. was there as well. He was clearly anxious. He kept watching me, as if he wanted to say something. Suddenly he said, "Go home quickly. Don't go into the street tonight. You are in great danger. But you will live, you are not going to die. I don't know what it is, but I see you high up, maybe on a roof, maybe on top of a wall, in the snow, I hear shots.... There are deaths.... You will be very frightened, you will be on the run, but you will certainly live."
> "I'll only have a fright then?" I asked with a forced smile.
> "Yes," said the clairvoyant. "You will live through a great danger."
> "Then perhaps I should stay away from home tonight?"
> "No," said O. "There is no threat to you at home. At home you will be safe. The danger is in the street.... Something will happen in the street, in various streets. You will be saved by a woman, a young, beautiful woman. There will also be an old man, a very honest man."
> Jacyna then goes on to relate the events of that night. He rushed home (a rented room in an apartment at Żurawia 25), drew the curtains and stayed in. He read till late but eventually fell asleep. His landlady woke him up in the night and told him to run—a German had been killed outside the main gate, and all the men in the building, including her husband, had ran away.
> The Germans were already outside the gate. Jacyna ran. His escape involved climbing, with a group of other people, through a disused toilet in the courtyard, over the roof of an extension, into the courtyard of the apartment block next door, where the caretaker let them out into the street. However, being in the street during curfew, in the center of Warsaw, was almost as deadly as staying behind. The group kept dodging patrols, had to run from an apartment block where the tenants refused to help them, and in the end found shelter at Marszałkowska 37, where the old caretaker had already taken in the other refugees from their block, at great risk to himself. Only one of the refugees was killed by a

patrol (in the Three Crosses Square). Jacyna ends his account by saying that the only thing missing was the beautiful woman.

But perhaps O. "saw" Jacyna's landlady, who was only in her twenties, with a different eye.

***

Influence at a Distance?

Case 1: Szmurło (undated)

Source: Ossowiecki, 1933, pp. 185–188. Reprinted report by Prosper Szmurło. originally published in *Ilustrowany Kuryer Codzienny* (unconfirmed).

Stefan Ossowiecki ... told me that if he wants, he can, at a distance, force even a total stranger seen for the first time to approach him or to carry out some action.... However, a little while later, more or less two years ago, I had the opportunity to witness it myself.

We arranged with Ossowiecki to go together to a performance by some Polish fakir [Szmurło, making good use of time spent waiting for a delayed performance, asked Ossowiecki to psychometrize a letter].

"All right, I will try, although I doubt if I can manage it under these conditions. Any idea who this might be?" he added, pointing to a tall lady, aged about 30, a stranger to me, who went past us, entered a box about 20 meters away, and greeted the people who awaited her there. "I have no idea," I answered. "I have never seen her before."

"An interesting type. I wonder who she might be," said Ossowiecki.

The orchestra interrupted our conversation.

Ossowiecki kept turning my envelope in his hands, from time to time glancing at the box where the lady sat turned sideways to us and not looking at us at all. During the break, before the next part of the performance, Ossowiecki gave me back the envelope, saying he was not in the mood and would prefer to put it off till later, but he still managed to mention a few correct facts about the author of the letter, his appearance etc. He then started to talk about the lady again.

"I am so intrigued by this lady that I should like to carry out an experiment with her. I shall make her introduce herself to us. You will see something new."

"But really, under such conditions, with this deafening orchestra, when you cannot concentrate, it's bound to fail."

"I have been working on it for a while," said Ossowiecki.

During the break the lady went past us. We saw her say good-bye to her companions, and she seemed to be leaving the circus.

"Oh well, it didn't work," he sighed.

However, after a very short while an usher approached Ossowiecki and whispered, "Sir, somebody is waiting for you in the hall and asks you to come out for a moment."

"For me? Who might that be?" said Ossowiecki, and followed the usher. After a minute he returned, accompanied by the lady, and introduced her to me, saying:

"Well, what do you know? It worked after all. I persuaded the lady to come back, though she has already said her farewells to her companions in the box, so that you could see for yourself. I have apologized to her and explained that this is about an interesting experiment we have been discussing."

The lady told us that even while she was still at the circus she began to experience an inexplicable desire to meet Ossowiecki, whom she not only did not even know by name but had never seen before. On her way towards Nowy Świat she suddenly felt that she would know no peace until she had managed it. After an internal struggle, against all social conventions, she asked to have Ossowiecki called out, pointing out our box from behind the curtain. When he came she was embarrassed and had no idea how to explain her behavior.

Ossowiecki calmed her down by explaining that it was an experiment in tele-suggestion.

I saw this for the first and so far the only time in my life.

Case 2: Zaremba—1999

Source: Elżbieta Witkowska-Zaremba. Reported orally to Zofia Weaver.

Ossowiecki's autobiography contains another, quite spectacular, account of the clairvoyant influencing a person's action at a distance. In this context it is worth mentioning an account given to me by a close friend and contemporary. Although we have known each other most of our lives, I only recently found out that her grandfather and Ossowiecki were friends. My friend has no interest in the paranormal and knew nothing about Ossowiecki except the few stories which became part of family history and which she related to me . One of these involved a great aunt who was very skeptical about the clairvoyant's powers. The family legend has it that Ossowiecki made her kneel in front of him at a party, thereby providing convincing proof of the reality of his gift. This information is, of course, purely anecdotal, but it does provide unsolicited support for the above account

***

4

Answers and Questions

Mary Rose Barrington

Having seen what Ossowiecki was able to demonstrate under experimental conditions, and taking account of the tests and incidents reported in the autobiography, and elsewhere, by apparently responsible named persons, the time has come to attempt some insight into ways and means. As the above title implies, any explanations offered will be the sort of explanation that give rise to further questions. The first explanation to be examined (and, one hopes, discarded without any serious misgivings) is that all these reports must be attributed to trickery by the psychic, complicity by the donors and/or the experimenters and misreporting on a scale that would have to imply deception, lies, willful blindness, intellectual dishonesty, defective intelligence and other human frailties on the part both of scientific investigators and of respectable citizens on a scale that may be unprecedented in modern history.

In psychical research, where effects depend on rare individuals and therefore cannot be repeated by others who do not have access to the same individuals, there is clearly strength in numbers, especially in numbers of experienced and generally respected investigators; for it is their work that makes it reasonable to broaden the perspective and give some degree of credence to the reports from the wider circles of friends and strangers; so it is on the formal experiments that concentration must initially be focused. That the reports in the *Revue Métapsychique* were authored by ten different researchers makes the totality more convincing than if the Ossowiecki *oeuvre* were to be founded entirely on the word of just one, however creditworthy.

Some of the target donors were highly regarded researchers in their own right—such as Dingwall and Besterman from the Society for Psychical Research and Santoliquido from the Italian society; in other cases people unconnected with research were asked for targets, some of them names unknown to us, some public figures such as Marshal Piłsudski. Perhaps one need not labor the point to exhaustion to be able to eliminate the idea of a widespread conspiracy to deceive, involving scientists and various evidently normal citizens from the worlds of literature, theatre, politics and business.

If a reasonable consideration of all the facts, including the absence of the instant communication systems of today, leads one to exclude complicity with the medium by the donors of target material, the next question to ask is whether the medium acting alone (for in most cases he was unaccompanied by anyone who might have assisted him) could have deceived his experimenters. It seems almost insulting to common sense to ask whether Ossowiecki could have opened sealed envelopes or packages, noted the contents and re-sealed them while supposedly under observation by the experimenter. In the case of undeveloped plates this would not have provided any useful information, and even in the invisible ink test with Geley, when he failed to reproduce the target contents, Ossowiecki still was able to give an account of the sentence structure; and conjuring tricks with envelopes would not help him to describe a scene in which a book of a certain size was taken down for a sentence to be copied from it and a man with moustaches interrupted the writing. If psi-deniers elect to reject the reports as good evidence of paranormal cognition one should credit them with grounds that are not so manifestly absurd as ascribing the results to simple legerdemain.

We must turn to the hypotheses of defective intelligence taken together with willful blindness. So far as intelligence is concerned there can be no doubt that the major players were all highly talented and respected in their own professional fields, so we are talking about a specifically directed lack of intelligence that manifested itself particularly *vis á vis* the study of the paranormal. It has to be conceded that very clever people can indeed show conspicuous stupidity in spheres other than their own specialty, so one must take this possibility into account. The question of whether there is evidence of serious naivety can be judged best by appraising how the researchers concerned seem to have tackled the subject, whether with reckless enthusiasm or step by step caution. We see that in their initial encounters they may not have been expecting Ossowiecki to live up to his reputation, and they were not prepared with carefully planned tests—though Richet had taken the precaution of equipping himself with two indistinguishable targets.

By the time they were ready for a second visit to Warsaw it was a very different matter, and one can see how Geley thought out various ways of eliminating possible loopholes, bringing with him material the contents of which were unknown to him, and exploring the limits of Ossowiecki's capacities with multiple targets and with a sealed lead pipe for a container. These steps look like the fruit of a systematic plan implemented by rational people. From people's writings it is possible to feel a bond of acquaintance with the writer, and to form a judgment about how far they can be relied on. Reading through Chauvet's rather diffuse account of his dealings with Ossowiecki, how many people would feel that he was not to be trusted to give a sincere and substantially authentic account of his evening at the Institut Métapsychique International?

It is a truism that most people get some details wrong; if we could see the contents of Chauvet's room with its various souvenirs of travel we might find that some of them were in another room. Other details that did not go to the heart of the matter may have been erroneous. But when the presumed quota of faulty detail has been stripped away from an honest narrative the core usually remains intact and valid. The core here is that Ossowiecki reproduced a hidden target drawing with great facility, failed interestingly to decipher the words that explained the drawing and even more interestingly described two one-franc coins that made him share the discomfort Chauvet had felt when he had obliterated them with molten wax and had assumed that they had been expunged from existence.

The point can be fairly made that everyone concerned with these researches wanted them to succeed, and wanted their success to stand as solid evidence in support of paranormal cognition. So like most researchers the scientists of the IMI had a preference. A bias of that sort is not special to researchers into the paranormal. There are certainly situations in which a person carrying out an experimental procedure has no preference for one result rather than another; a forensic chemist, for example, may not care whose bloodstain he is about to identify, because he is performing a commissioned task, and in this he is hardly distinguishable from his apparatus. But in creative research the experimenter is seldom indifferent to the outcome of his investigations; he therefore has to be aware of his bias and ensure that it does not influence his actions or judgment.

Psychical researchers are for the most part acutely aware of their preference for a positive outcome, especially knowing that it will always be urged against them with greater vehemence than if they were reporting something consistent with the accepted scientific paradigm—such as a small blip on a chart tracing that could be interpreted as a fleeting particle of anti-matter, the sort of research that, like paranormal investigations, cannot in practical terms be repeated by other scientists;. they have to rely on specialist reporting, and a blanket skepticism to all results not open to their personal scrutiny would not be taken as a mark of high intelligence and critical acumen.

The bias in the case of psychical researchers is often deemed to be of irresistible force because acceptance of the paranormal leads (it is said) immediately to intimations of immortality, a state to which everyone aspires, and hence the power of the paranormal to overcome the normal balance of the mind, making the rational irrational, the careful careless and the honest man blind to his dishonesty. It has to be agreed that the more profound the implications that go into each person's interpretation of the evidence, the more attractive is the paranormal thesis, and the more dominant the preference. This again is no news to the researcher. One is aware of the partiality, and of the exaggerated view of it often taken by some critics, and is also aware of the need to give fair consideration to all reasonable arguments that might be urged against a paranormal interpretation of data.

Though preference for an outcome favorable to psychical research is conceded, it should be noted that survival was not foremost in the minds of the French researchers; Geley, who was in fact always convinced that mind subsisted outside space and time (Geley, 1919/1920), never profited by his association with Ossowiecki by asking him to carry out any experiment that could be interpreted as supporting a survival hypothesis. Osty and Richet, Richet especially, did not consider paranormal cognition to be anything other than a human faculty and an unexplored facet of science (Richet, 1923/1995). Does one see any pattern suggesting that the results reported by Richet were significantly different from those reported by Geley? Geley was concerned in a greater number of experiments, but Richet was just as successful.

These arguments could be indefinitely extended, perhaps to the point of tedium. So let us bring down the guillotine—but not before remarking that bias is not only one way. A reader whose preferred explanation at the start of this chapter was in terms of error, malobservation, deception, or something, indeed anything rather than the reality of paranormal cognition, will not undergo a change of mind after reading the points urged so far, and would not be any more convinced by further exhortation. Others will be impatient and prefer to move on.

There is however another preliminary hurdle to be cleared, which is the familiar, and reasonable, complaint that there is no Ossowiecki available for testing today. This has all the semblance of a stumbling block, and it is one that many people of good will and open mind feel to be insurmountable. There are however reasons that can be put forward. First of all, let us remember that Ossowiecki was an educated man in a western European country of advanced culture, enjoying a social position that enabled him to put his psychic gifts at the disposal of articulate researchers. There may be hidden away in less favorable conditions a hewer of wood or drawer of water, or his wife, who can tell their fellow toilers about events happening in the next village, or where to find a lost bracelet; but we are not likely to hear about it. If we do hear about it, then in the absence of personal observation or reports from unimpeachable sources such rumors seep away and leave no useful trace.

It is equally possible that the ability to demonstrate paranormal cognition consistently and reliably is exceedingly rare, and may occur only (say) once in a hundred years. In early nineteenth-century France from 1835 to 1850, Alexis Didier, in a state of hypnotic trance, demonstrated psychometry with the same degree of reliability as Ossowiecki, and if anything his clairvoyance was even more remarkable. But though there are excellent records of experiments carried out and reported by highly reputable sitters both in France and in England Didier preceded the age of learned societies dedicated to psychical research, so that he has slipped into relative oblivion—from which he has recently been reclaimed (Méheust, 2003). Perhaps a European clairvoyant spectacularly gifted and available to researchers is now due to make an appearance.

There are other sorts of people with singular gifts. The frequency of testable mediums may be of the same order as the frequency of calculating *idiots savants*, who can immediately tell the day of the week if you specify a date such as midsummer day 529 B.C. Within the last decade 12-year-old, Stephen Wiltshire, somewhat impaired in general intelligence, showed himself able to observe complex buildings and then, from memory, make skilful, accurate and artistically informed drawings of them, complete with architectural detail (BBC 1987). Among prodigies brought to public notice he may be unique, and as an infant prodigy he no longer exists, having grown to adulthood. Ossowiecki is pre-eminent rather than unique. Few, if any, rational people doubt the authenticity of the prodigy cases, nor do they argue that such people do not exist because they have not personally encountered one.

There is also a distinct possibility that the paranormal manifests in response to the demands of the *Zeitgeist*, if the *Zeitgeist* makes sufficiently clear demands. If indeed telepathy is a fact of life (life rather than of the research laboratory) then it may be far more pervasive than would appear from formal experimentation. In this case it would be natural enough to expect psychics to respond to what people want of them, as perceived by their psychically sensitive subconscious minds. In the 1880s people were feeling lost and lonely in a world that was being stripped of God the Father and His assurances; their mediums gave them phenomena that *prima facie* suggested life beyond the grave. The next generation asked for more subtle and intellectual evidence, and were rewarded with the cross-correspondences, intricate puzzles pointing obliquely to the authorship of purported *post mortem* communicators, redolent with elusive clues requiring scholarship for their elucidation—also requiring patient study from affluent, leisured, intellectually questioning ladies and gentlemen of a class that became extinct after 1918.

After World War I, researchers of the then recently constituted IMI in France distanced themselves sharply from survivalists (especially the followers of the popular Allan Kardec) by treating the paranormal strictly as a department of science; they obtained these very clear demonstrations of the extended human mind. They were also in the habit of arranging for selected sitters to ask professional mediums for advice about such matters as health, property and their business affairs, these professional psychic advisers enjoying a much higher status than the English fortune teller at the end of the pier (who was also likely to attract attention from the law if she claimed to predict the future), and Osty's psychometrists seem to have made quite specific predictions that proved to be correct (Osty, 1923).

This is an area of research virtually nonexistent in English language research; the French had other interests and expectations. Other French specialties were the tracking down of criminals by mediums who followed the trail from the scene of the crime rather like bloodhounds (suggesting a decidedly sensory approach to paranormal cognition) and the delivery of hypnotic commands at a distance. Different societies have different requirements, and have received different paranormal responses accordingly. If this does not sound like a scientific state of affairs, that is because it is not. When approaching the paranormal it is important to bear in mind that the cosmos as perceived and delineated by science is not to be equated with the entire scope of reality.

In the 1930s and 1940s American ideas became dominant, and the world stage was taken over by parapsychologists, led by J.B. Rhine, who believed that every citizen could demonstrate a useful quantum of psi (the general term for paranormal cognition of any kind), and that this controllable psi-flow would lead to manipulation and theoretical advances comparable to those in the field of electromagnetism. At first these methodologies were highly successful, and on a statistical basis the whole enterprise has produced impressive results (Radin, 1997); but they have not led to the expected mastery, and reduced confidence has in general been matched by reduced performance. New techniques for eliciting a paranormal response are devised from time to time, but so far the analogy with science has not led to the sort of control that is the aim of scientific endeavors. There are some new initiatives emerging, though whether these green shoots will lead to a twenty-first-century Ossowiecki coming forward remains a hope rather than an expectation.

As one would expect, mediumship is sensitive to the influences of the intellectual and social climate, and for some time now cultural confusion has reigned, so that we get pickled sheep as art and people are expected to take seriously 4½ minutes of silence as a contribution to music. This widespread state of affairs must be demoralizing for genuinely creative minds, and mediums, who at their best must be regarded as creative artists, find themselves in an unfavorable climate. With mediumship at a low ebb, psychical researchers are not at all sure what to do next.

The conclusion to be drawn from this short digression into the diverse and changing forms of mediumship is that the absence of anyone today who can match the performance of Ossowiecki should not be regarded as invalidating the reports about the man himself. The shifting nature of mediumistic response leads to further considerations. How reasonable is it to apply the canons of scientific validation to phenomena that vary in their effects according to which side of the Channel or the Atlantic they are observed to take place? If the paranormal manifests in ways fundamentally different from those associated with the regularities of physics and chemistry, it follows that the postulated analogies with scientific methodology are of limited validity, and history may provide more useful models for psychical research. The study of history does not depend on goals, but on observation and interpretation of the way things were and are.

History also furnishes a more relevant mode of verification; one proves that English royalty spoke French in the twelfth century and German in the nineteenth not by trying to devise an experiment to repeat the effect but by studying the sources, i.e. the testimony and any accompanying exhibits, and making a judgment as to whether or not the facts have been established to one's satisfaction. This is in fact the way most things that happen in the world are established as veridical, and this is the way that the authenticity of paranormal cognition falls to be "proved"—by examining reports of events said to have occurred and assessing the strength of the evidence.

It is rather fashionable to set oneself up as a resolute 'skeptic,' taking pride in rejecting testimony, if it testifies to the paranormal. But the dismissal of solid evidence does not necessarily indicate an impartial, rational approach; it may rather indicate unwillingness to listen, an *a priori* bias or just poor judgment. Denial is not an inherently superior attitude. A fair skeptic will keep an open mind in the face of unusual material, and be prepared to accept any incident as authentic if the evidence is good enough, however repugnant it may be to intuitive or learned ideas about what is possible. A closed mind is in danger of remaining shackled to a flat earth and other limited concepts. But let the point not be hammered to exhaustion. All the foregoing arguments could be greatly expanded, but perhaps enough general ground has been forked over to permit a brief return to the three researchers, Richet, Geley and Osty, who theorized about what Ossowiecki was doing and how he was doing it.

Reference has been made in the text and commentary to telepathy, clairvoyance, retrocognition, precognition and psychometry; in the context of the experiments the meaning of these words has, one hopes, been comprehensible. But before advancing into more generalized discussion a useful preliminary will be some amplification of these terms. The exercise of telepathy, which the experimenters were often at pains to exclude from possible operation, is often equated with thought-reading. In fact it covers a wider field, and is better understood as a form of transitory mind-to-mind bonding in which data that belong in one mind come to the surface of the other mind, whether in the form of knowledge, an unexplained compulsion to take action, a hallucinatory vision, spoken words, dramatic scene or other manifestation indicative of image- feeling- thought- or memory-fusion between sender and receiver (agent and percipient, in the customary jargon).

Within the ambit of telepathy, one can distinguish between the perception of sensory imagery on the one hand and the reception of abstract thought or ideas on the other. Perception of material in someone else's mind *has* to be interpreted as telepathy only if it is self-generated, i.e. not due to an external stimulus; once an external source is present, telepathy can no longer be presumed with certainty, because the stimulus would be available for clairvoyance, i.e. direct extra-sensory perception of environmental data, unmediated by the mind of an observer. That it cannot be presumed with certainty does not mean that interpretation as telepathy is unlikely; if at a time when the agent is drowning the percipient feels he is being suffocated, this suggests telepathic empathy rather than a clairvoyant vision of a seascape with a swimmer in difficulties.

While unequivocal tests for clairvoyance can, as we have seen, easily be set up, the operation of telepathy can be deduced rather than demonstrated experimentally, because the setting of a target in order to obtain a corresponding response can be based only on targets that remain for ever unrecorded except in the mind and memory of the target-setting agent, and it is far from satisfactory to have to rely on the word and memory of the agent. There is however abundant evidence from spontaneous cases and from non-experimental mediumship to validate the operation of telepathy, and some instances have been noted in passing where Ossowiecki seems to have picked up the thoughts of his sitters . It is very likely that some demonstrations of telepathy are mis-attributed to clairvoyance, which is difficult to exclude, and some cases may be mis-attributed to telepathy because there happens to be an observer/agent present. In cases of paranormal cognition where there is no way of excluding one faculty or the other it is convenient to resort to the use of the general term ESP (extra-sensory perception).

Precognition (apparent sightings of future events not deducible from facts known to the claimant) and retrocognition (apparent sightings of past events unknown to the claimant) must also be considered, and again there is a great deal of evidence to support the authenticity of spontaneous premonitions and experimental predictions. Precognition is a very complex subject, since it can take many forms; it can concern the prediction of events in the world that are not connected with anyone making, receiving or being the subject of the prediction, and who may or may not be present when the corresponding event takes place. Or it might concern personal events affecting the predictor, the sitter or any other person who either has or will have some connection with the event. In some cases of clairvoyance a person aware of a prediction may be in a position to assist in its realization, and bizarre theories have also been propounded to the effect that when events have been convincingly predicted they are actually brought about by efforts of will known as psychoboulia. This alarming power is considered by some people to be preferred to the concept of a foreseeable future.

There are in fact several fairly painless ways of accommodating precognition with a future not entirely set in stone. On one view, an unconscious awareness of every factor operating at the present moment could be extrapolated to predict the most probable outcome; whether that is more or less likely than precognition is an open question. If the glimpse of the future is only on a probabilistic basis, then the precognitive vision that gets the facts slightly wrong, whether or not due to intervention by the forewarned precognizer, can be fully accounted for without any concerns about determinism *versus* free will, backward causation or other paradoxical notion.

As precognition was not one of the faculties frequently demonstrated by Ossowiecki, and the evidence for it is less robust than in the case of present/past time clairvoyance, these complexities need not be examined in depth, except to point out that the few predictions recorded by or about him are entirely concerned with personal life events, such as the re-marriage of the singer Smirnov to a Russian called Lydia who would be encountered in America (p. 120, *Premonition/Precognition? Case 2—Jaroszewicz Smirnov*). It is of some value to bear in mind that though Ossowiecki denied any ability to make predictions, Jacyna says that Ossowiecki could sometimes foretell the future. This is of interest because there is a lot to be said about precognition's partial mirror image, retrocognition, though at present it is enough just to note that the mirror image is partial in that retrocognitive sighting of the past is paranormal only when it relates to events at which the psychic was not present. The mirror image of personal-experience precognition is of course one's own memory, and Osty conceived precognition to be in effect "memory" of a person's own future.

So far as psychometry is concerned, this is sometimes referred to as if it were a faculty in the same class as telepathy or clairvoyance and alternative to them; but it is better understood as a facilitating mechanism used to establish contact with a person who has owned or been in contact with a link object. That, as Geley pointed out, is a description, not an explanation. Psychokinesis (PK), or telekinesis, applies to paranormal action brought to bear directly on the environment, causing objects to move around without any normal force being applied, or causing even odder manifestations that do not concern us here, as Ossowiecki did not demonstrate materialization or other outlandish PK effects except (according to his own statement) the movement of objects.

To describe any or all paranormal effects, whether cognitive or physical, the word *psi* is used, this unadorned letter of the Greek alphabet being free of all implications beyond the indication that paranormal action is presumed to be connected with some function of the psyche or mind. The essential terms now defined, we can look first at the main issues that evoked comment and speculation from the principal researchers, i.e. whether any of the experiments could be interpreted as indicating the exercise of telepathy, and what was the role of link object (envelope or article) that Ossowiecki invariably chose to handle to obtain rapport with the sitter, the target object or with an absent owner.

It has been very clear from start to finish that most, and perhaps all, of the foregoing experimental results could have been obtained without any obvious form of thought-reading, and that many of them must have been. If a person unknown to Ossowiecki supplied the experimenter with several sealed envelopes or containers, and one was selected at random, then the donor of the articles had no way of knowing which target had been chosen, so that she would not have had any useful thoughts in her head. Even supposing that Anna de Noailles and Richet were in useful telepathic contact she would also have had to exercise clairvoyance to know which target was in the envelope he had selected before she could have had this information picked out of her mind by Ossowiecki. In cases where the identity of the donor was unknown to Ossowiecki and where even the experimenter did not know which donor was in question, a hypothetical chain of telepathic interchange would be even more tortuous. The whole concept is grossly uneconomical, and it is easy to agree with Geley and Richet in ruling it out.

Osty, however, had some rather different ideas, probably because (as has been mentioned) he worked with several remarkable psychometrists whose talents lay in prediction of their sitters' future life events, many of them extraordinarily precise. Reviewing his experience, Osty noted that if his psychics were asked to report on '*the* future' there would be no useful response; they could not, as it were, wind on the videotape of things to come and describe future events in the world at large. They could make a useful response only if they were asked to view future events that were going to be experienced *by the inquirer*. His conclusion was that every person has inside his mind knowledge not only of his own past but also of his own future, and that the psychometrist gained access to this information from the sitter's mind.

So though Ossowiecki was giving clear demonstrations of clairvoyance, Osty had to reconcile this with his views on the supposed all-embracing faculty of telepathy. His speculations were omitted from the reports in the sixth issue of the 1925 *Revue Métapsychique*, but they merit attention at this point. His comments arise out of the ingenious experiment devised by Szmurło using one out of four undeveloped photographic plates supplied by two different photographers. It was, like so many of the rigorously conceived experiments, intended to screen out telepathy. After complimenting Szmurło on his interesting and well designed protocol, Osty continues as follows.

> If they believe that they succeeded in their objective [exclusion of telepathy] by virtue of the conditions under which it was carried out, I think I am right in asserting that this is an illusion. I say this because of my own experience in experimental research and I also deduce it from the report itself. The experiment shows—and it can be shown quite easily—that when one puts into the hands of a person endowed with psychic abilities, such as M. Ossowiecki, an article that has been touched by someone, or which belongs to that person's immediate surroundings, the contact with or the proximity of the article promotes an unconscious inter-mental collaboration between the two minds whether they are close by or at any distance apart. As between the near and the more or less distant there is a difference only in facility and quality of the information perceived.
>
> In any case, is it not remarkable that, according to the report, while M.

Ossowiecki gave only a vague description of the undeveloped image on the photographic plate held in his hands, he showed considerable knowledge of the scene that took place around M. Bakierowski at the time when the photograph of the picture was taken.

After remarking on the scale of the hypothesized mind-to-mind collaboration, Osty continues:

> I hope it will be clear that the only way of excluding information attributable to telepathy is the unusual experimental condition in which no living human mind is consciously or unconsciously aware of the material that the psychic is asked to communicate.
> Even this elimination of a telepathic source of information is strangely complicated by that dual state of things to which I tentatively draw attention:
> 1. We do not know the extent of the human mind or of its latent cognitive powers.
> 2. If there is telepathy in space, things happen, experimentally, as if there were also telepathy in time. And there we arrive at the most obscure of human mysteries.
> Let us guard against illusions and prejudices, the progenitors of hasty explanations that set back the progress of research.

It must be said first that Osty, while cautioning against illusion, prejudice and hasty explanations, makes no attempt to meet the point raised above, namely, that even supposing an inter-mental collaboration between, say, Sarah Bernhardt and Ossowiecki, she did not possess the vital information needed for the test to succeed, which was the identity of the target that had been selected at random for the experiment.

On a broader front, it will be remembered that Osty's 'unusual experimental condition' was in fact realized in the experiment carried out by the very same Szmurło after the death of the target donor, Deniose Jonky. (pp. 80–84). Later in his career Osty found himself the recipient of a case in which a medium who (unfortunately in his view) claimed to operate by receiving communications from deceased persons, was asked to locate a missing estate worker, presumed dead. Apparently guided by the deceased man's directions she successfully traced his route and located the corpse, which had been overlooked by an extensive search party well acquainted with the terrain. Osty, who like many of the IMI researchers, found the notion of survival an intellectual embarrassment, then had recourse to his telepathy in space and time. Unfortunately he did not make it entirely clear either here or then what he actually meant by these concepts.

It is possible that he was hinting at an idea familiar to adherents of religion, spiritualism and other branches of speculation that would certainly make Osty recoil—the Akashic records of theosophy, the Liber Scriptus of Revelation or, perhaps more to Osty's taste, Jung's collective unconscious—where all thoughts, ideas and actions are recorded and can be abstracted by one who has the art of abstraction. The enduring past (Sheldrake, 1988) is an idea that has also had some attention from liberal science in recent years, and it may be remembered that Rupert Sheldrake's, *A New Science of Life* (Sheldrake, 1981), was described in *Nature* as 'a book for burning.' The equally enduring future is also a concept known to science and philosophy, and these concepts will have some relevance to ideas that will be explored after the theories put forward in the *Revue Métapsychique* by Richet and Geley have been considered.

Richet himself ventured on a fairly hasty explanation in 1922 (*Revue Métapsychique* No. 3) when he declared "Everything indicates that awareness of things comes to Ossowiecki by touch; it is a tactile hyperaesthesia, but an immensely potent hyperaesthesia that we do not understand. One must even postulate that the written letters carry in themselves some property other than the external properties perceptible by our normal senses…. It is rather like the emanations that come from underground water and provoke movements in the divining rod…. In other words, due to an emanation coming from the writing, and by means of an unknown tactile sense (cryptaesthesia) with which he is endowed, Ossowiecki acquires knowledge of graphic forms but not of ideas."

Richet was encouraged in this idea of emanation from handwriting by Ossowiecki's inability to perceive material that was printed or typewritten. But later in his career Ossowiecki learned to do this, one of the few cases where a medium acquires greater skills in the course of time; more usually psychic powers decline rather than strengthen. However, there are many other failings in Richet's tactile theory; he himself pointed out that it was only a provisional explanation and that it was one that Ossowiecki did not accept. Apart from other considerations one has to consider how Richet would deal with targets other than writing, such as the two fish scales, which though not identified as such, were clearly described by Ossowiecki (pp. 58–59).

There is also the fact that touch did not necessarily involve contact with the target or target container itself. The incident related by Gravier about documents stolen from the bank safe involved contact only with the interior of the container where the target had been but no longer was (p. 106, *Missing Property, Case 3*); the same is true of the similar incident, the location of a brooch (p. 104, *Missing Property, Case 1*). Contact with the place on the coat where the brooch had been pinned seemed to work, almost literally, like magic, but unless one counts residual particles of brooch left on the coat the contact was not with the target.

However, the observation that "awareness of things comes to Ossowiecki by touch" is undoubtedly correct, though not the whole answer. One could hardly come to any conclusion about Ossowiecki's modus operandi without taking his apparent need for contact of some sort into account, and Geley, writing a few months before Richet in the *Revue Métapsychique* 1922 No. 2, declares that "In short, M. Ossowiecki's gift is to be ascribed mainly to psychometry Though that, it is true, does not amount to an explanation. Despite the excellent work reported on psychometry, especially those of M. Bozzano and M. Oesterreich, this form of clairvoyance remains a total enigma."

It was in fact Osty who was to become, over the next two decades, the leading authority on psychometry, and he came to various firm conclusions about its effects, though without shedding much light on its causes. He was convinced that touch was the essence of the matter, so that if an article was handled by A, passed on to

B, who passed it on to C, who brought it to the psychometrist, she (most of his psychometrists were women) would first of all describe and talk about C and his life or problems, then about B, and finally about A, rather as if she were working her way down through layers of DNA richly impregnated with coded information. It is a thoroughly mechanistic depiction of a process that would be entirely acceptable to a conventional scientist, which Osty considered himself to be, apart from his acceptance of paranormal phenomena.

Osty derived these ideas from extensive observation of his talented psychometrists, but before one accepts his experience as decisive of the matter, one should pause to consider the entirely inconsistent experience of Gustav Pagenstecher (Pagenstecher, 1923), a medical practitioner, who wrote extensively and contemporaneously about his many experiments in psychometry with a non-professional psychic who had no idea that she had any paranormal gifts until he put her into a state of hypnosis as an aid to pain relief. Pagenstecher, heavily inclined to belief in survival, was rewarded with astonishing psychometry by his Señora Zierold, who, when presented with articles belonging to deceased persons, and *regardless of intermediate handlers*, leapt headlong into personal participation in the crisis that (for instance) led to the death of the article's owner, and she sometimes produced vivid descriptions of incidents that were later confirmed. Her psychometry fits a model more akin to the article operating as a sort of mobile telephone calling a number stored in its memory and receiving a graphic message from the person whose number has been dialed. This is much more compatible with the notion of survival than Osty's model, which would be more attractive to a scientist concerned with extending the boundaries of biology.

So despite the experience of two researchers with extensive and assiduously classified data we are still left with what Geley fairly described as an enigma. For though they conscientiously recorded the observations that prompted their theories, they did not address, still less elucidate, some fundamental questions. Does the link article play an objective role? If so, how? Or does it act by boosting the psychometrist's confidence in appearing to offer a quasi-physical mechanism as an aid to a dauntingly non-physical task? Or is its sole and crucial purpose to define the designated person that the psychometrist is required to contact?

The one certainty so far is that Ossowiecki's clairvoyance was undoubtedly assisted by psychometry, and it is interesting to remember what he did on one occasion when his confidence was undermined by what the sitter, a medical conference delegate, described as a total failure (p. 32, *Experiments 4, 5, 6*): when the next delegate presented himself for a sitting Ossowiecki told him to hold the target envelope in his own hand while he took the sitter's hand. This tells us at least that we can dispense with Richet's idea about emanations from the writing, or emanations from any other target article. But the larger questions remain.

Psychometry will prove to be a key issue, but for the time being we must return to the mainstream telepathy/clairvoyance debate. One must bear in mind that Richet was always pleased to dispense with telepathy, mainly because English researchers, in their efforts to obtain material that could be identified as coming only from the mind of a deceased communicator, naturally attributed any such mediumship to telepathic communications from the deceased, clairvoyance not offering itself as an alternative hypothesis. Richet, ever anxious to distinguish his researches from those of seekers after immortality, rejoiced in the results of experiments such as the one where he wrote the word *TOI* (p. 41, *Experiment 4*), to have it not only interpreted as *T and zero and 1*, but also to have a description of the two down strokes he had placed on the bar of the T before screwing the paper into a ball. One must agree with Richet that nothing could be more demonstrative of clairvoyant perception of forms and nontelepathic reception of ideas.

When it comes to the vivid descriptions of the donor, the room where he created the target, in some cases incidents in the life history of people entirely unknown to him, and even of their friends, Osty's argument that this has to be telepathy looks more promising. But against these demonstrations of telepathic-like resonance with persons distant and unknown, or relative strangers such as Prof. Barrington-Emerson, how do we reconcile Ossowiecki's failure to grasp ideas from donors either well known or very sympathetic to him, who were presumably willing him to understand the ideas that they wanted to get across to him.

There were the fish-scales that Geley, present and aware of the target, must presumably have been beaming at him telepathically whether consciously or unconsciously, but without success (pp. 58–59). Another notable example is Ossowiecki's lack of telepathic insight into the mind of Chauvet, to whom he had taken an immediate liking. Though he was aware of the pain Chauvet was suffering, Ossowiecki still did not connect it with the drawing (*Reception at the IMI*, pp. 45–54). We may note in passing how little he seemed to have picked up in the way of clues and cues from the presence of people who were aware of the target.

From the *Revue Métapsychique* articles alone one could conclude that there is nothing that called for interpretation as telepathy, though some incidents are suggestive, e.g., the "second triangle" that troubled Ossowiecki when one target was a triangle and the other was a rope with 12 divisions. He might have received straight from the target donor's mind the idea that the rope could be used to construct a triangle; but as an engineer his unconscious perception of the 12 divisions (which did not get incorporated into his own drawing) might also have given him this idea (p. 79, *Experiment 4*). Charpentier, who drew a mouse, was told that he had intended to draw something round (p. 91, *Experiment 15*) and confirmed that his first idea had been to draw a curled up cat. On such vague generalizations one could not base an argument for telepathy; but there are reports about people who were told more precisely about their intentions, e.g. the Latvian "skeptic" who heard Ossowiecki talk about the swastika he had intended to draw before making a W instead (pp. 99–102, *Experiment 28*).

These go beyond guesswork, and they cannot be attributed to clairvoyance, as they never got further than the mind, or perhaps the mind's eye. This certainly looks like telepathy, or perhaps clairvoyance of the mind's imagery, if that can be regarded as a distinguishable psi faculty amounting to a telepathic sort of clairvoyance, or a clairvoyant sort of telepathy; for there is still nothing to suggest the transmission of an idea as opposed to an image. This might, of course, be due to a particularly visual trait in Ossowiecki's mind, so that telepathy in his case would always manifest as imagery, and never manifest as nonsensory input. Be that as it may, we are definitely driven to the slightly untidy conclusion that as well as clairvoyance, i.e. a form of ESP that bypassed the minds of people who had a lot of useful information available in their minds (useful to the perception of the target material), Ossowiecki also occasionally picked up relevant images from people, sometimes total strangers, who were not particularly motivated to part with the information.

This conclusion is not so untidy as it looks. The clairvoyant faculty that Ossowiecki had more or less under control was applied to the experimental challenges put before him, while the occasional flashes of telepathic insight came unsought, and these were not in any way under his control. This makes sense, for this is how telepathy usually seems to operate in the real world; someone in a crisis involuntarily externalizes an emotion and the telepath picks up some glimpse of his predicament. We have not reached the end of the telepathy road, but first we need to examine in depth the clairvoyant faculty most decisively demonstrated in the controlled experiments, and the role played by psychometry.

The particular aspect of Ossowiecki's clairvoyance that must be examined in depth is retrocognition, the sighting of past events that shows up most clearly in experiments such as the visit to the medieval dungeon (pp. 161–62, *Archaeological Experiment 5*), where the whole purpose was to explore the past. But looked at closely, retrocognition will be seen to pervade all the experiments, even those where there is nothing to suggest operation in the past rather than the present, and it may prove to be the key to a general mechanism for the realization of paranormal cognition. The ideas of Geley, Richet and Osty have been explored to some degree, but an important voice has not yet been heard, that of the clairvoyant himself. Following the experiments reported in the *Revue Métapsychique* 1922 No. 4 and after further speculations about Ossowiecki's powers, Geley concludes with the following wise words:

> Better to admit our impotence at the present time to understand the mechanisms of lucidity. We have however sought to obtain the opinion and impressions of M. Ossowiecki himself. Here are the very interesting observations that he has sent us about himself....
> Pictures rise up in front of me; usually of the past. I see the man who wrote the letter and I know what he has written. I see the object at the moment when it is lost, with all the details surrounding the event; or I know, I sense the history of some object that I have in my hands.

No one seems to have taken this at face value, but perhaps one should. It sounds like an exercise in retrocognition. When one looks back at Ossowiecki's utterances when he is groping his way towards apprehension of a target, he often sounds like a person rewinding a videotape, scanning backwards and forwards around the target area, glimpsing the target as the image comes and goes, not apparently being able to halt the motion so as to enable him to take in every detail in an orderly way. Sometimes he might feel that he has had a clear sight of the target and does not struggle for greater precision; it gets confused with other memories, and a right-facing trout comes out as a left-facing plaice. Ossowiecki knew that what his experimenters wanted was a plain answer to the problem set, i.e. the content of the target material, and his scene-setting was not taken to be the measure of successful performance. That so many of his utterances were directed to the donor, the time and the place of the target's inception was a matter of interest, but a straight description of the target was the desired outcome. Certain observations can be made.

1. Ossowiecki often started by establishing what one might call the space-time co-ordinates, i.e. the place where the target was prepared and the time of day;
2. his rovings around the target preparation often occurred when he appeared to have difficulty in clarifying his vision of the target;
3. talking about what went on at the scene where the target was prepared seemed to assist him in keeping the communication channel open;
4. it was at times, and perhaps always, easier for him to do this than to focus on the target;
5. his perception of the target material and all its details was furthered by his retrocognitive reconstruction of the scene that took place when it was created;
6. the scene setting also led on to his cognition of the appearance, characteristics, life events and close associates of the target donor or of other persons connected with the donor or the target.

From these observations it would seem possible to draw a conclusion, namely, that Ossowiecki came to know what the targets were by a process analogous to rewinding a videotape of life, finding the scene where the target was prepared, and (to take the simplest hypothesis) taking a look at it, or a series of looks. The rewinding and forward scanning by a person who has an unreliable battery in a capricious remote control would result in disorganized, fragmentary perceptions and odd details that might be picked up as an image comes and goes. Here are some examples, with material related to the target, or which could have been derived from its content, in bold print, and comments about the target donor, more remote persons and the environment in italics.

Experiment series 1, April/May 1921,
 First experiment (RM 1921 No. 5), p. 28

> **There is talk about a lady called Berger.** *It's a gentleman 50 years of age who wrote this letter,* **which is a reply to a letter from Prof. Richet. This letter does not come from Paris;** *it comes from a place near the sea.* **It's about various matters. It's an invitation. There is something about this lady called Berger.** *She is 33 years of age. She is married.* **I can't read this. It was written very quickly, it's confused, it digresses.** *It's a musical man who wrote it.*

By effectively "re-winding" to the preparation of the target Ossowiecki will see a man who looks about 50, and perhaps he saw a musical instrument in the room, but *he will not see the lady called Berger,* because she is not present, and it is difficult to believe that she is referred to as aged 33 in the letter. (That she is married will of course be obvious if she is described as Madame). Switching metaphors, has Ossowiecki's boat, rapidly navigating the course of the 50-year-old musical letter writer's life, turned off down a side stream to find out what the lady called Berger looks like? And, as Osty would insist, does he do this by entering the mind of the letter-writer?

Experiment series 2, Experiment 7 (RM1921 No 6), pp. 32–33

> *A lady ... years of age (here Mme. Geley's exact age) wrote this letter.* **The letter is addressed to me.... It is an affectionate sort of letter. It expresses her feelings of admiration and good wishes....** *One of her daughters was at her side while she was writing. It was written on the second floor. The lady looks tired. She wrote this in the office where there are chairs covered in dark leather....* **The letter was written on 22nd August. This lady, in her admiration for me, is happy to know me, and expresses the hope that she will see me soon....** *The letter was written between 4 and 5 o'clock in the evening.*

From one viewpoint Ossowiecki must have felt very confident about his reading of this target letter, because it was one of those occasions on which he returned the letter to Geley, saying he would give his response on a later occasion (the next day). He had already divined that it came from Geley's wife and consisted of compliments and an invitation. This expansive sort of target called for précis rather than word by word transcription, which is actually a more exacting intellectual task than (so to speak) taking dictation. This may account for the lack of fluency, compared to more immediate response to some simpler targets, and therefore account for the resort to scene-setting.

Let us note in passing that in the 10th experiment in this series (p. 34), very little scene-setting was needed to facilitate a precise description (after a shaky start) of the drawing and caption on a sheet of paper sealed inside a lead pipe. Ossowiecki's only remark about the target donor was that a woman had written something. But we are told that after the initial difficulty and the remark about the target donor the mentation came 'more readily.'

Reception at IMI, (RM 1923 No. 5), pp. 45–54

When Stephan Chauvet handed Ossowiecki his prepared target envelope Ossowiecki never got round to describing the contents because he was taken away to meet other IMI members, but what he had to say about the preparation may be remembered for one very remarkable feature.

> *I see two coins; they are one-franc pieces; French money; yes, French; these coins give me a feeling of embarrassment;* **but still I see a sheet of paper with a phrase written on it;** *it was written by a woman, 30–35* [actually 38] *years of age; tall; dark; distinguished; intelligent; she has been divorced, she is a doctor's wife; she looks at the desk, there are very varied things from foreign countries; some antiquities; she tries to think what she should devise; she has decided on a concept; it is something impersonal, something elevated, an ideal* [pp. 50–51].

The remarkable features are:

1. The one-franc pieces, which probably had no clear physical existence at the time, having had hot wax dropped over them and a fresh seal imprinted on the wax. They remained in the mind of Chauvet, whose mind had however had signally failed to transmit the simple message of 'My life' to accompany Ossowiecki's reproduction of his cross; they remained in the mind of the lady who had created them with a one-franc piece (just one coin, but two seals), and one wonders why her mind should have been more accessible than Chauvet's (the feeling of embarrassment was presumably common both to Chauvet and to her); the two 'coins' also remained in the past, at the scene where the offending images were created.

2. An idea of Chauvet's decor, and of the patient's age, looks, even intelligence could be gained by an observer present in Chauvet's consulting room at the time, who could also perhaps note that the woman had paused and then taken down a learned book to copy out a phrase, but how could the same observer know that she had been divorced and was now married to a doctor? That implies some further probing of the past, an excursion either into Chauvet's knowledge, the woman's own memories or a train of events leading back from the target envelope to the woman who provided it, and thence further back into her own life events.

The next experiment in date order where ostensible retrocognition plays a prominent part is the one carried out by Geley in June/July 1924 when for the first time Ossowiecki was confronted with a target written in invisible ink. But this calls for extended comment and will be dealt with last in this group. We pass on to the equally challenging undeveloped plates.

Experiment series 5 (RM 1924 No. 2), p. 60

> *It's a photo made inside, not out of doors. There are two people in the room.... A girl came in and went out after taking something. She is blonde or auburn, small.*
> **I see it.... It is the photograph of a woman....**
> *The gentleman who took this is very nervous; rather dark. He has a little clipped moustache; quite a lot of hair.*
> *The photograph was taken between 1 and 3 o'clock.... There are a lot of pictures or portraits in the room....*
> *It is on the third floor or thereabouts.*
> *One of the gentlemen is in a hurry.... He leaves immediately after the photograph has been taken.*
> *The second one arranges the plate in its black packaging.... I have the impression that it is the second one who has done everything.... The first one is pale, tired.*

It will be remembered that this is the experiment that was evaluated after Geley's death, and while the target almost certainly was a photograph of a woman seated quietly, much as described by Ossowiecki, it could theoretically have been the one that was smashed beyond recognition. It may be fair to say that even if the target plate had in fact been one of those destroyed in the crash the correlation with the surviving plate is remarkable in itself, and if it had not been the true target the explanation might well have been the proximity of the three target plates.

Ossowiecki's error about the location of the room on the third floor decreases the possibility that he was able to guess the identity of the photographer and that he was acquainted with the studio. Ossowiecki described the presumed target photograph very well after the first four observations, and was not able to add any further details (such as the chin resting in the woman's hand) despite all the further scene-setting that followed; but as ever it seems to have acted as a way of keeping a channel open.

Experiment 15 (Charpentier) (RM 1925 No. 2), p. 91

In cases where Ossowiecki was given a spontaneous target he did not seem to need an excursion into the past in order to describe the target, but in some cases he did a little mild showing off, making it clear that an excursion had in fact been made. Without hesitation Ossowiecki described and drew a mouse, closely resembling Charpentier's, and having done so he added:

> You settled down at the far end of the hotel cloak room, I followed you; you didn't sit down, you knelt on a stool, drawing on a little table. You thought at first of drawing something round."

Experiment 9 (RM 1925 No.6), pp. 74–76

This was another undeveloped plate target, and one that might have been either of two plates taken by either of two photographers. Ossowiecki needed a lot of help from whatever quarter he was able to derive it.

> **This is a photographic print, taken in an apartment....** *Yes! One thing is for sure, this photograph was taken in an enclosed place.... I see a nicely furnished room.... A lot of ornamental objects ... framed portraits....* **I don't understand what this has to do with a chateau....** *At the moment when this photograph was taken I see three people ... a woman and two men.... I see as if through a fog. I see a tall man, slim, with a long, thin face. The second is rather small, stocky, with a round face ... and I think he has a beard. One seems very strong, the other rather delicate, much weaker.... One is in military uniform.*
> **I don't understand what the chateau signifies and what it has to do with everything I am seeing ... but I see it all the time....** *The room is very beautiful ... portraits ... a desk ... no, it's bigger, more robust.... I see a sculpture on it ...* **the chateau again!**

Osty pointed out the contrast between the "vague" description of the target photograph (which was in fact focused mainly on a chateau) with the copious and mostly accurate description of the scene and those present at it. He deduced that this indicated the operation of telepathic rapport between Ossowiecki and the persons present at the scene; this far from self-explanatory assumption will be examined later. For the time being it merely illustrates once again that when Ossowiecki feels confused he tries to steady himself by (somehow) using the target-creation scene as his *point de repère*.

Before returning to the invisible ink test, which will also have bearing on the telepathic hypothesis, the last case to be recollected for evoking scenes from the past is the unique experiment with the packet prepared by the provident engineer Deniose Jonky, carried out nearly seven years after his death and after the last reported Paris experiment. The heading *Paranormal cognition of things unknown to anyone living* poses a challenge to simple notions of telepathy.

Experiment 11 (The Jonky case) (RM 1936 No. 1), pp. 80–84

This was a very extended reading over two sessions. There had, however, been an earlier session at which 'almost nothing' was said. However it may have assisted Ossowiecki to some extent enabling him to start at once on some general remarks about the wrapped target box and its contents. But having remarked that:

the wrapping, the paper the box get in the way....

He then talked about Jonky:

I see the owner of this object. He is no longer alive. [This is the only time he made this comment, or had occasion to make it.] *He has been dead a long time, tragically* [it may be recalled that no tragedy attached to Jonky's death, but tragic deaths were related in a cutting enclosed in the box] *he had done well for himself, he had a house.... But the tide of success ebbed away.... He was an old man, with a gray beard, and he had a wife. He was a man of great spiritual worth, of wide culture, highly educated, especially knowledgeable with regard to the paranormal.... He used to arrange séances, and experiments, he read and wrote a lot, he traveled a lot. The package has been sent to someone who looked very much like M. Gravier. It was in his apartment; the package stayed there, I see it down there in the bookcase.*

So spectacular was Ossowiecki's description of the contents of the box that Szmurło, whose report is fairly lengthy, may have felt it unnecessary to comment on every detail of this mentation, so we cannot be sure about Jonky's spiritual worth, nor does he confirm that Gravier was one of the experimenters who was given the box in order to obtain other readings, or if he kept it in his bookcase; but there is at least some veridical material, and when Ossowiecki had delivered it he went straight on to describe the articles inside the box. Then, dramatically, he appears to follow the "volcanic mineral" into its past, eons back in time before the lifetime of the donor.

There is something here that pulls me away to other worlds ... towards another planet. Now I am seeing a huge planet, immense, a distant world quite unconnected with ours. It is rushing headlong through outer space. It collides with another body. There is a catastrophic cosmic event. **Something breaks away, breaks up, shatters into small pieces. They rush on, they fall to earth in various places.... Yes, yes, they are pieces of meteorite.**

We can be sure that the box and its contents were prepared by an elderly man with a gray beard who knew a lot about the paranormal, and that somehow Ossowiecki was able to be aware of this man who had made up the target. Can we be so sure that Ossowiecki pursued the object back into the distant past when it developed as a meteorite? There are obviously other interpretations, such as the imagination of the medium, who when faced (i.e. clairvoyantly faced) with an article, vividly imagines its genesis, whether in outer space or, as he described on other occasions, being dug out of the earth or made up in a factory. It is a more economical interpretation, so perhaps that is where the matter must rest. If however, it were to be found one day that Ossowiecki's archaeological pronouncements showed knowledge more consistent with current findings than with those of 1940, we might have to think again about how far an object held in the hand of this powerful psychometrist could guide him to its origins in space and time.

Experiment 7, The Besterman Report—1933, pp. 65–70

A less dramatic but even clearer excursion into the past is shown with startling clarity in the experiment reported in the *SPR Proceedings* in which Theodore Besterman prepared the target. He did this with certain objectives in mind. One was to see if Ossowiecki would show any telepathic insight into the notion of 'swan,' i.e. the black swan that formed a significant part of the Swan Ink trademark. As we saw, there was in fact nothing in Ossowiecki's response about a bird, or water, or fountain pen (Swan being a well-known brand).

Besterman also arranged that the word SWAN was folded over on itself, whereas INK was unfolded. (In the reproduction of the drawing the fold appears as a line through the SWAN). But it will be remembered that Ossowiecki dealt more fluently and accurately with "Swan" than he did with "Ink." We must bear in mind that Ossowiecki could not "read" illegible handwriting such as that of Sarah Bernhardt and Chauvet. A word folded over on itself would be even more unintelligible, but Ossowiecki was able to reproduce it. This shows with something like certainty that his clairvoyant viewing related not to the folded paper of "now" that he held in his hand, but to the target paper as it was "then," when created by Besterman. This surely has to point to retrocognition, an excursion into the past to the point where the target appeared in its original form.

The last example, held over from the experiments carried out by Geley in 1924, is the most remarkable in its implications.

Experiment series 5—June/July 1924 (RM 1925 No.2), pp. 55–57

This was Geley's invisible ink test, where Ossowiecki started with a detailed description of the various layers of enveloping, and having clairvoyantly peeled off the outer wrappings found himself "obstructed" and saw nothing. **"You could say that there is nothing to see."**

From there he turned his attention to the target-creation scene.

> *There is a man, it's not you, another man who collaborated in this experiment. You talked with someone. I see this man; he has moustaches and a lot of hair. He reminds me a little of [René] Sudre. You had a conversation with him toward evening time, at 5, 6 or 7 o'clock. He is a little taller than Sudre.*

Geley confirmed that all the details were correct. We must ask, of course, how acquainted Ossowiecki was with Geley's assistants, and whether he could have guessed at this one. It is difficult to see how he could have guessed that a conversation took place with him around 5 to 7 p. m. while the experiment was in preparation (for he speaks of collaboration). If Ossowiecki made inspired guesses about Geley's assistants, he made another one, again after making a few correct observations about the target writing, and then becoming stuck again:

> *'The man who gave you the sympathetic ink is very young; he looks younger than he is.* [Correct.] *He interrupted you while you were preparing the experiment. I see you leave your office; then come back.'*

All this was also correct, so guessing now seems implausible, and we can be reasonably sure that this is an example of Ossowiecki using retrocognitive scene setting to help him with a difficult target reading.

As to the reading itself, it should be noted that though he never obtained a clear "sight" of the text, he was able to describe eight features about it that were correct, but just as one can have subliminal vision if an image is presented in brief flashes so it looks as if he had some measure of subliminal clairvoyant perception. But the method by which he obtained his subliminal perception is the most extraordinary feature—by observing and striving to interpret the pen strokes made by Geley when he wrote the text using invisible ink.

So while it has become a familiar feature of Ossowiecki's mediumship that he would visualize himself back in the past—and it will be remembered that this is exactly what he said he did—there was no clear sign indicating just how he used his presence in the past to gain knowledge of the target. Here we have a precise description: he watched the pen as it wrote the words, and if they had been written in normal ink he would have had a clear, if fluctuating, image of the text. This is highly compatible with other cases such as that of Charpentier, who drew a mouse; Ossowiecki described how he "followed" him and saw how he knelt on a stool at a table instead of seating himself. If Ossowiecki can follow him into the room, he can certainly look at the drawing, though in his glimpses of the target it may not have been clear even to him that he was, in effect, looking over Charpentier's shoulder. The sight of the drawing may have come to him in close-up, so to speak, with no contextual background.

Returning to the invisible ink writing, the second striking feature is the entire lack of telepathic rapport in this case. Apart from Ossowiecki's failure to pick any ideas out of the mind of Geley, present and willing, he also failed to read the mind of Geley having traced him back into the past. He felt himself clairvoyantly in Geley's office, watching him take down a book of a certain size (correctly described) and copying a passage; he could gather a certain amount of information from watching the pen strokes, but he could not focus on the printed text from which it was being copied because *he was not inside Geley's mind*, and therefore could not view the scene through Geley's eyes. But he was able to operate effectively at once when Geley, giving up all hope of getting a clear account of the target writing while it remained invisible, went into the adjoining room and wrote down the text from memory, not with total accuracy. In its visible (albeit enveloped) state Ossowiecki was able immediately to grasp the four essential words, including the "deism" substituted by Geley for the original "philosophy" of Pasteur.

It is difficult to imagine a more conclusive demonstration of clairvoyance and failure of telepathy than this, and it is tempting to hypothesize that where attempts are made to invoke paranormal cognition experimentally (and an experiment is not confined to a place designated as a laboratory), the percipient is the active party, and that he goes about the task by using retrocognitive clairvoyance, or in some cases (not those studied here) precognitive clairvoyance. The clairvoyant percipient does not have to know that this is the *modus operandi*, and might be surprised at the idea of searching the past when the task is conceived of as scrutinizing a target in the here and now. But it takes little reflection to understand that everything that happens, the moment it has happened, every word uttered or target created or observed, in fact the whole of the real world, is in the past, and the only things not in the past are those that have not yet happened. The present moment is as elusive as a geometrical point, a quasi-imaginary line between the real world of the past and the unrealized future.

It may well be that telepathic communication, predicated as it is on immediacy and spontaneity, and often manifesting as brief flashes of insight, makes use of this infinitely narrow bandwidth; but this is a large subject that cannot be pursued here. Without venturing too far into the realms of the unprovable one can readily understand that while the gift of clairvoyance may in rare cases be brought under control there is no corresponding "right" to pry into another person's mind and take information from it unless, in some stressful situation, it gets exteriorized and projected.

We are approaching the rationale of the link object, the enigma at the heart of the mystery, and are able to conclude that it may have an objective role that goes beyond defining the target person and encouraging the psychometrist to believe that he is holding a useful tool in his hand. The link object may be performing the same sort of role as Ariadne's thread, which served to guide the wanderer back to the place from which he started; so the link object may lead him back to one of the significant places from which *it* started. The psychometrist can be seen to trace the link object back into *its* own past, where he sees the drawing made, or sees the message written; from there he can latch on to the person who created the target, or who was sufficiently associated with the time and place where it was made, and not only describe those people, but go back into *their* lives, beyond the point where the link object came into existence.

Though the point has already been argued and rejected, it is still tempting to say that Osty must be right, and that Ossowiecki, once put in touch with the Chauvet's patient by the link object, must then have gained this knowledge from the woman's mind, and out of her entire stock of self-awareness he picked certain items. But why should he be able to pick things out of *her* mind if he could not pick what he wanted from the mind of his experimenters? One might develop a thesis that he felt it was bad manners to read the minds of his friends, like reading their diaries, but he would not mind rifling the mind of a stranger. Though this idea may fit some of the facts, it does not convince.

Or one might speculate that he could not mind-read any item that was actually in the conscious mind of the agent. This idea might recommend itself in the case of a five or ten minute test that was given up when an immediate response was not forthcoming. But the invisible ink experiment was carried out over several days, and there must have come a time when Geley was thinking about his dinner, and Ossowiecki was also in an idle phase; that would have been the time for the words and ideas of Pasteur to come to him if telepathic rapport was operating. So that idea does not stand up. Better surely to cross the boggle-threshold and return to the thesis that once guided firmly into the past by the link object, Ossowiecki can then use the target donor as a secondary link object and search not her memories, but her past—go clairvoyantly further back in time, tracing her to her own surroundings where he *sees* that she is married to a doctor, and if he does not learn about her divorce from some clue at that point, he goes yet further back in her life story.

Most of the argument so far has been based on the solid rock of the IMI experimental research, but it might be misleading to ignore evidence that comes mainly from reports or letters cited by the psychic himself or by a member of his family. The stories relating to theft and sabotage are particularly interesting in the light they throw on incidents highly suggestive of telepathic awareness. Ossowiecki's usual psychometric clairvoyance could account for his ability to identify wrongdoers; the extra factor that could not be explained by clairvoyance is his assertion in one case that the thief would return the stolen money (the Loth narrative) and in the other that the industrial saboteur would not offend again (the Wedel factory manager's story).

In the case of the thief, one may surmise that having identified the person—and from the language used it sounds as if it might have been a woman—Ossowiecki himself might have spoken to her and received assurances, but in the case of the saboteur Ossowiecki made his assertion on the spot, and whereas he might have been influenced by his interview with the man, this would make him an exceptional judge of behavior as well as an exceptional psychic. But the inevitable question must be asked again, why should he have come into telepathic rapport with the saboteur when he remained so firmly outside the minds of Geley, Chauvet and Richet?

The alternative speculation here is that he believed himself capable of impressing his own ideas into the minds of other people, as opposed to lifting their ideas into his own mind. If this was his belief, then it appears to have been justified in the Wedel case, where most people would have shared the misgivings of the factory manager about the future conduct of a hitherto ruthless saboteur. There is some support for the "willing" hypothesis in the article by Szmurło about Ossowiecki apparently drawing a woman to introduce herself to him (pp. 122–23, *Influence at a Distance, Case 1*). It will be remembered that Szmurło was responsible for some very well planned experiments; Geley and Osty thought well enough of him to publish his reports in the *Revue Métapsychique*, so he does not sound like the sort of person who would make up an eminently disbelievable story when he would certainly have had a good store of more readily acceptable anecdotes available to him.

Again, the "willing" faculty might have been responsible for the remarkable meeting between Ossowiecki and the man who picked up Aline de Glass's brooch. Ossowiecki may have felt that, compared with some of his property restorations, he had not given the best possible service to Mrs. Glass, merely telling her that she had better advertise the loss of her brooch (presumably naming a reward), and he may well have brought his mind to bear on how to locate it. The subconscious mind of Ossowiecki may have responded to his desires by bringing the man in question to the right place at the right time.

There are then several strands to Ossowiecki's paranormal repertoire, of which the many times repeated psychometry-mediated retrocognitive clairvoyance is the most manifest and incontrovertible. It seems to have been under control to a remarkable degree. There are the occasional flashes of telepathy, when an image in the mind of the sitter is picked up, and he tells the sitter what he meant to draw. Then there are the occasional instances of something like reverse telepathy, where he seems to put material into someone else's mind. It was postulated that telepathy is uncontrollable because we have an inhibition against snooping around in someone else's mind; Edmund Gurney and Frederic Myers felt that *mind-reading* sounded so caddish that they coined *telepathy* to take its place, so altering the concept to one of sympathetic resonance. But isn't putting items into someone else's mind an even greater liberty? And to some degree Ossowiecki may have had this under control.

Giving rather than taking may be an intrusion, but is not actually a breach of privacy. In a case where putting something into another person's mind amounts to a compulsion to take action, this becomes difficult to distinguish in practical terms from some form of telepathic hypnosis. We have been told about several occasions on which Ossowiecki succeeded in imposing his will, but there may have been other occasions on which the recipient refused delivery. The dramatic experiment reported by Ossowiecki in which Geley supervised his 'appearance' to a woman who cried out his name at the moment when he had the subjective experience of projecting into her room was an intrusion in another guise; for while the incident could be interpreted as Ossowiecki visiting the lady in his astral body, the more conservative view would be that he performed some operation on his mind that acted on her mind so as to cause her to hallucinate a phantom figure looking like him (pp. 118–19, *OBE? Case 1*). These externalizations may be the vestigial remains of the psychokinetic powers that he claimed to have had when young, and which subsided when he developed mental mediumship.

We have no satisfactory corroboration of his early physical mediumship, so it may be time to turn back from the further end of the Ossowiecki spectrum where the evidence is relatively thin and revert to those areas where the evidence is abundant and (in pragmatic terms) incontestable. The conclusion on the narrow front must be that when Ossowiecki was set a task in paranormal cognition he carried it out by using the faculty that was extensively under his control, i.e. retrocognitive clairvoyance. On a wider front, it is more than possible that this is the primary *modus operandi* of every psychic who is presented with an experimental target, whether that target is words, a drawing, an article, a question, a life history, or any other subject matter, other than a future event requiring the exercise of precognition.

If one relates these excursions into the past to the workings of memory then there are analogies to be drawn with normal thought processes. Short term memory can be equated with using the link object to find the target donor, the missing person, or whatever; the excursions into that person's life and past is more like long term memory. Most of our life disappears down a black hole of forgetfulness, but everyone has indelible memories, some going back to early childhood. While the expendable memories, constituting most of one's life experience, may become irrecoverable with the passing of years, it takes no greater time or effort to recall an ineradicably etched memory from the distant past than to recall one from a more recent time. This may have some relevance to Ossowiecki's glimpses into significant events in the distant past of complete strangers; he would have 'seen' key incidents that had made an indelible mark in that person's remembered life story.

That brings us to the heart of the larger problem. One may talk of rewinding the video cassette, or consulting the Akashic records, or in other metaphorical terms. But if the past is still in ontological existence, or sufficiently in existence to be on view, where is it? This is, of course, rather like asking where heaven and hell are supposed to be located. Whether or not physics that can accommodate the past somewhere in space and time (or elsewhere) is not the point. Even supposing this to be so, no one outside science fiction is actually going to *go back* into it. The only way to revisit the past is within a memory system. We have seen that when Ossowiecki took himself back to the scene where the invisible ink pen strokes were made, he did not make telepathic use of Geley's mind, so he was not in Geley's memory. So whose memory did he use? Are we not driven to deducing the existence of an observer, an entity or at least a consciousness with a memory, who, or which, saw and remembered what Geley did, though not necessarily what Geley thought; or if the stored memory did include the thoughts as well as the deeds, they were stored in a folder of the memory not accessible to any one other than the person whose private thoughts they were.

The concept of a common consciousness, or of smaller minds as cells within larger minds, is far from original, and not very fashionable, whether expressed as the gorgeous palaces of Shakespeare, Berkeley's thoughts in the mind of God, or any other image conveying the notion that our whole experience of existence is a dream (or nightmare) suffered by an enveloping mind. But the retrocognitive clairvoyance demonstrated on so many occasions by Ossowiecki points to such a mind. Strictly speaking the only concept called for to accommodate retrocognition is a memory, and a memory could, arguably, be as unmindful as the memory of a computer, a computer put together by a blind computermaker. But a memory without a mind is rather like a grin without the Cheshire cat, and it is difficult to see how or why a memory should come into existence except as a necessary component of an associated mind.

One person's idea of a logical deduction is another person's idea of a wild speculation, and neither viewpoint can be conclusively vindicated. This sort of determination belongs in the realm of physics, and the paranormal reality proposed here lies outside that realm, not outside as a small, separatist fringe territory making itself a nuisance and demanding independence, but more literally outside as an encompassing macrocosm. This elusive but comprehensive reality includes the cosmos so efficiently mapped by science, with all the regularities that give us solid ground under our feet and a world that we can recognize every day as being more or less the same as it was the day before; what is suggested by glimpses of the paranormal is that while the truth of science may be nothing but the truth, it is not the whole truth.

If this conclusion seems larger than is warranted, it must be said that the psychometry of Ossowiecki is only the tip of a very large iceberg, a tip of exceptional brilliance and clarity. But the corpus of mental mediumship is not the only anomalous hulk submerged in the ocean of experience; alongside is a large body of soundly based reports detailing cases of crisis telepathy, precognitive dreams and much more. Ossowiecki's early exploits in moving heavy objects round by willpower rest on his own word, but there is an impressive array of testimony (mostly from scientist researchers) verifying telekinetic effects produced by various physical mediums, and indeed testifying to even more outrageous phenomena, such as materialization and poltergeist effects. When the full extent of well-evidenced paranormal material is taken into account (see bibliography), the idea of a more comprehensive reality to accommodate events that do not belong in the normal world becomes not only plausible but necessary.

This review of the Ossowiecki material promised that the answers would raise fresh questions, and that promise has doubtless been fulfilled. Accessing the data stored in an encompassing memory has been proposed as a *diagnosis* rather than an explanation, because explanation implies an analysis of method and a prescription for performance. An explanation in these terms might come closer to realization if a time comes when the location of our own memories (whether in the brain or elsewhere) and our means of access to them is satisfactorily expounded. But the mechanism for access into the hypothesized great storehouse of memory external to ourselves is not likely to be in prescriptive, mechanistic terms, and may be in terms that are beyond the reach of our understanding. Considered another way, requesting an explanation might be to commit a category error, like asking how, in a dream, when you were riding a bicycle one moment and then found yourself immediately riding a horse, how did you get from the bicycle to the horse? The answer will not be in terms of time and motion.

It can be annoying to have it implied that something real may nevertheless be outside one's grasp, and a very natural reaction is to say "Speak for yourself." But even when apologies have been tendered, it must be said that some questions are more answerable than others. "How deep is the ocean?" is answerable by science, and when the inventory is complete the answer will give satisfaction. But what sort of response can you give to "How high is the sky?" It looks as if the scope of the paranormal may indeed be as high as the sky, and no answer will ever entirely satisfy anyone, including the person who puts it forward.

Afterword
IAN STEVENSON

Should we call Ossowiecki unique? So far as I know, he has had no successors, at least of his quality. He did, however, have predecessors, and it will help our appraisal of him if I briefly review their accomplishments. I exclude from this review mediums, who claimed to transmit messages from discarnate personalities. Instead, I will consider the group of persons best known by the word *clairvoyant*. Many of them used psychometry, the touching or handling of an object or the cover of a concealed message or sketch. Reports of Ossowiecki's clairvoyance show his frequent, but not invariable use of contact with a relevant person, object, or covering.

The literature of clairvoyance and psychometry includes accounts of numerous clairvoyants (and psychometrists) whose talents no one systematically investigated. Some were unknown or little known outside their own region. Knut Rasmusson Nordgarden, known as "Wise-Knut," who lived in Gausdal, Norway, from 1792 until 1876, belongs in this group (Björnson, 1908). Nordgarden could, for example, find missing persons and detect dishonesty.* Leaving such persons aside, I propose to consider in relation to Stefan Ossowiecki ten persons whom investigators observed with some control over the conditions.

Alexis Didier was the earliest of these persons. His talent for clairvoyance drew favorable attention in France and England in the 1840s and 1850s (Méheust, 2003; Osty, 1934). Beginning as a youth he satisfied critical observers that he could sometimes discern the contents of fully concealed objects. Skeptics found unconvincing Didier's correct statements about a single word written on a piece of paper and concealed in an envelope, especially if someone present knew the word concealed. Didier often spoke hesitantly, expecting and receiving responses from his audience as he seemed to grope toward the correct word that he would finally reach. In doing this he might have learned the word from the responses of the person who knew it.

Didier, however, had a much more extensive repertoire. He sometimes described objects, such as a bone, that experimenters had concealed. Of such objects he could

---

Zofia Weaver has told me of an autobiographical book by a Polish priest, Father Czesław Klimuszko (1906–1980), who exhibited a type of clairvoyance, including the ability to read the past, similar to that of Ossowiecki. Polish investigators tested him, with success.

also sometimes give the history (Elliotson, 1845). He could state the previous activities of someone not personally known to him. For example, one report credits him with accurately recounting unusual events occurring two days earlier in the life of an Englishman resident in Paris (Elliotson, 1849). On another occasion he described in detail an obscure episode that occurred in 1812 during the Peninsular War in Spain; this happened some 30 years before Didier's correct and later fully verified description of the episode (Elliotson, 1845, 1846). Didier also demonstrated a kind of "travelling clairvoyance" during which he would describe the location and the contents of distant houses he could never have seen. His statements about the interior of the houses he visited in this way sometimes included details of paintings hung on the walls (Elliotson, 1845; Lee, 1866).

For the exhibition of his phenomena a regular mesmeric magnetiser (J.B. Marcillet) put Didier into a kind of trance. Didier's perceptions improved when he held the covering of an object he sought to describe or held the hand of the person who consulted him. He did not find such contact necessary, because he sometimes traced missing persons. He sometimes spoke immediately and fluently. At other times he spoke more slowly; for example, when trying to read a word concealed in an envelope, he might say some of the letters of the word individually before perceiving the whole word. At times he experienced the strong emotions of an event he described. He could also achieve a kind of identification of a person he described to the extent of imitating unusual but habitual movements that person would make.

In his ordinary waking state, Didier had no paranormal powers. Indeed, in that state he seemed amnesic for what he had said and done when hypnotized.

Didier and his magnetiser charged fees, which allowed skeptics to attribute his successes at billet reading to previous preparations for such tests or the assistance of confederates. No one has proposed that such explanations could possibly account for either Didier's correct statements about a stranger's past or his travelling clairvoyance. Dingwall (1967) provided an excellent summary of reports on Didier's phenomena.

In the 1850s and later, William Denton, a geologist, investigated several subjects with clairvoyant powers. Typically he would give the subject to handle a small piece of stone, a piece of tufa, or a tile from an ancient mosaic. The subject would then state the origin and history of the stone, sometimes with stunning accuracy. Denton referred to his studies as "psychometric researches."* His sister Anne succeeded well with him, but his wife, Elizabeth, proved even more successful. She contributed an important section of autobiographical comments to Denton's principal book (Denton and Denton, 1863). Denton became convinced that everything of the past continues to exist and that some persons can discern it and describe images from it.

If we proceed chronologically we come next to the Polish-American Bert Reese (1851–1926). He claimed extraordinary clairvoyance, and numerous persons, some of them eminent and reputedly competent, testified to his talents. He sometimes

---

Although not the coiner of the word psychometric *in this sense, which is etymologically incorrect. Denton popularized the term. Later clairvoyants and investigators have commonly used the term whenever the clairvoyant has physical contact with a target object or person.*

styled himself "professor," although Moll (1926) described him as a "salesman." He specialized in the reading of words or a line of words written on small pieces of paper, which were then folded to become small pellets or billets. Reese convinced some investigators that he had an important gift for clairvoyance (Carrington, 1928; Richet, 1922). It seems probable, however, that he covertly obtained the pellets, exchanged them, read unobserved the writing on them, and then communicated the words read as if he had learned them clairvoyantly (Dessoir, 1931; Dingwall, 1926; Moll, 1926; Prince,1932).

Ludwig Kahn, a German born in 1873, attracted attention from investigators in the first decades of the twentieth century. Like Reese he seemed able to read words written on small pieces of paper. (Sometimes he reproduced simple sketches.) While Kahn remained in another room, or at least out of range of normal vision, the person testing him would write a few lines or words on a piece of paper. He (the experimenter) would fold this into a small compact state and hold it firmly in a clenched hand. Kahn sometimes touched the tester's hand, and he occasionally held the billet briefly in his fingers; at other times he was thought not to have touched the billets.

Kahn did not have an unblemished character (Schellinger, 2002). He was crassly commercial, especially in attempts to predict winners of horse races. He advertised himself as "Professor Akldar." He favorably impressed Schottelius (1913) and later Osty and Richet (Osty, 1925). Others, however, considered him only a clever conjuror. Moll (1926) and Dingwall (1926) bracketed Kuhn with Reese, unfavorably. Kahn and Reese had in fact known each other when both were living in the United States. Kahn once acknowledged that he had learned what he knew from Reese and had even been Reese's assistant for a time (Moll, 1926).

Moll's (1926) critique of the 1925 experiments with Kahn in Paris angered Richet, who responded testily by objecting that Moll had himself never experimented with Kahn or observed others doing so. Richet based his conviction on experiments he had conducted when he and Kahn were entirely alone (Richet, 1926, 1927). Moll ridiculed such loose circumstances, maintaining that a person handling a test object cannot at the same time adequately observe the subtle movements of an accomplished prestidigitator. One may perhaps reproach the French investigators with not having become suspicious that Reese and Kahn only exhibited their claimed powers when reading a few words on billets. Unlike genuine clairvoyants they could not read the past. Moreover, Kahn could sometimes read concealed words without understanding their meaning. Oesterreich (1916), in a critique of Schottelius (1913), drew attention to this limitation and also to the restriction of Kahn's "thought-reading" to discerning words written on pellets. Richet (1926) became aware that Kahn could read words without understanding their meaning and contrasted this with the talent of Ossowiecki, who could both read concealed words and get a general sense of their meaning; but Richet's awareness of this difference did not make him suspicious of Kahn.*

---

*Readers unfamiliar with the trick of billet (or pellet) reading can find descriptions of it in Bird (1925), Dessoir (1931) and Meyer (1914). Typically, the billet-reader works with three or four pellets, as did Reese and Kahn.

We can best appraise Reese and Kahn by calling them neither black nor white, but Dalmatians, that is, black and white. They may have reversed the behavior of some professional mediums by falling back on paranormal powers when they found conditions inappropriate for conjuring. I do not consider them forerunners of Ossowiecki.

In the early 1920s Gustav Pagenstecher and W. F. Prince reported observations of the clairvoyance of a Mexican, Maria R. Zierold. She had consulted Pagenstecher, a practicing physician, for medical reasons, and he hypnotized her therapeutically. Quite unexpectedly, he found that during hypnosis she showed knowledge outside her normal perceptions. He then began systematic experiments with her.

In one experiment Pagenstecher let Maria Zierold handle pieces of pumice stone that had previously been treated differently; for example, one piece had been exposed to a high temperature, another placed for a time inside the frame of a large clock. When used as test objects the separate pieces seemed indistinguishable to normal senses. Maria Zierold correctly stated the several different "treatments" given to the pieces of pumice (Pagenstecher, 1920).

In a later experiment, Maria Zierold read a letter concealed in an opaque cover. The letter had been found in a bottle washed ashore in the Azores. The writer of the letter had been on board a ship that was sinking, and he just had time to scribble a few lines sending his love to his wife and children. Maria Zierold described with strong emotion the circumstances of the letter's writer. She described his physical features, including a large scar above his right eyebrow. Proper names in the letter led to the writer's identification. He was a Spaniard living in Cuba and a political refugee, who had been trying to return to Spain from the United States. His wife had last heard from him when he wrote to her from New York early in 1915. He was presumed to have drowned when crossing the Atlantic Ocean as a passenger on a ship torpedoed by a German submarine as happened at that time. His wife confirmed the correctness of Maria Zierold's description of him, including the scar above the right eyebrow (Prince, 1921).

Maria Zierold experienced emotions, sometimes strong ones, corresponding to the events she narrated, if these had been stressful to the person connected to the object or message she was holding. She had no paranormal powers when not hypnotized.

In the 1920s investigators, first in France and then in England, published numerous reports about the clairvoyance of Pascal Forthuny (pseudonym for Georges Cochet). According to Osty (1926a) Forthuny discovered a gift for psychometry by accident when Mme. Geley (whose husband, Gustave Geley, was a principal investigator of Ossowiecki) passed a fan to him and asked him what he could say about it. Forthuny said he had a sensation of suffocation and heard "Elisa." The fan had belonged to a friend of Mme. Geley who had died seven years earlier of "pulmonary congestion." During her illness she had thought that using the fan had eased her breathing. She had been cared for by a friend called Elisa. Mme. Geley then asked Forthuny what he could say about a walking stick that she gave him to hold. Forthuny said it made him think of army maneuvers somewhere in the East. He mentioned a young officer and said that the officer's ship had been torpedoed when he was returning to France. This was all correct. The stick had belonged to a young French army officer who participated in the Franco-British campaign in Greece (during World War I). During his return voyage to France the officer's ship had been torpedoed.

Forthuny often exhibited his clairvoyance in the presence of a group of people, sometimes of as many as 40 persons or more. He would move among the group until he became aware of a connection with someone to whom he then spoke the information that came to him clairvoyantly or perhaps clairaudiently. It sometimes happened that what Forthuny said made no sense to the person addressed; then another person nearby, who had overheard Forthuny, would say that the statements correctly applied to him (or her). Although Forthuny sometimes made statements true of many persons, his statements to "nearby" persons had adequate specificity. It appears from such instances that some persons have greater perviousness for clairvoyance than others.

Eugene Osty, who succeeded Geley as director of the Institut Métapsychique International in Paris, conducted a series of experiments with Forthuny (Osty, 1926b; Sudre, 1926). In 1930 the Society for Psychical Research invited Forthuny to demonstrate his clairvoyance in London. He had some success there, but less than he had in Paris, perhaps because of being in a different culture (Woolley, 1931). Forthuny wrote a lengthy autobiographical statement about his ideas concerning the process of clairvoyance (Forthuny, 1926).*

Olga Kahl, a native of Russia, was an approximate contemporary of Forthuny. During the 1920s and later, she lived in Paris, where she practiced as a professional clairvoyant. Although Besterman (1930a) justly described her as "quite indifferent to the scientific point of view," she lent herself willingly to numerous careful investigations by scientists. Osty (1929, 1932) wrote especially detailed reports of his investigations, but others have left us valuable accounts of her phenomena (Besterman, 1929, 1930; Efron, 1944, Grondahl, 1930; and Toukholka, 1922). She did not read the past, but specialized, we might say, in ascertaining names and simple designs that were set for her as targets. In two features her clairvoyance differed from those of other persons I am considering here. First, she sometimes stated names that had been thought but not written down. She would thus demonstrate telepathy without the possibility of clairvoyance (strictly speaking). Second, the names or designs would often appear on her skin in distinct red lines, presumably made by slight expansions of arterioles. These lines usually occurred on one of Olga Kahl's forearms, but occasionally on her upper chest. Sometimes the red lines would spell a name without Olga Kahl being consciously aware of it. The process seemed then to bypass the conscious levels of her mind. The process also sometimes transmogrified the names, as normal memory may do.

Osty, during his tenure as director of the Institut Métapsychique International

---

In 1930 the French magazine Psychica *published an accusation of fraud against Forthuny. He was said to have planted in a group attending one of his demonstrations an accomplice who signaled information to him about a designated target for his clairvoyance. Forthuny denied any wrongdoing (Besterman, 1930b), and the allegation had no influence on the continued sponsorship of Forthuny by the* Institut Métapsychique International.

(1924–48) investigated many clairvoyants, whom he called métagnomes (Osty, 1923). About most of these he furnished little information. One of them, Raoul de Fleurière, supplied this omission by writing a thoughtful autobiographical account of his clairvoyance (de Fleurière, 1926). He much marveled at the powers of his subconscious mind, especially in enabling him to speak without thinking such details as the name of a person in whose presence he found himself (without any introduction or other normal knowledge of the person's name). He seemed especially skilled also in reading the past of a target person. His description of the state in which he achieved clairvoyance somewhat resembled that described by Ossowiecki: the experience of being in communication with a different level of awareness, while not completely oblivious of the world of normal perceptions.

Rafael Schermann was an Austrian graphologist whose description of the personalities of writers far exceeded what ordinary graphology could reveal (Fischer, 1924, 1934a). He merely glanced at the writing on a piece of paper shown to him and sometimes made accurate statements about the writer from handling an envelope in which some writing was concealed. Schermann's psychometry seemed limited to handwriting; he could not manifest it when holding some other object. According to Fischer, Schermann could accurately describe a person when Fischer merely held an image of that person in his mind. Schermann could accurately describe the person's face. Fischer wrote that Schermann was the first clairvoyant to permit his faculty to be systematically investigated.

Unfortunately, Fischer did not write down in advance the characteristics—physical or behavioral—of the person whose handwriting Schermann tried to read. The correspondence between Schermann's statements and the writer he described depended solely on Fischer's judgment after he had heard Schermann's statements (Dessoir, 1931). Schermann became a professional graphologist and toured in the United States with a manager and fanfare. Prince (1924) carefully analyzed Schermann's readings of the handwritings of six persons unknown to Schermann. They were, however, persons of eminence in American and British history, which Schermann could have inferred. Schermann's statements were never specific and generally were either totally off the mark or referred to attributes common to many persons. Schermann may have had some paranormal ability, but I cannot rank him as an important forerunner of Ossowiecki.

Otto Reimann, a Czech born in 1903, had an equal or greater talent for psychometry than Schermann of whom he was an approximate contemporary. As a young man Reimann became interested in graphology, but never underwent any formal training in it and never practiced professionally as a graphologist. His family was wealthy, and he worked as an employee of a bank.

From just glancing at a piece of paper, Reimann could describe the writer's appearance, surroundings, and to some extent the past of his life. For example, of one item presented to him he said correctly that the writer had behaved like a madman and had to be locked up. Of another item he said correctly that the writer was blind in his left eye (Schmidt, 1930). In another test the target, concealed in an envelope, was some writing in Chinese. Reimann said the writing was Chinese and then himself drew characters on a piece of paper that with fair closeness resembled some of the Chinese characters of the target (Sünner, 1930). When Fischer gave Reimann a medicinal capsule as a test object, Reimann first said that it had contained a lethal poison; at the same time by bringing both his hands near his throat he seemed to suggest death by strangulation. Fischer told Reimann that poison was incorrect. Reimann then said death had occurred by self-strangulation, but he thought this impossible. In fact, he was correct. A doctor had owned the capsule, which had contained a lethal poison. He had had a premonition of having a stroke and intended to kill himself with the capsule if that happened. He did have a stroke, but at that time nurses watching over him thwarted his plan to swallow the capsule. A little later, when the nurses left him briefly unwatched, he strangled himself with his shirt (Fischer, 1934b).

Reimann could develop and communicate information about the history of objects, such as weapons and the lethal capsule I mentioned, that he was allowed to hold. Given a test object he would speak immediately and fluently (Schmidt, 1930). In this respect he differed from Ossowiecki, who sometimes took minutes, even hours, to obtain information about a test object. In another respect, however, he resembled Ossowiecki; he had some capacity for introspection, and at a meeting of physicians in 1930 he tried to describe the process of psychometry. His information about the target did not come to him, he said, as one piece altogether, like a photograph. Instead, as metaphors of the process he preferred those of slowly building a mosaic from tiny pieces of stone or painting a portrait by repeated applications of pigment to a canvas (Schmidt, 1930).

I now return to the word *unique* as possibly applicable to Ossowiecki. The foregoing summaries of earlier clairvoyants leave no doubt that he had predecessors. Several of them may have attained his ability as a clairvoyant. If we deduct Reese, Kahn, and Schermann, as I think we should, we have at least seven persons who qualify to be in Ossowiecki's class. These are Alex Didier, Elizabeth Denton, Maria Zierold, Olga Kahl, Pascal Forthuny, Raoul de Fleurière, and Otto Reimann. Of these seven all but Olga Kahl could read the past of a target object or person.

Investigators studied these forerunners, but they did so less thoroughly—less exhaustively, one might say—than their contemporaries and successors studied Ossowiecki. For example, the reporters of Didier's clairvoyance seemed rarely to have planned tests in advance; independent verification of Didier's accuracy occurred equally rarely. We must agree with Fischer's identification of Schermann as the first clairvoyant investigated in a systematic manner. Unfortunately, Schermann seems never to have gained the interest of other investigators besides Fischer. We may grumble also that Maria Zierold had only two investigators and Pascal Forthuny had few. In contrast, a large number of persons observed Ossowiecki perform under controlled circumstances; their number impresses me more than their eminence in other walks of life.

In another respect also Ossowiecki seems pre-eminent among clairvoyants. I refer to his intelligent interest in the process of clairvoyance. Our best hope for eventually understanding clairvoyance surely lies in the introspections of the few persons who have this faculty well developed. Ossowiecki not only provided important demonstrations of clairvoyance; he described the condition of his remarkable lucidity, and in doing so he showed why so few persons have achieved it. We learn this from his statement to Gustave Geley:

> I begin by stopping all reasoning, and I throw all my inner power into spiritual perceptions. I affirm that this condition is brought about by my unshakable faith in the spiritual unity of all humanity. I then find myself in a new and special state in which what I see and hear exists outside time and space [Geley, 1922, pp. 254–255].

The last decade of the twentieth century was celebrated as the "decade of the brain." Let that be so; then the present one may be the decade of the mind. The phenomena of Ossowiecki and a few other gifted persons show that minds may sometimes function independently of brains. They show, too, that the past continues to exist. I doubt whether scientists can discover any more important facts than these.

Appendix I
Archaeological Experiments

Although the archaeological experiments carried out with Stefan Ossowiecki cannot be subjected to satisfactory verification and therefore are not considered in the main body of the book, they are of interest for a number of reasons. Firstly, most of them are very well documented and corroborated, and it may be the case that archaeologists will uncover evidence confirming Ossowiecki's visions; therefore they should be kept on record, especially as at least one account (p. 161, Archaeological Experiment 5) contains what appears to be a spectacular hit—an accurate description of wall engravings covered by clay and revealed only after Ossowiecki identified their location. Secondly, some of the accounts (such as Archaeological Experiment 11 reported here, p. 163) give a vivid insight into how far Ossowiecki entered into and identified with his visions. Thirdly, they offer an illuminating sidelight on how experimental design can be affected and perhaps distorted by the interests of the researchers involved.

A number of experiments with Ossowiecki involving archaeological objects were recorded. Some, which sound quite informal, dating from the 1920s, are related in his autobiography. However, the main series of between 31 and 33 sittings took place from 1935 to 1944 and was designed by professor Stanisław Poniatowski, professor of ethnology at Warsaw University. The participants were prominent academics, the target objects were chosen with care from museum collections and other academically acceptable sources and, judging by the extracts which are available, the sittings reported in a detailed and professional manner.

There is no doubt that the 1935–1944 sittings took place as described; this has been confirmed by a number of independent sources. The full Polish manuscript which reports them, now in private hands and unpublished, seems to have been delivered to Ossowiecki's widow in a mysterious manner after the Second World War. Its author, Stanisław Poniatowski, died in 1945. Mme. Ossowiecki distributed a number of extracts from the manuscript among researchers; some of them have been published in Polish publications, some translated and published in English (Goodman, 1978, Schwartz, 1978). The problem both with the sittings arranged by Poniatowski, and the earlier, less formal experiments, is the difficulty of verifying Ossowiecki's statements except on a very basic level. This problem was recognized by the investigators in the 1920s, and it should be pointed out that the later experiments give the impression of having been designed not so much as a test of Ossowiecki's psychic powers, but as a creative and innovative aid to archaeological research, with the reality of Ossowiecki's gift taken for granted. Without access to the full manuscript it is impossible to say to what extent the author took account of the possibility of coincidence or the power of Ossowiecki's imagination when asked to supply visual detail. It is also not known whether the experimental designs included plans for seeking confirmation of Ossowiecki's statements through further research into the objects and the sites from which they came.

The published accounts of reasonably well documented archaeological experiments are briefly summarized below in chronological order.

Experiments Reported in Ossowiecki's Autobiography

Archaeological Experiment 1 (Source: Ossowiecki, 1933, pp. 212–13)

1925 (1 November). The experimenter placed a relatively large gray stone in Ossowiecki's hands. Ossowiecki described another planet, with plains and rocks of purple color, strange cypress-like black trees and transparent forms similar to humans, enormous expanses and rusty-iron colored giants flying through space, scattering into small pieces. After the session the experimenter revealed that the stone was a meteorite; in fact none of the experiments described here exclude the possibility of telepathy being involved.

Archaeological Experiment 2 (Source: Ossowiecki, 1933, pp. 211–12)

1925 (27 November). The object given to the clairvoyant was a piece of dried mud wrapped in a rag. Ossowiecki described, in some detail, a place which was destroyed suddenly, being deep down—possibly in the cellars, a one-story white house where gatherings used to take place with both men and women taking part, a kind of church with everyone singing. The piece of mud came from the temple of Mithras from under the church of St Praxeda in Rome.

Archaeological Experiment 3 (Source: Ossowiecki, 1933, pp. 212–14)

1926 (3 January). The experimenter put a marble fragment into Ossowiecki's hands. Ossowiecki's description included details of architectural features of a large building, the altar, the ceremony taking place and the appearance of the participants. The stone came from the ruins of the temple of Castor and Pollux, and according to the experimenter Ossowiecki's account was consistent with the historical evidence.

Archaeological Experiment 4 (Source: Ossowiecki, 1933, pp. 214–15)

1926 (probably 14 January). On being given a few pieces of earth crust to hold, Ossowiecki described a town which had been destroyed by natural disaster and buried in the mass of the same material. The experimenters, who gave Ossowiecki a piece of lava from the Vesuvius eruption, had hoped to have a description of the geological events taking place during the volcanic explosion.

Archaeological Experiment 5 (Sources: Ossowiecki, 1933, pp. 133–137; Zag. Met. Dec. 1926)

1926 (27 May). In this experiment Ossowiecki was asked for his impressions of a medieval dungeon during the excavations at the Royal Castle in Warsaw. This location was chosen by Szmurło (the experimenter) because nobody had entered it for a very long time and the public were not allowed access. An impression of this session can be gained from the following extract from Szmurło's report:

> We [there were five investigators] all went down a ladder, aided by the light of an electric lamp. We saw unplastered walls, built of large bricks of a thickness one no longer encounters, covered with a layer of clay and sand. Stefan Ossowiecki knelt by a wall on a coat, leaning with his palm on one of the bricks, and started talking at once:
> "This is a prison, a prison; here the unfortunate condemned carved coats-of-arms, gallows, using nails or sharp stones." The hardened sand and clay were cleared from this part of the wall and we did in fact see, at the level of human height, some signs probably scratched with a nail or a piece of stone, in a number of places. It was very dark, but by bringing the electric light closer we could make out coats-of-arms, letters, gallows, traces of the former inhabitants of the dungeon. Ossowiecki concentrated; we checked the time, it was 6.50 p.m. He stayed silent for 10 minutes, then at 7 p.m. he started speaking haltingly and with pauses, and two of us were taking notes....
> "I can see now, I see people ... there were two of them.... One bald-headed, with a long beard, wearing a garment with a red collar and such patches on the sleeves, he carved this sign, the gallows [this was where the psychometrist's palm was resting at the time]. The entrance was here, the door was high up, and the prisoners were lowered from there [he points with his hand]. They were brought in by soldiers in armor with long pikes, wearing odd helmets. The top was round [the vault] ... how black it is ... as if soot.... I also see elongated openings in the wall, which allow the air in.... Some iron bars ... [he points with his hand] there was a kind of niche, in which the guard sat. There [he points] I see many armed men with pikes. Some steps. [Steps were indeed found on checking.] Food was lowered here.... They stood by the wall ... waited.... It was a long, long time ago. So many impressions, pictures, it is difficult for me to put it all into words. There was one lying here, wearing just a shirt and trousers, without any shoes; sometimes there would be many of them, six to eight people. Further on there [he points] some long, low passage—a dungeon, you almost have to crawl on your stomach, and there was water there. [It did in fact turn out on closer inspection that there was a very narrow passage leading into the wall. Professor Skórewicz says that in the days Ossowiecki is talking about there was water there—the river Vistula.]

Ossowiecki continues:

> I see a monk in a black coat with an uncovered neck. I have the impression that he blessed and said farewell to the condemned who were taken from there to their death. [Indeed, at the indicated location there were what seemed to be

bricked up doors and from there a long corridor to the left leading to a room next to the dungeon.] And here, behind the wall [where the psychometrist was sitting] you may find something: I can see something metal, it shines, perhaps a helmet ... still.... No, I cannot do any more, I am tired.

Professor Skórewicz [the person in charge of the operation] says that Ossowiecki described the Castle as it was at the end of the fourteenth century, in the times of Mazovian princes, before the majority of the present buildings came into existence. The dungeon where the experiment took place is situated under the old Grodzka Baszta (Tower), where members of the gentry were imprisoned as a punishment. The Vistula, which later changed its course, in those days flowed right next to the castle walls and most probably at the point indicated by Ossowiecki there was a secret passage through the walls which he described. The tower was then separated from the Castle itself by a courtyard, where there usually would be the armed castle guards he mentioned. There also must have existed steps leading onto the defense wall which linked the tower and the castle.

A breakdown of the statements made by Ossowiecki shows that the verifiable "hits" relate to correct pinpointing of the physical features of the location, such as the presence of the steps, the narrow passage and the proximity of the river; since this information was confirmed by Professor Skórewicz, telepathy as the source cannot be excluded. Some of the other features, such as soot on the ceiling, might be expected in a very old building, and its use as a prison would be a likely guess. However, the carvings on the wall, revealed in the place indicated by Ossowiecki and matching his description cannot be explained so easily. It makes one wonder whether the detailed and vivid descriptions of the people and their clothes, which create such a dramatic effect, may be accurate, even if unverifiable.

Other Sources

Archaeological Experiment 6 (Source: Boruń & Boruń-Jagodzińska, 1990, p. 113, Schwartz, 1978, pp. 75–6.)

1935 (14 February). Ossowiecki correctly identified a mummified human foot presented to him in a metal foil box wrapped in paper. The only thing known by the experimenter (Witold Balcer) was that the object was a part of a mummy recovered in Egypt around 1927.

Archaeological Experiment 7 (Source: Boruń & Boruń-Jagodzińska, 1990, p. 113; Schwartz, 1978. pp. 77–8.)

1935 (18 March). The same mummy's foot was identified by Ossowiecki as belonging to a pretty, high-bred young woman who died in childbirth, whose funeral he went on to describe. No archaeologists or historians were involved at this stage. Mention is made of Ossowiecki's exhausted and confused state after the experiment.

Archaeological Experiment 8 (Source: Boruń & Boruń-Jagodzińska, 1990, pp. 119–25.)

1926 (October). This involved Ossowiecki in an unusual attempt at historical research rather than archaeology. An astronomer writing a biography of Copernicus hoped that Ossowiecki might supply suggestions explaining doubtful details relating to Copernicus's personal life, particularly the fate of some books which had belonged to Copernicus. Ossowiecki created a very vivid picture of the Copernicus family, Copernicus himself and the people and emotions associated with the books he was given to handle. An extended account of this experiment can be found in Boruń (1990); it makes fascinating reading but, as Boruń points out, apart from statements and images which sound probable, there are also clear factual errors and much of the story remains unverifiable.

The Poniatowski Series

Archaeological Experiment 9 (Source: Schwartz, 1978, pp. 82–3.)

1936 (23 April). In the presence of a number of prominent academics Ossowiecki described the impressions gathered from a small flint tool some 10,000 years old. He talked about a forest and gave a description of a microlithic culture, people and customs. Those present agreed that the vision was accurate as far as it could be judged.

Archaeological Experiment 10 (Source: Schwartz, 1978, pp. 85–88, Bugaj, 1994.)

1936 (May). Under conditions similar to those in Experiment 9, Ossowiecki described the impressions associated with a stone club relating to early *Homo sapiens*. The stone had a complicated history: the rock had been part of a hearth ring, a portion of the doorway to a primitive stone house, then after reworking it became a weapon. Most information belonged in the possible but unverifiable category. However, Ossowiecki claimed that he could see the ocean (between Belgium and Normandy shores), whereas Poniatowski thought the object came from central southern France. On checking the next day Poniatowski found that the source, Abbeville, was within sight of the ocean.

Archaeological Experiment 11 (Source: Schwartz, 1978, pp. 88–91.)

1938 (21 October). Ossowiecki described an ancient culture, correctly identifying the site. He became agitated and anxious that he would not be able to return when he started to observe in vivid detail a couple making love, but calmed down when able to move on to a description of some animals.

Archaeological Experiment 12 (Source: Schwartz, 1978, pp. 100–105.)

1939 (6 November) Having handled a Magdalenian engraving tool, Ossowiecki described a cremation and burial of ashes in an urn. The description did not agree with what was known of Magdalenian funerary customs; however, see Experiment 13.

Archaeological Experiment 13 (Source: Schwartz, 1978., pp. 100–101.)

1941 (22 October). Poniatowski gave Ossowiecki the same object to handle as in Experiment 12. Ossowiecki's impressions were the same as in that experiment. It has been suggested that later archaeological developments tend to support Ossowiecki's interpretation.

Archaeological Experiment 14 (Source: Imich archives, unpublished.)

1941 (5 March). Having been given a tool from the Chalk Plateau in Kent, England, Ossowiecki comes up with a very detailed description and some drawings of a settlement with round houses, water in the distance, the appearance of the people, and a prehistoric animal being hunted.

Archaeological Experiment 15 (Source: Imich archives, unpublished.)

1941 (19 March). Another session with the tool from the Chalk Plateau in Kent. Similar to Experiment 14 in the detailed description, including drawings. The descriptions relate to the structure of houses, what seem to be underground caves; people, their tools and what they eat.

Appendix II
Chronology and List of Cases

Cases included in this book appear in bold type.
Cases not included appear in italics.

22 August 1877	Born in Moscow in a well-to-do family, father a chemist, owner of a paints factory.
1891	Evidence of telepathy as a 14-year-old.
1894	Graduated from Third Cadet Corps in Moscow at the age of 17.
1895–1898	Telepathy evolves into "mediumistic abilities," objects moving, writing in unknown languages.
1898-1899?	Meeting with Wróbel in Homel.
1899	Completion of studies at Petersburg Institute of Technology. Development of psychokinesis, powers developing and increasing, moving very heavy objects. Witnesses' names given but no formal records. Physical mediumship diminished as clairvoyant faculty increased.
1899-1900?	Year and a half of practical experience at Cassel plants at Frankfurt am Main. *Possibly the encounter with the mysterious stranger in hotel whose past he recounted in a letter to her.* Working in factories, then on the boards of family factories in Russia.
1913	*Jacyna's report on psychokinetic feat "witnessed" by Olgierd Missuna, guests were allowed only to view the result.*
1914	Death of father, Ossowiecki becomes the head of the large chemical plant which the family inherited.
1917	Member of the council of Military Association of Poles in Moscow. Imprisoned for some months in horrific conditions under threat of death.
1918	Arrives in Warsaw, lives at Trębacka 11.

1919-1925	Sales manager for Żyrardów Plants Association.
1920	Active in the Polish Red Cross.
1920s	"Astral" projection, supervised by Geley, confirmed in a statement by the woman "visited."
1920	Reading of a chess gambit from Marshal Piłsudski, confirmed by letter from Lieutenant Cz. Świrski.
early 1920s	*Sosnkowski & Plater, answering a question written by a guest at a party without seeing it.*
early 1920s	Telepathy with Marshal Piłsudski; living at Piękna 5, a damp "hole" and where his "hand ached badly."
early 1920s	*Writing down words sent to each other with Piłsudski.*
1920s	*Ossowiecki tells a friend how and where he lost a document from his pocket.*
1920s	Account by Proffessor N. Tugan-Baranowski in letter of 10.07.1928. of various experiments:. 1. "102"-Ossowiecki saw a smudge on the zero. 2. Ossowiecki identified his name as target. 3. £1note-Ossowiecki identified the note. 4. Ossowiecki described drawing in wallet, unknown to NTB,. 5. "NON"-Ossowiecki said it was a three figure number, with zero in middle.
25 April 1921	Reports by Geley:. 1. Read first five letters of signature,. 2. Text in English "I consider you are wonderful."
26 April 1921	Reports by Richet. 3. "Never does the sea look grander than when it is calm." 4. Read four-digit number.
01 April 1921	Reports by Geley. 5. Richet's letter of invitation from Mrs. Berger. 6. Richet's text on muezzin call to prayer.
12 September 1921	Reports by Geley. 1. "Good luck at Warsaw."
14 September 1921	2. "Man....is a thinking reed."
21 September 1921	3. Five targets, including left/right-facing fish.
September 1921	Three tests with Warsaw medical congress participants. 4. "China is a charming country." 5. Dr. Bergeret said that SO was entirely wrong. 6. "Love is the child of Bohemia."
23/24 September 1921	7. Letter from Mme. Geley praising SO.

25 September 1921	8. Printed material from Sudre.
27 September 1921	9. Elephant and crocodile target.
28/30 September 1921	10. Drawing of "perfect gentle knight" (Piłsudski) enclosed in a lead tube.
Winter 1921	Account by S. Byszewski (22 October 1932) of how his wife "saw" Ossowiecki who next day confirmed his "astral" projection.
1922	Marriage to Alietta de la Carrierre.
19 April 1922	Reports by Richet. 1. Cross with spots in corners.
20 April 1922	2. Rostand quotation from Anna de Noailles. 3. "Life seems good... ephemeral" from Sarah Bernhardt. 4. "Toi" read by Ossowiecki as "T 0 1."
May 1922	Geley's report on second Anna de Noailles target, praising Richet.
06 June 1922	Finding lost brooch for Alice de Bondy de Glass, confronting finder/taker while visiting his bank.
02 February 1923	*Answering question-target set by General Rybak where the Marshal was at the time.*
12 March 1923	Reports by Szmurło. 1. One of 4 boxes made up by outsider, urn fragment. 2. Crossed swords drawing.
25 May 1923	Sokołowski and two witnesses verify accurate description of the inside of a watch.
12 June 1923	*Afternoon experiment with Charles Richet junior- Yacht drawing.* Article by Dr. Stephan Chauvet describing evening reception at the Institut Métapsychique. Further articles by Chauvet in La Vie (1 September 1923) and Le Mercure de France (1 October 1923). Reports by Chauvet.
12 June 1923	1. Crucifix titled (illegibly) "My life." 2. Envelope prepared by patient and sealed with coins. 3. Mme. X-her question about a voyage answered.
15 June 1923	4. d'Anglard-Where shall I be this time next year?. 5. d'Anglard repeated the same target. 6. d'Anglard drew Tyrolean hat/helmet. 7. SO told d'Anglard he had planned to draw triangles.
June 1923	Ossowiecki saved drowning soldiers seen clairvoyantly; his arrival at the scene and rescue by boat confirmed by Z. Kozieł.

Appendix II

28 August 1923	Second International Metapsychical Congress in Warsaw. **Dingwall's wine-bottle target presented publicly at the Warsaw Congress.**
05 September 1923	report by Neumann & MacKenzie.
15 September 1923	**Report by J.A.Kimaczyński-Ossowiecki traced a bracelet, giving accurate description of house, occupants and their activities.**
11 May 1924	Ossowiecki identified target as name and address of bishop.
11 May 1924	Ossowiecki described wounding and death of letter donor's brother.
11 May 1924	Ossowiecki gave information about death confirmed only later.
11 May 1924	*Ossowiecki identified thief of stolen watch, given empty box as target.*
15 May 1924	Report by Szmurło-four undeveloped plates from two photographers-Ossowiecki described target chateau and people present.
04 June 1924	Report by Osty of experiments initiated by Geley-portrait of a woman target taken at random from three undeveloped photographic plates.
22/24 June	Report by Geley-Experiment using quotation copied from
07 July 1924	Pasteur written with invisible ink; Ossowiecki "saw" pen moves.
13 July 1924	Report by Geley-Carp scales contained in a box that once held pharmaceutical products-Ossowiecki identified medicine labels etc. and thin, round, transparent "mica" but did not recognize scales.
1924	*Report by Szmurło-Ossowiecki traced his movements around town, as described by Szmurło in "The Illustrated Courier."*
1924	Report by G. Charpentier, League of Nations Delegate, SO reproduced Charpentier's mouse and described his actions.
03 November 1924	Editorial report on experiment with Santoliquido-SO reproduced "Francesco" in Santoliquido's handwriting.
1924	Account by M. Szpyrkówna, secretary of the Psychopysical Society, of Ossowiecki describing murder, murderer and where victim would be found.
1925-1927	Administrative director, Widzew Manufacture.
1925	Becomes a council member of the Spiritual Unity League in Warsaw.

29 October 1925	Report by Sokołowski on letter from Cobo Martinez; diamond drawing and detailed description of house and people.
01 November 1925	Ossowiecki identified a meteorite provided by A. Czubryński (Archaeological Exp. 1).
27 November 1925	Ossowiecki identified a mud specimen, archaeological experiment with Czubryński (Archaeological Exp. 2).
03 January 1926	Ossowiecki identified a stone provided by Czubryński (Archaeological Exp. 3).
14 January 1926	Ossowiecki identified a piece of lava provided by Czubryński (Archaeological Exp. 4).
27 May 1926	Report by Szmurło-Archaeological clairvoyance at the Royal Castle; some statements verifiable and correct (Archaeological Exp. 5).
October 1926	Tracing the fate of books which supposedly had belonged to Copernicus. (Archaeological Exp. 8).
07 January 1927	*Ossowiecki described the home of an Italian general, reproduced target "Mussolini" in General's writing; confirmed by Father C. Oraczewski.*
April 1927	Report by Gravier-Ossowiecki identified the thief of missing shares in the PS Bank in Warsaw, after placing his hand in the safe.
1927	Account by A. Jaroszewicz of Ossowiecki predicting to D. Smirnov that he would meet and marry a Russian in USA. Confirmed.
1928	Account by Professor Barrington-Emerson of Ossowiecki doing successful experiments and giving detailed life reading.
1928	*Account by Archbishop Ropp of how Ossowiecki gave accurate description of island from specimen of tree bark.*
21 November 1928	Account by Vice Prosecutor O. Missuna, Ossowiecki tracing missing father, to a Chinese ship; appearance, illness etc. Confirmed 17 January 1930.
December 1928	*Reading for named Appeal Court judge; printed matter unread, but signature of Justice Minister reproduced, with description of him.*
December 1928	*(i) Ossowiecki's drawing conflated female head that W. thought about with eagle which he drew, (ii) Ossowiecki described previous owners of ring.*
02 June 1929	*Account by St. Ziejewski of how SO told Hindu visitors correct details about their family history.*

06 October 1929	*Account by Professor Władysław Witwicki of two tests: Zentralblatt für Okkultismus.* *1. SO picked out two target papers from 60 upturned sheets.* *2. SO gave approximate reading of "Who stole the spirit?"* *(The date refers to the article by Witwicki).*
1929	*Letter to editor of "The Bugle" describing him and his misfortunes, all confirmed in his reply.*
1930	*Divorce from Alietta.*
1930-1934	*Operates an employment cooperative for disinfecting telephones using his and his business partner's invention.*
17 January 1930	**Account by G. Godejski of Ossowiecki giving a mother news of her son, on a French ship; all details confirmed by letter of 12 February 1930.**
20 March 1930	*Ossowiecki told singer Titta Ruffo about his past.*
Autumn 1930	**Ossowiecki identifying a saboteur at the Wedel factory, and correctly stating that he would not offend again (confirmed by letter from F. Pintowski).**
October 1930	**Ossowiecki described an enveloped photograph confirmed by K. Kallenberg, Sweden.**
November 1930	*Ossowiecki reproduced drawings by Artur Rubinstein and a violinist.*
November 1930	*Ossowiecki reproduced Minister for Transport's triangle with circle inside it.*
November 1930	*Archaeological case where Ossowiecki accurately tells the experimenter how the object was obtained.*
1930	*Ossowiecki willed pianist Orlov to come to a friends' house and described Orlov's actions, Orlov confirming actions and compulsion on arrival. Witnesses included composer Szymanowski.*
1930s	*Professor Leon Petrażycki (a convinced sceptic) deeply upset because Ossowiecki correctly identified target ("Birch tree") though LP tried to mislead him.*
1931	*Approaching one of the guests at a party, giving a correct diagnosis of ailment and advising him to seek medical help (Ossowiecki, 1976 [Chicago edition], pp. 326-7).*
16 May 1931	**Stanisław Szpotański's account in "The World."** *(I) a wrong piece of clothing presented as target.* **(Ii) SO reproduced triangle with cross inside.** (Date refers to publication).
May 1931	**Account by Francisco Madrid (3 June 1932) of Ossowiecki giving a detailed description of a lady's house in Oslo and family members.**

09 November 1931	Account of Ossowiecki "visiting" a house in Riga and reporting on Baroness Luder's mother's health. Three witnesses.
13 November 1931	*Sealed drawing confirmed by the Rev. J. Belton and another witness.*
November 1931	Account by Konrad Strauss, art historian, from Berlin, of how Ossowiecki related his life events in great detail, 95/100 facts correct.
Winter 1931	Account by detective Bachrach of how Ossowiecki traced movements of a missing lawyer, including train journeys and attempted drowning.
1931-1932?	*Account by Jacyna of Ossowiecki finding the body of a kidnapped child and identifying the murderer; rich industrialist in Germany involved.* *Unconfirmed.*
14 January 1932	Account by Civil Engineering Society Chairman (letter of 14 March 1932) tells of Ossowiecki locating missing documents for the Polytechnic.
05 February 1932	Account by M. Mohuczy of Ossowiecki locating and describing state of health of a missing relative in the Belgian Congo.
18 May 1932	Account by Stefan Rzewuski of Ossowiecki reading targets consisting of incorrect arithmetical equations.
18 May 1932	Follow on from previous experiment-another experiment with concealed numbers, excluding telepathy, e.g., $3 \times 5 = 18$.
1932	Account by J. Jacyna of Ossowiecki having impression of J. with his head and face swollen; two weeks later J. was attacked round the face by bees.
27 August 1932	*Account by Baron N. Kruzensztern & Wanda Badior of Ossowiecki reproducing drawing, and also drawing house and head that K. intended to draw.*
15 September 1932	*Ossowiecki reproduced cross with drawings in each segment, and correctly told C. Vorstelman, an Englishman, that he meant to draw a circle.*
19 October 1932	*Account by Metapsychical Society chairman of experiments with Tarot cards, including getting one participant to identify a designated card.*
12 November 1932	*Account by Professor A. Gravier of various experiments, including identifying a coin that had appeared at a sitting.*
21 November 1932	*Account by Chief Architect of Warsaw of Ossowiecki identifying provenance of a ring, describing purchase at a Far East bazaar.*

23 November 1932	Account by five witnesses of Ossowiecki describing a postcard of a painting, also giving details of the postcard sender.
23 November 1932	Same witnesses confirm reading of "Le Roi de Rome 1811–1832." in which Ossowiecki also reproduced the handwriting.
1933	Publication of Ossowiecki's autobiography.
September 1933	Report by Theodore Besterman of SO reproducing the SWAN INK target set by in July and sent to Warsaw; paper folded over Swan but not Ink.

September 1933	Report by Osty on experiments with Dulché using four envelopes prepared by target setter in Paris, contents unknown to Dulché —
	    1. five-point star, reproduced by SO with 4 points.
	    2. Triangle and rope with 12 knots; SO drew two triangles and rope.

1934	Report by Osty of two experiments in Warsaw—
	    1. SO failed to read undeveloped photographic plates.
	    2. Mongel set tears, cross and coffin; partial success.

1934-5	Affair with a friend of Jacyna, unconfirmed.
14 February 1935	Archaeological experiment in which Ossowiecki correctly identified a mummy's foot (Archaeological Exp. 6).
18 February 1935	Archaeological experiment with mummy's foot continued (Archaeological Exp. 7).
1935	Report by Szmurło of Ossowiecki reading a sealed packet containing meteorite, etc., prepared by Jonky (by then dead) in 1927.
1936	Account by F. Loth of Ossowiecki identifying but not naming a guest who stole money, stating correctly that it would be given back.
April 1936	Archaeological experiment with Poniatowski (one of 33). (Archaeological Exp. 9).
May 1936	Archaeological experiment with Poniatowski (one of 33) (Archaeological Exp. 10).
1936	*Gordon Bennet Cup-balloon disaster over the USSR, Ossowiecki supposedly locating survivors, unconfirmed.*

November 1937	Report by M. Wojdyłło (30 November 1937) outdoor experiment.
	    1. Elliptical shape (pentagonal solid).
	    2. W—drawn by skeptic, who had intended to draw a swastika.

February 1938	Account by Prof. W. Doroszewski of Ossowiecki describ-

	ing condition of patient about to undergo operation and predicting outcome.
1938	Becomes co-founder and honorary member of the Polish Parapsychological Society, amalgamated from various other societies.
1938	*Account by Szomański of Ossowiecki locating the site of crash of a Polish LOT flight from Warsaw to Athens (unconfirmed).*
July 1939	Marriage to Zofia Skibińska (Świda by first marriage).
September 1939	Move from Polna 32, destroyed by bombing.
24 September 1939	**Account by Maria Bołtuć of Ossowiecki correctly describing her officer husband receiving neck wound, his movements, pinpointing his location and describing his companions.**
October 1939	**Account by I. Rowecka-Mielczarska of Ossowiecki being unable to give information about a resistance officer who did not want to be located.**
06 November 1939	**Archaeological experiment with an engraving tool (Archaeological Exp. 12).**
end December 1939	**Account by Jacyna of Ossowiecki warning him about danger on the street, having to climb and being saved by a young woman.**
September 1940	**Account by J. Olewiński of Ossowiecki using map divining and then on site locating body of officer buried underneath other corpses.**
1939-1944	Engaged in occasional trade in animal feed and iron goods. Main source of income-coffee bar run by his wife and her family. Giving most of his time to people with missing or imprisoned relatives.
05 March 1941	Impressions from a tool (Archaeological Exp. 14).
19 March 1941	Impressions from a tool (Archaeological Exp. 15).
22 October 1941	Repeat of an archaeological experiment conducted in 1939. (Archaeological Exp. 13).
April 1943	**Account by Dr. T. Gliwic of Ossowiecki relating circumstances of father's arrest and death.**
05 August 1944	Murdered in a large group of people in German reprisals for the Warsaw uprising. Body never found.

Undated Reports

Ossowiecki read a sealed target and then told an American banker, Ob-deyk [presumably Updike] details about his house, his wife, his dog and illness of a grandchild not then known to Updike.

Four witnesses named.

Account by Major X (signed but identity withheld) of how Ossowiecki traced his missing son, with "minutest details," including blistered feet and loan of money from a young man wearing spectacles.

Ossowiecki traced missing sons for a Mrs. Lewicki, saying one was dead but the other would return from Russia in two to three months, as he did. Ossowiecki assisted "present" District Court Prosecutor and named detective to apprehend murderers of an entire family. Ossowiecki helped Prosecutor Sima by locating missing documents that had been misplaced.

Account by Szmurło of how Ossowiecki willed a an attractive woman (a stranger) to approach him at a theatre;

Account by Dr. Wilhelm Neumann of Ossowiecki reproducing his drawing of an asymmetric ace of hearts; eight witnesses present;

Account by Professor Chojecki of Warsaw University, who used six targets unknown to him; Ossowiecki picked and identified "Speech is silver, silence is golden";

In the next experiment, Chojecki set "Nel mezzo del cammin di nostra vita." SO said "… Italian… Nelli….nostra vita" and C. said "That's good enough for me";

Account by Prof. Witkowska-Zaremba of Ossowiecki forcing a woman who doubted his powers to kneel down in front of him at a party.

Appendix III
Biographical Profiles of the Experimenters

BESTERMAN, Theodore (1904–1976)

Besterman, who provided and evaluated the significant "Swan Ink" target, was a world renowned bibliographer, who was associated with the University of London School of Librarianship. He became Librarian of the Society for Psychical Research, producing its Library Catalogue in 1927, and served as its Investigating Officer from 1927 until 1935 and was also Editor of the Society's *Proceedings* and *Journal* He was a prolific author in several fields, his publications on psychical research including *The Divining Rod: an Experimental and Psychological Investigation* (1926), written in collaboration with Sir William Barrett FRS, and *Some Modern Mediums* (1930), which he edited.

DINGWALL, E[ric] J[ohn] (1890–1986)

Dr. Dingwall, who provided the target drawing for Ossowiecki's Warsaw Conference demonstration and used his expertise to make it tamper-proof, was Director of the Department of Physical Phenomena at the American Society for Psychical Research 1921–1922, and Research Officer for the (London) Society for Psychical Research 1922–1927. Among his activities he was an anthropologist, Hon. Assistant Keeper of printed books at the British Museum and a member of the Magic Circle. His publications include *Some Human Oddities* (1947) and *Abnormal Hypnotic Phenomena* (4 vols.) 1967–8.

GELEY, Gustave (1868–1924)

Geley was a physician who became a full time psychical researcher. He was a founder of the Institut Métapsychique International and the first editor of its journal, the *Revue Métapsychique*. His first book, *L'Être Subconscient*, published in 1899, showed him diverging from the prevailing materialistic philosophy of contemporary scientists in France. His two later books, *L'Ectoplasmie et matérialisation* and *De l'inconscient au conscient* were both translated into English as *Clairvoyance and Materialisation* and *From the Unconscious to the Conscious.*

GRAVIER, Alphonse (1872–1953)

Gravier was a Frenchman by birth, who settled in Warsaw after the First World War. An architect by profession, he organized a School of Building of which he was the Head; he also lectured at the prestigious Warsaw Polytechnic (one of the top higher education establishments in the country). He designed and built many of the important buildings in Warsaw. He was very active in the Towarzystwo Badań Psychicznych (Society for Psychical Research) in the 1930s, including being its President. Eventually he was elected President of the Society for Parapsychological Research in 1938, which replaced all others when the various Polish organizations decided to amalgamate. (Sources: *Polish Biographical Dictionary*; Szczepański, 1936.)

MISSUNA, Olgierd

Like many of the Polish investigators, Missuna was a professional man of high standing, but he has no entry in any of the biographical dictionaries consulted, and information about him has been gathered from a variety of sources, including his own publications. He was a relative of Ossowiecki, a lawyer by profession and State Prosecutor from 1930. This meant that he was involved in working closely with the police in investigating, securing evidence and determining the motives in criminal cases. In the 1960s he published two volumes of reminiscences about his career, which show the author as a clear-headed man, with a good understanding of human nature.

OSTY, Eugène (1874–1938)

Osty was, like Geley, a physician who came to devote most of his life to the Institut Métapsychique International, succeeding Geley as its Director and Editor of the *Revue Métapsychique*. His main publication was *La connaissance supranormale*, translated as *Supernormal Faculties in Man*. He is one of the few researchers to have written extensively about psychometry, especially as utilized by professional psychics specializing in precognition. He later became celebrated for research with the physical medium Rudi Schneider, detecting an effect on infra-red radiation when acted upon by telekinetic force.

PIŁSUDSKI, Józef (1867–1935)

Piłsudski was the Commander of the Polish independence army during the First World War, and the first Head of State after Poland's re-emergence as an independent state in 1918. In 1926 he headed a coup, as a result of which his role within the state became one of "overseeing" the functioning of democratic institutions; he retained this role until his death in 1935. He was a very popular if controversial leader, with a charismatic and powerful personality. His interest in the paranormal and his psychic abilities (he has been credited with powers of precognition, telepathy, psychokinesis and a great power of suggestion) are mentioned in a number of independent sources. (Sources: *Polish Biographical Dictionary*; Szczepański, 1937.)

(POLISH) SOCIETY FOR PSYCHICAL RESEARCH
See (WARSAW) PSYCHOPHYSICAL SOCIETY

PONIATOWSKI, Stanisław (1884–1945)

In his youth Poniatowski was a conspirator and freedom-fighter in the movement pursuing the cause of Poland's independence. His academic career involved teaching at various higher education establishments, including a professorship of ethnography at Warsaw University; he was also a member of many Polish and foreign scientific associations. His main interests were anthropology, ethnology and investigating the material culture of past civilizations. During the Second World War he was active in the resistance movement; arrested by the Germans in 1942, he died in a concentration camp. (Source: *Polish Biographical Dictionary*.)

RICHET, Charles (1850–1935)

Richet was Professor of Physiology at the Faculty of Medicine in Paris, 1881–1925, and winner of the Nobel prize for physiology in 1913. He was originally incredulous and scornful *vis-à-vis* psychic phenomena, but when confronted by the evidence of personal experience he retracted his views and expressed regret for having doubted the word of scientific colleagues such as Sir William Crookes and Sir Oliver Lodge. He wrote extensively about physical mediumship, describing the process of materialization as seen and handled by him. Certain as he declared himself to be about these effects, he said that insofar as there were degrees of certainty he accorded the highest degree to the clairvoyance of Ossowiecki. His most comprehensive work was his *Traité de Métapsychique*, translated as *Thirty Years of Psychical Research*.

RZEWUSKI, Stefan

It has unfortunately proved impossible so far to discover any biographical information about this investigator. He was the Secretary of the Warsaw Psychophysical Society, and a very active researcher, but even then one whose work was mostly of a "hands-on" practical nature, with the descriptive part being left to others. However, his original contributions to experimental design and painstaking investigations of claimants (as in eventually unmasking a physical medium who used his teeth to produce the séance phenomena) speak for themselves.

SOKOŁOWSKI, Tadeusz (1877–1950s)

President of the (Polish) Society for Psychical Research at one stage, and an active researcher, Sokołowski also had a busy medical and academic career. A professor and doctor of medicine, expert in psychotherapy and hypnotism, he was the Chief Administrator and Supervisor of Warsaw hospitals before the Second World War. During the Second World War he fought with the Polish army formed in the then Soviet Union. After the war he returned to Poland and worked as a surgeon and was Head of an Operating Clinic in Szczecin, in northern Poland. (Source: Jerzy Woźniak, *Julian Ochorowicz,* in *Trzecie Oko* No. 4, 1984, p. 14.)

SZMURŁO, Prosper

Szmurło was the founder of the Warsaw Psychophysical Society, Editor of *Zagadnienia Metapsychiczne* and a very active and able researcher. Unfortunately it has not been possible to find any biographical information about him, except for one passing reference to his work as a tax inspector. However, he published a number of books on psychical research, which give us some insight into his views. His publications include: *Świat nadzmysłowy i metody jego badania* (The world beyond the senses and methods of its investigation); *Sen, jego symbolika i nadświadomość* (Dreams, their symbols and superconsciousness); and *Ze świata tajemnic* (The world of mysteries). This last volume was aimed at popularizing the subject of psychical research by explaining the terminology, describing some cases and making the reader aware of the need for adopting a critical approach and distinguishing between fact and belief.

(WARSAW) PSYCHOPHYSICAL SOCIETY [Warszawskie Towarzystwo Psychofizyczne]

This society, founded by Prosper Szmurło in 1921, was one of a number of organizations devoted to psychical research which functioned in Poland, mainly in Warsaw, in the period between the two World Wars. It existed alongside the (Polish) Society for Psychical Research (Towarzystwo Badań Psychicznych) founded earlier by, among others, Piotr Lebiedziński and Tadeusz Sokołowski. Also active in Warsaw were the Metapsychic Society (Towarzystwo Metapsychiczne) and the Polish Metapsychic Association (Polskie Stowarzyszenie Metapsychiczne). Since the members of the various societies all tended to publish their research in *Zagadnienia Metapsychiczne* (a quarterly published irregularly from January 1924 to December 1929 and edited by Prosper Szmurło) and to participate in experiments organized by other societies, it is often difficult to distinguish between them. It was thus a logical step for them to amalgamate, which they did in 1938, forming the Polish Parapsychological Society (Polskie Towarzystwo Parapsychologiczne). Its president became Alphonse Gravier, with Szmurło and Sokołowski among the vice-presidents, and Ossowiecki among the founder members.

More important than their organizational structure was the range of activities undertaken by members of these societies, and the vigorously scientific approach they adopted when investigating paranormal phenomena. Their research also had a truly international flavor, involving cooperation and collaboration with, among others, organizations in France, Germany, Greece and England.

Glossary

General Terms

Medium (mediumship)   A practitioner of the paranormal [the practice]
   (1) *Mental medium*   One who specializes in mental phenomena [in some cases a medium who purports to transmit messages from deceased communicators]*
   Mental phenomena   Paranormal cognition [i.e. psychic perception or awareness]
   (2) *Physical medium*   One who specializes in physical mediumship
Physical phenomena   Material effects attributable to paranormal causes (such as materialization of phantom forms, movement of objects)
Paranormal   Seemingly mind-related phenomena that transcend the usual physical and biological limitations
Parapsychology   An alternative term for *psychical research*, but particularly used in reference to the experimental side of the field
Psi   Paranormal events and faculties of all kinds
Psychic [a psychic]   [A person] gifted with the faculty of paranormal cognition
Psychical research   The study of the paranormal
Séance/sitting   A session during which a medium demonstrates paranormal cognition to sitters, who may be researchers and/or members of a circle. *Séance* is used more often for displays of physical mediumship or Spiritualist-style clairvoyance.

Specific Terms

Akashic records   term used to describe the concept that the universe contains "memories" of all that has happened since the beginning of time
Aura   A "halo" of coloured light some psychics claim to see around the head and/or body of people
Cryptaesthesia   see *Hyperaesthesia*
Extra-sensory perception   *ESP* covers clairvoyance, precognition, retrocognition and telepathy
*Clairvoyance**   Paranormal cognition of things concealed or events happening else-

---

*In Spiritualist circles *a* demonstration of clairvoyance *means a public display by a medium practising this branch of mediumship.*

where, the latter also called *distant* or *remote viewing* (Richet's term *lucidité* is sometimes translated as *lucidity*)

Precognition   Paranormal cognition of future events

Retrocognition   Paranormal cognition of past events

Telepathy   Paranormal cognition of material in another person's mind

Hyperaesthesia   Sensitivity of the subconscious to stimuli beyond the scope of conscious awareness

Psychokinesis (PK)   Causing things to move by force of will (also called *telekinesis*)

Psychometry   Handling an article to establish rapport with its owner, origin, history or location

Bibliography

BBC (1987). *The Foolish Wise Ones,* documentary program *QED,* British Broadcasting Corporation; and see Oliver Sacks, *Foreword* to Stephen Wiltshire, *(1991) Floating Cities,* London: Michael Joseph

Beloff, John (1993). *Parapsychology: A Concise History.* London: Athlone.

Besterman, T. (1929). Report of a four months' tour of psychical investigation, *Proceedings of the Society for Psychical Research* 38:413–33.

———. (1930a). *Some Modern Mediums.* London: Methuen.

———. (1930b). Notes on periodicals. *Journal of the Society for Psychical Research* 26:87.

———. (1933) An experiment in "clairvoyance" with M. Stefan Ossowiecki, *Proceedings of the Society for Psychical Research,* XLI Part 132, pp. 345–51.

Bird, J.M. (1925) Commentary to Osty, E. A man of paranormal cognizance. *Journal of the American Society for Psychical Research 19,* 545–570.

Björnson, B. (1908). *Wise-Knut.* Bernard Stahl, translated. New York: Brandu.

Boruń, K., and Boruń-Jagodzińska, K. (1990). *Ossowiecki — zagadki jasnowidzenia.* Warszawa: Epoka.

Borzymowski, A. (1965). Experiments with Ossowiecki, *International Journal of Parapsychology,* vol. 7, pp. 259–280.

Braude, Steven E. (1979). *ESP and Psychokinesis: A Philosophical Examination.* Philadelphia: Temple University Press.

Bugaj, R. (1994). Nieznany eksperyment, in *Nieznany świat* 9/1994, pp. 14–17 and 10/1994, pp. 22–25.

———. (1994a). *Fenomeny paranormalne.* Warszawa: Oficyna "Adam."

Carrington, H. (1928). Correspondence. *Journal of the Society for Psychical Research 24,* 337–338.

De Fleurière, R. (1926). Comment je sens fonctionner ma faculté de clairvoyance. *Revue métapsychique* 343–54.

Denton, W. and Denton, E. (1863). *Nature's Secrets or Psychometric Researches.* London: Houlston and Wright.

Dessoir, M. (1931). *Vom Jenseits der Seele.* Stuttgart: Ferdinand Enke.

Dingwall, E.J. (1924). An experiment with the Polish medium Stephan Ossowiecki. *Journal of the Society for Psychical Research,* vol. XXI, pp. 259–63.

———. (1926). Notes on periodicals. *Journal of the Society for Psychical Research 23,* 93–95.

———. (1967). *Abnormal Hypnotic Phenomena: A Survey of Nineteenth-Century Cases.* Vol. 1. France. London: J.&A. Churchill.

Efron, D. (1944). Telepathic skin-writing. (The Kahl case). *Journal of Parapsychology* 8:272–86.

Elliotson, J. (1845). Reports of various trials of the clairvoyance of Alexis Didier, last summer, in London. *The Zoist, 2,* 477–529.

———. (1846) More of Alexis Didier. *The Zoist, 3,* 389–397.

_____. (1849) Clairvoyance of Alexis Didier. *The Zoist*, 6, 417–420.
Fischer, O. (1924). *Experimente mit Rafael Schermann*. Berlin: Urban und Schwarzenberg.
_____. (1934a). Experimentelles. Zur Frage der Kriminaltelepathie. *Zeitschrift für Parapsychologie 5*, 193–201.
_____. (1934b). Experimentelles. Zur Frage der Kriminaltelepathie. *Zeitschrift für Parapsychologie 6*, 241–256.
Forthuny, P. (1926). Ce que je puis dire du travail de ma faculté métagnomique. *Revue métapsychique* 355–70.
Gauld, Alan (1982). *Mediumship and Survival*. London: Heinemann.
Geley, Gustave (1920). *From the Conscious to the Unconscious*. London: Collins (trans. from *De l'inconscient au conscient*, 1919, Paris: Alcan.
_____. (1922). La clairvoyance de M. Stefan Ossowiecki. *Revue métapsychique*, No. 4, 247–257.
_____. (1927/1975). *Clairvoyance and Materialisation*, London: T. Fisher Unwin, 1927; New York: Arno 1975, reprint, translated from *L'Ectoplasmie et la clairvoyance*. 1924, Paris: Alcan.
Goodman, J. (1978). *Psychic Archaeology*, London: Wildwood House, pp. 31–53.
Grondahl, I.C. (1930). A sitting with Mme Kahl. *Journal of the Society for Psdychical Research*. 26: 43–45.
Grzymała-Siedlecki A. (1962). *Niepospolici ludzie w swoim dniu powszednim*. Kraków: Wydawnictwo Literackie.
Inglis, Brian (1985). *The Paranormal: An Encyclopaedia of Psychic Phenomena*, London: Grafton Paladin
Jacyna, Jan (1926). *30 lat w stolicy Rosji (1888–1918)*. Warszawa: F. Hoesick.
Jacyna, Jerzy (1970–71). Fakty i Legenda o Ossowieckim, in *Tygodnik Demokratyczny* 28/1970-21/1971.
Lee, E. (1866) *Animal Magnetism and Magnetic Lucid Somnambulism*. London: Longmans, Green.
Marcinkowski, J. (Mustafa Akhara Jusuf) (1985). *Pamiętnik jasnowidza*. Warszawa: Ludowa Spółdzielnia Wydawnicza.
Marks, D., and Kammann, R. (1980). *The Psychology of the Psychic*. Buffalo, N.Y.: Prometheus Books.
Méheust, Bertrand (2003). *Un Voyant prodigieux: Alexis Didier 1826–1886*. Paris: Les Empêcheurs de penser en rond.
Meyer, R. (1914). Die "Hellseher." Ihre Tricks und Ihre Opfer. *Berliner Klinische Wochenschrift*. 51: 1521–23.
Moll, A. (1926). Der "Hellseher" Ludwig Kahn und seine Untersucher. *Zeitschrift für kritischen Okkultismus 1*, 161–179.
Nowak Zbigniew (1997). *Ocean Czasu*, Warszawa: Fundacja Biomed.
Oesterreich, K.T. (1916). Psychologische Bemerkungen zu dem von Max Schottelius publizierten Fall eines "Hellsehers." *Journal für Psychologie und Neurologie 22*, 75–83.
Ossowiecki S. (1933) *Świat mego ducha i wizje przyszłości*. Warszawa: Dom Książki Polskiej; second edition (1976) Chicago: Astral Editorial Office.
Osty, E. (1923). *La Connaissance supra-normale: étude expérimentale*. Paris: Félix Alcan. (English edition: *Supernormal Faculties in Man*, translated by S. de Brath. London: Methuen, 1923).
_____. (1925). Un homme doué de connaissance paranormale: M. Ludwig Kahn. *Revue métapsychique* No. 2, 65–79.
_____. (1926a). *Une Faculté de connaissance supra-normale: Pascal Forthuny*. Paris: Félix Alcan.
_____. (1926b). Un Métagnome, M. Pascal Forthuny. *Revue métapsychique* No. 1, 28–61; No. 2, 91–115; No. 3, 171–214.
_____. (1929). Ce que la médecine doit attendre de l'étude expérimentale des propriétés psychiques paranormales de l'homme. *Revue métapsychique* No. 2, 79–148.

____. (1934). N'assignons pas de limites aux pouvoirs surnormaux de l'esprit: A propos d'Alexis Didier, prodigieux clairvoyant. *Revue métapsychique* No.5, 285–320.

Pagenstecher, G. (1920). A notable psychometric test. *Journal of the American Society for Psychical Research* 14, 386–417.

Pagenstecher, Gustav (1923). *Past Events Seership (A Study in Psychometry)*. W.F. Prince, *Proceedings of the American Society for Psychical Research* 16, Part 1.

Pajewski, J. (1995). *Budowa Drugiej Rzeczypospolitej 1918–1926*. Kraków: PAU.

Piłsudska, A. (1989). *Wspomnienia*. Warszawa: Instytut Prasy i Wydawnictw "Novum."

Polski Słownik Biograficzny (1979). Wrocław: Polska Akademia Nauk, Ossolineum

Prince, W.F. (1921). Psychometric experiments with Señora Maria Reyes de Z. *Proceedings of the American Society for Psychical Research* 15, 189–314.

____. (1924). Testing Rafael Schermann. *Journal of the American Society for Psychical Research* 18: 537–561.

____. (1932). A sitting with Bert Reese. *Journal of the Society for Psychical Research* 27, 249–254.

Radin, Dean. (1997). *The Conscious Universe: The Scientific Truth of Psychic Phenomena*. San Francisco: Harper Edge.

Rhine, Louisa E. (1981). *The Invisible Picture*, Jefferson N.C.: McFarland.

Richet, C. (1922). *Traité de métapsychique*. Paris: Félix Alcan. (English edition: *Thirty Years of Psychical Research*. Translated by S. de Brath. New York: Macmillan, 1923.)

____. (1926). Une Critique inopérante: M. Albert Moll et la cryptesthésie de Kahn. *Revue métapsychique* No. 3, 215–218.

____. (1928/1995). *Notre Sixième Sens*. Paris: Montaigne. (English edition. *Our sixth sense*. London: Rider, 1928.)

Roszkowski, W. (1983). *Mesjanizm a masoneria okultystyczna w Drugiej Rzeczypospolitej*, in Przegląd Powszechny, 2/1983, pp. 209–24.

Rowecka-Mielczarska, I. (1985). *Ojciec: Wspomnienia córki generała Stefana Grota-Roweckiego*, Warszawa: Czytelnik.

Schellinger, U. (2002). Faszinosum, Filou und Forschungsobjekt: Das erstaunliche Leben das Hellsehers Ludwig Kahn (1873–ca.1966). *Die Ortenau: Veroffentlichungen des Historischen Vereins für Mittelbaden.* 82:429–468.

Schmidt, A. (1930). Experimente mit dem Metagrahologen Otto Reimann-Prag. Im Auftrage der "Berliner Aertzlichen Gesellschaft für Parapsychische Forschung." *Zeitschrift für Parapsychologie* 10, 600–615.

Schottelius, M. (1913). Ein "Hellseher." *Journal für Psychologie und Neurologie* 20, 236–252.

Schwartz, S.A. (1978). *The Secret Vaults of Time*. New York: Grosset & Dunlap, pp. 57–107.

Sheldrake, Rupert (1981). *A New Science of Life: The Hypothesis of Formative Causation*. London: Blond & Briggs; and see *Nature* Vol. 293, 24 Sept. 1981, p. 245.

____. (1988). *The Presence of the Past*. London: Collins.

Sudre, R. (1926). A new clairvoyant: The French writer, Pascal Forthuny. *Journal of the American Society for Psychical Research* 20, 65–77.

Sünner, P. (1930). Experimentelles. Die phenomenale psychometrische Begabung des Herrn Otto Reimann aus Prag. *Zeitschrift für Parapsychologie* 2, 709–716.

Szczepański, L. (1936). *Medjumizm współczesny i wielkie media polskie*. Kraków.

____. (1937). *Cuda współczesne*. Kraków.

Szmurło, P. (1928). *Świat nadzmysłowy i jego badania*. Warszawa.

____. (1928a). *Ze świata tajemnic*. Warszawa.

____. (undated) *Sen, jego symbolika i nadświadomość*.

Toukholka, S. (1922). Expériences de clairvoyance avec Mme. Olga Kahl. *Revue métapsychique* 429–33.

Tymowski, M. (1995). *Najkrótsza historia Polski*. Warszawa: Trio.

Weaver, Z. (2002). Poland—home of mediums. *European Journal of Parapsychology*, Vol 17, 54–71.
Woolley, V.J. (1931). The visit of M. Pascal Forthuny to the Society. *Proceedings of the Society for Psychical Research 39*, 347–357.
Woźniak, J. (1984). Julian Ochorowicz. *Trzecie Oko*, 4/1984, p. 14.

Index

Abramowicz, Mlle. 78
Akashic records 3, 133, 148, 179
Albrecht, Mr. 90
Alexander III, Tsar 8
Aura 8, 19, 179
Automatic writing 7

Bachrach, Detective 111, 171
Badior, Wanda 171
Bakierowski, Mr. 133
Barrington-Emerson, Professor 93, 94, 95, 136, 169
Barrett, Professor Sir William, FRS 175
BBC 127
Belton, the Rev. J. 171
Benedict XV, Pope 15
Berger, Mrs. 28, 138, 139, 166
Bergeret, Dr. 32, 166
Berkeley, Bishop 148
Bernhardt, Sarah 40, 41, 133, 143, 167
Besterman, Theodore 23, 65, 66, 67, 68, 77, 124, 143, 155, 172, 175
Bird, J.M. 153
Björnson, B. 151
Blake, William 1
Bluhmen, Mr. and Mrs. 112
Bołtuć, General Mikołaj 115
Bołtuć, Mrs. 115, 173
Bondy, Mr. 104
Boruń, Krzysztof 7, 9, 11, 13, 19, 115, 116, 162, 163
Boruń-Jagodzińska, K. 7, 9, 11, 13, 19, 115, 116, 162, 163
Borzymowski, Andrzej 19
Bozas, Count Guy du Bourg de 34
Bozzano, E. 37, 134
Bugaj, Roman 163
Byszewski, Stanisław 119, 167

Carrierre, Alietta de la *see* Ossowiecka, Mme. Alietta
Carrington, H. 153

Chamski, Mr. 88
Charpentier, G. 91, 136, 141, 144, 168
Chauvet, Stephen 45, 47, 48, 50, 52, 54, 55, 78, 125, 126, 136, 139, 140, 143, 145, 146, 167
Chłobowski, R. 81
Chmieleński, A. 107
Chojecki, Professor Artur 102, 174
Chyr, Mlle. Z. 81
Clairvoyance: definitions of 179–180; types of 129–137; *see also* Lucidity; Psychometry; Retrocognition; Telepathy
Conan Doyle, Arthur 75
Copernicus, Nicholas 163, 169
Crookes, Professor Sir William, FRS 177
Cryptaesthesia *see* Hyperaesthesia
Czengery, Barbara 80
Czubryński, A. 169

d'Anglard, Monsieur 49, 51, 52, 54, 55, 167
Dante 103
Denton, Elizabeth 152, 157
Denton, William 152
Dessoir, M. 153, 156
Dickens, Charles 24
Didier, Alexis 127, 151, 152, 157
Dingwall, Dr. E. J. 22, 62, 63, 64, 65, 66, 124, 152, 153, 168, 175
Doroszewski, Professor Witold 113
Dreyszer, Monsieur Z. 81
Drzewiecki, Monsieur 93
Dulché, Monsieur 78, 79, 172
Duma 5

Efron, D. 155
Elliotson, J. 152
Epictetus 46, 51
Evelyn, John 66, 67, 70
Extra-sensory Perception (ESP) 23, 130, 137, 179

First World War 5, 6, 155, 176
Fischer, O. 156, 157

Fleurière, Raoul de 156, 157
Forthuny, Pascal 154, 155, 157
Fossombrone (painter) 99
Fulda, Robert 100

Geley, Professor Gustav 1, 9, 14, 20, 22, 26, 27, 29, 30, 31, 33, 35, 36, 37, 38, 40, 42, 43, 44, 45, 47, 49, 54, 55, 57, 59, 60, 61, 62, 70, 85, 87, 104, 118, 119, 125, 126, 129, 131, 132, 134, 135, 136, 137, 139, 140, 143, 144, 146, 147, 148, 154, 155, 158, 166, 167, 168, 175, 176
Geley, Mme. 30, 32, 33, 36, 60, 61, 139, 154, 166
Géo-Lange, Monsieur 27, 29
Gilius, Professor 19
Giżycki, Mr. 81
Glass, Aline de 43, 44, 104, 146, 147, 167
Gliksman, Dr. 32
Gliwic, Professor Hipolit 116
Gliwic, Dr. T. 116, 173
Godejski, G. 110, 170
Goniec Warszawski 7, 9, 18
Goodman, J. 159
Górzyński, Dr. S. 97, 112
Gravier, Alphonse 66, 67, 68, 69, 70, 81, 82, 106, 134, 142, 169, 171, 176
Grondahl, I. C. 155
Grot-Rowecki, General Stefan 115
Grzymała-Siedlecki, Adam 10
Gurney, Edmund 147
Guzik, Jan 16, 30

Hoene-Wroński, Józef 16
Hoori, Monsieur 95
Hope, Lord Charles 66, 67, 68, 70
Hyperaesthesia 35, 38, 41, 42, 44, 134, 179, 180

Ilustrowany Kuryer Codzienny 15, 86, 97, 122
IMI *see* Institut Métapsychique International
Imich, Alexander 9, 11, 115, 116, 164
Immortality *see* Survival
Institut Métapsychique International 14, 26, 45, 55, 62, 74, 91, 125, 126, 128, 133, 139, 146, 155, 156, 167, 175, 176

Jack, J. 59, 60
Jacyna, Jan 6, 8, 9, 11, 86, 87, 88
Jacyna, Jerzy 8, 9, 10, 11, 19, 20, 23, 24, 86, 106, 109, 112, 113, 115, 116, 121, 122, 131, 165, 171, 172, 173
Jacyna, Wiktoria 87, 121
Jankowski, Józef 16
Jaroszewicz, A. 120, 131, 169

Jelski, Stanislas de 34
Jonky, Deniose 24, 80, 81, 82, 84, 133, 142, 172
Journal of the Society for Psychical Research 65, 175
Jundziłł, Count Antoni 120
Jung, Carl Gustav 133

Kahl, Olga 155, 157
Kahn, Ludwig 153, 154, 157
Kaliński, Dr. C. 81
Kallenberg, Professor 99, 170
Kamielski, Professor 113
Kammann, R. 21, 23
Kardec, Allan 128
Kątkowski, General 81
Kimaczyński, Jan Alfons 104, 168
Klimuszko, Czesław 151
Koneczna, Halina 113
Koneczny, Władysław 113, 114
Kopeć, Adolf 90
Kozieł, Zenon 119, 167
Krieger, General 104
Krieger family 23
Krokiewicz, Professor 113
Kruzensztern, Baron N. 171
Kunc, Major 115
Kwiatkowski, Captain 115

Lachenko (painter) 75
Langard, Unni 96
League of Nations 91
Lebiedziński, Piotr 178
Lee, E. 152
Leszczyńska, Miss 118
Lewicki, Mrs. 174
Life after death *see* Survival
Listowski, General 105
Lodge, Professor Sir Oliver, FRS 177
Loth, Felicjan 108, 109, 146, 172
Lubomirski, Prince S. 30, 31, 32, 34
Lucidity 27, 37, 38, 43, 44, 45, 137, 157–158, 180
Luder, Baroness Maria 98, 112, 113, 171
Łukaszewicz, Professor 113

Mackenzie, William 103, 168
Madrid, Francisco 96
Magnin, Monsieur 30
Marcillet, J.B. 152
Marcinkowski, Józef 24
Marks, D. 21, 23
Martinez, Dr. Cobo T. 92, 93, 169, 170
Mazerat, Commandant de 91
Méheust, Bertrand 127, 151
Mendeleyev, Dmitry 7
Mental mediumship *see* Clairvoyance

Le Mercure de France 45, 167
Metapsychic Society [Towarzystwo Metapsychiczne] 178
Meyer, R. 153
Michael, Grand Duke 8
Mickiewicz, Adam 98, 99
Milewska, Mrs. 110
Missuna, Olgierd 22, 23, 81, 110, 165, 169, 176
Moczarski, Kazimierz 117
Mohuczy, Monsieur 112, 171
Moll, A. 153
Mongel, Monsieur 77, 172
Moniuszko, Mrs. 104, 105
Mościcki, Professor 111
Myers, Frederic W.H. 147

Napoleon (painting of) 76
Nature 133
Neuman, Mme. 87
Neumann, Wilhelm 63, 103, 167, 174
Nicholas II, Tsar 8
Niesiołowski, S. 81
Nieznany Świat 15
Noailles, Anna de 38, 39, 42, 43, 132, 167
Nordgarden, Knut Rasmusson 151
Nuksa, Monsieur 73

Oesterreich, Konstantin 37, 134, 153
Olewiński, Janusz 116
Olewiński, Jerzy 116, 173
Oraczewski, Father C. 169
Orlov, Mr. 170
Ossowiecka, Mme. Alietta 10, 47, 54, 71, 167, 170
Ossowiecka, Zofia 10, 20, 81, 115, 116
Ossowiecki, Stefan: abilities, range of 1, 3, 8–9, 20–21, 117–123; archaeology, experiments with 13, 137, 159–164; beliefs 2, 6, 12, 16–18, 44; detective work *see* psychic detection; experimental conditions 1, 4, 12, 16, 21–24, 26–31, 41, 63–64, 70–1, 72–73, 80, 85–87; experiments, types of *see* Target objects; failures 23–24, 29, 32, 36, 62, 77, 78, 115–116, 135; influence at a distance 122–123; out-of-body experiences 118–119; personality 2, 7, 9–12, 13–14, 18–19, 49; rapport with experimenters 2, 16, 46, 49; remote viewing 112–114; spontaneous scene-setting, examples of 104–105, 111–112; states of consciousness 2, 11, 44, 49, 158
Osty, Eugene 1, 49, 59, 60, 61, 62, 66, 74, 76, 77, 78, 81, 85, 91, 106, 126, 128, 129, 131, 132, 133, 134, 135, 136, 137, 139, 141, 145, 146, 151, 153, 154, 155, 156, 168, 172, 176

Pagenstecher, Gustav 135, 154
Pascal, Blaise 30, 157
Pasteur, Louis 55, 57, 144, 146, 168
Patek, Minister 118
Petrażycki, Professor Leon 170
Physical mediumship *see* Psychokinesis
Piery, Dr. 32
Piłsudska, Aleksandra 117
Piłsudski, Józef 6, 9, 14, 26, 34, 35, 87, 88, 117, 124, 166, 167, 176
Pintowski, F. 106, 170
Plater, Mr. 166
Polish Metapsychic Association [Polskie Stowarzyszenie Metapsychiczne] 178
Polish Parapsychological Society [Polskie Towarzystwo Parapsychologiczne] 178
Polish Society for Psychical Research [Towarzystwo Badań Psychicznych] 42, 66, 77, 176, 177, 178
Polskie Stowarzyszenie Metapsychiczne 178
Polskie Towarzystwo Parapsychologiczne 178
Poniatowski, Stanisław 13, 159, 163, 164, 172, 177
Ponikowski, Professor Antoni 88, 89
Precognition 19, 34, 119–122, 129–131, 145, 147–149, 176, 180
Prévost, Marcel 49
Prince, W. F. 153, 154, 156
Proceedings of the Society for Psychical Research 66, 143, 175
Przybyszewski, Z. 88, 89, 90
psi 125, 128, 131, 136, 179
Psychic detection: dead man's footsteps 115, 116–117; lost objects 2, 20, 21, 23, 43, 104, 105; missing body 116; missing persons 2–3, 90, 110, 111, 112, 115–116; murder case 109; sabotage 106–107; stolen objects 106, 107, 108–109
Psychokinesis 7, 8, 15, 16, 23, 30, 77, 131, 147, 149, 165, 176, 177, 179–180
Psychometry 15, 37, 43, 44, 72, 73, 127, 129–137, 147–149, 151, 154, 156, 157, 176, 180

Radin, Dean 128
Rasputin 8
Red Cross 11, 91, 95, 166
Reese, Bert 152, 153, 154, 157
Reimann, Otto 156, 157
Retrocognition 129–137, 140, 143, 145, 147, 148, 180
Retrocognitive dissonance 65
Reutiner, Miss A. 66, 67, 70
Revue métapsychique 26, 28, 35, 37, 41, 42, 45, 52, 56, 57, 59, 62, 70, 72, 74, 76, 79, 80, 84, 86, 87, 91, 93, 95, 104, 106, 118, 124, 132, 134, 136, 137, 138, 139, 140, 141, 142, 143, 146, 175, 176

Rhine, J.B. 128
Richet, Professor Charles 1, 14, 20, 22, 26, 27, 28, 29, 35, 37, 38, 39, 40, 41, 42, 43, 44, 52, 59, 74, 85, 125, 126, 129, 132, 134, 135, 136, 137, 138, 146, 153, 166, 167, 177
Richet, Charles, Jr. 74, 167
RM *see Revue métapsychique*
Roman Catholic church 15
Ropp, Archbishop 169
Rosicrucian movement 16
Rostand, Edmond 38, 39, 40, 167
Roszkowski, Wojciech 16
Rowecka-Mielczarska, Irena 115, 173
Rubinstein, Artur 170
Ruffo, Tita 170
Russian Revolution 5, 6
Rybak, General 167
Rzewuska, Mme. H. 81
Rzewuski, Stefan 15, 22, 74, 81, 97, 171, 177

St. Petersburg Institute of Technology 7
Santoliquido, Rocco 91, 92, 124, 168
Saszkiewicz, Lieutenant 87
Schellinger, U. 153
Schermann, Rafael 156, 157
Schmidt, A. 156, 157
Schneider, Rudi 176
Schneider, Willi 63
Schottelius, M. 153
Schrenck-Notzing, Baron von 22, 62, 63, 64, 65, 85
Schwartz, S.A. 159, 162, 163, 164
Second World War 6, 12, 19, 87, 88, 115, 159, 177
Shakespeare, William 148
Sheldrake, Rupert 133
Sikorski, General Władysław 87
Sima, Prosecutor 174
Skibińska, Irena 98, 99
Skibińska, Zofia *see* Ossowiecka, Zofia
Skibiński, Leon 98
Skórewicz, Professor 161, 162
Skorupka, Dr. 114
Ślósarski, Michał 90
Smirnov, D. 120, 131, 169
Society for Psychical Research 62, 63, 65, 66, 68, 77, 124, 155, 175
Sokołowski, Dr. T.E. 88, 92, 167, 169, 177, 178
Sosnkowski, General 87, 166
SPR *see* Society for Psychical Research
Strauss, Konrad 97
Sudre, Mme. 34
Sudre, René 30, 33, 36, 56, 62, 143, 155, 167
Sünner, P. 157

Survival 15–16, 26, 80, 81, 126, 133, 135–136
Swan Ink *see* target objects
Świda, Marian 11
Świda, Zofia 98, 112; *see also* Ossowiecka, Zofia
Świrski, Lieutenant C. 88, 166
Szajkiewicz, Mr. 88
Szarska, Irena 110
Szawernowski, Piotr 112
Szczepański, Ludwik 15, 176
Szelążek, Bishop Adolf 89
Szmurło, Prosper 2, 14, 22, 70, 71, 73, 74, 76, 80, 81, 122, 132, 133, 142, 146, 161, 167, 168, 169, 172, 174, 178
Szomański, Monsieur 173
Szpotański, Stanisław 96, 98, 99, 170
Szpyrkówna, Maria 109, 168
Szymanowski, Karol 170

Target objects: concealed in lead pipe 29, 34–35, 43, 44, 57, 125, 139; concealed writing 7, 27, 28, 29, 30, 31, 32, 33, 34, 38, 39, 40, 41, 42, 43, 46, 50–51, 52, 63–64, 87, 88, 89, 90, 92, 93, 94, 95, 96, 97, 98, 99, 102, 103, 108, 138, 139, 153, 154, 156; contents of box 71–72; drawing 31, 34, 35, 37, 47, 48, 49–50, 53–54, 63–64, 72, 73, 77, 78, 79, 91, 92, 93, 94, 95, 96, 100, 102, 103; fish scales 58–59; invisible ink 55–57, 143; metal case, inside of 88; personal reading 94, 97; photograph 25, 82, 98, 99; printed material 3, 33, 36, 43, 44, 58, 59, 72, 83–84; Swan Ink experiment 65–70, 77, 143, 172, 175; undeveloped photographic plates 59, 74–76, 77, 141; unknown to anyone living 80–84
Telekinesis *see* Psychokinesis
Telepathy 7, 15, 26, 38, 41, 44, 71, 72, 73, 74, 76, 81, 93, 99, 102, 103, 117, 127, 129–137, 142, 145, 147, 149, 155, 160, 162, 165, 166, 171, 176, 180
Theosophy 2, 16, 133
Thomas, Valentin 79
Thought reading 36, 45, 62, 130, 132; *see also* Telepathy
Toukholka, S. 155
Towarzystwo Badań Psychicznych 42, 66, 77, 176, 177, 178
Towiański, A. 99
Tugan-Baranowski, Professor N. 95, 96
Tutankhamen 17

Vallée, Professor 46, 47, 49
Vett, Monsieur 63
La Vie 45, 167
Vladimir, Grand Duke 8
Vorstelman, Mr. C. 171

Warcollier, René 55, 56
Warsaw (Polish) Psychophysical Society [Warszawskie Towarzystwo Psychofizyczne] 14, 74, 76, 80, 86, 109, 168, 177, 178
Warsaw University 13, 102, 108, 113, 159, 174, 177
Warszawskie Towarzystwo Psychofizyczne 14, 74, 76, 80, 86, 109, 168, 177, 178
Wawrzeniecki, Marjan 71, 72
Weaver, Z. 25, 123, 151
Wedel, Jan 106, 107, 146, 170
Wielopolski, Count 97
Wieniawa-Długoszowski, Colonel Bolesław 118
Wiltshire, Stephen 127
Witkowska-Zaremba, Professor Elżbieta 123, 174
Witwicki, Professor Władysław 170
Wodzińska, Mme 66, 67, 70, 77
Wojdyłło, Marian 99, 100, 172
Wolfke, Professor 117
Woolley, V. J. 155
Woroniecka, Princess 87
Woroniecki, Prince J. 70
Woźniak, J. 178
Wróbel 2, 7, 8, 16, 18, 165

Yudenich, General 90

Zagadnienia Metapsychiczne 13, 14, 15, 22, 70, 86, 92, 178
Ziejewski, Stanisław 169
Zierold, Maria R. 135, 154, 157

www.ingramcontent.com/pod-product-compliance
Ingram Content Group UK Ltd.
Pitfield, Milton Keynes, MK11 3LW, UK
UKHW050524150426
5217IPUK00026B/1786